Published by Aperitifs Publishing Company
Santa Rosa, California

Copyright: March 2023
Written by: Tim Higgins

Compiled & Published by John C. Burton
johncburton@msn.com
707-523-1611

ISBN: 978-1-7324530-6-7
Library of Congress Control Number: 2023903391

Printed in the United States of America

All rights reserved. No part of this book may be reproduced or transformed in any form or by any means, electronic or mechanical, including photocopying, recording or by any information storage and/or retrieval system without permission in writing from the publisher.

I, John C. Burton, on September 23, 2022, purchased the contents and rights to this publication from Tim Higgins of Jackson, California.

Tim Higgins made every attempt to provide accurate information on the following subjects.

ACKNOWLEDGMENTS

The author would like to thank the following for their contributions:

American Bottle Auctions, Sacramento, Cal.
Gary Antone, Livermore, Cal.
Steve Bava, Antioch, Cal.
Benicia Public Library
Mike Bryant, San Diego, Cal.
Dan Brown, Petaluma, Cal.
Wayne Bucholz, Santa Maria, Cal.
John Burton, Santa Rosa, Ca.
Jerry Dore, Pleasanton, Cal.
Gary Flynn, Brewerygems.com
Glass Works Auctions, Lambertville, N.J.
Rick Hall, El Cajon, Cal.
Steve Hubbell, Gig Harbor, Wash.
Dr. Tom Jacobs, San Rafael, Cal.
Donald King, Benicia, Cal.
Phil Kriess, Pioneer, Cal.
Lou Lambert, Sebastopol, Cal.
Rick Lindgren, Martinez, Cal.
Byron Martin, Angels Camp, Cal.
Ferdinand Meyer, Houston, Texas peachridgeglass.com
Bruce Mobley, Beer Bottle Library online site
Bob Quinn, Sacramento, Cal.
Rick Simi, Downieville, Cal.
Barbara Uhlich, Lodi, Cal.
Vallejo Historical Museum
Bob Welch, Santa Cruz, Cal.

A special thanks to Jerry Dore for some of the crown top photos and Byron Martin for some of the blob top photos that I could not track down. Their books on western beers inspired this one. And a big thanks to all the people who sent me photos of bottles and breweriana via the internet. Most of these people did not leave me a name, so I thank you all as a group. Glass Works supplied these. No internet sites such as ebay were considered here.

Rarity is based on a near mint bottle in average condition unless otherwise noted. I feel that rarity is better way to go that trying to put a dollar value on every bottle. Many small town bottles are very rare, but are only worth a lot to the local collectors. They may have a fraction of the value to collectors in other areas. Of course disirability comes into play with color and crudity a factor. One bottle that comes to mind is the Swan Lager. More than 50 exist, which would put this in the common category. But it still commands a high price, due to many people wanting one, and its age as the first San Francisco embossed beer.

Some abbreviations that may be used:

GWA - Glassworks Auctions
ABA - American Bottle Auctions
S.B. - smooth base
RE. - reverse
A.T. - applied top
T.T. - tooled top
B.T. - blob top
C.T. - crown top
Qt. - quart
Pt. - pint
ABM - automatic bottle machine

Rarity Scale
Unique -- 1
Ex. Rare -- 1- 10
Very Rare -- 10- 20
Rare -- 20 - 35
Scarce -- 35- 50
Common -- 50+

Updated Feb. 2020
The oldbottleman

Front: A. B. / SAN FRANCISCO

    Quart, Applied Blob Top
    Yellow Olive
    Rarity: Ex. Rare
    Note: No known whole specimens to date. This may have been a bottle from the Albany Brewery. It is of the right time span. The map below is circa 1899, fronting Natoma St. and ad in circa 1872. Brewery is on Everett St. Maybe they moved or it's a different Company/ The "AB" label was trade marked in 1892, by the Hagemann Brewing Co. S.F.

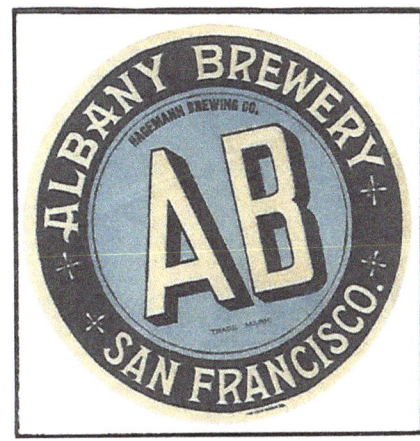

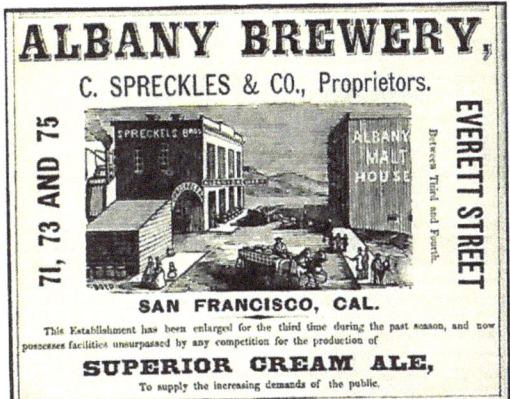

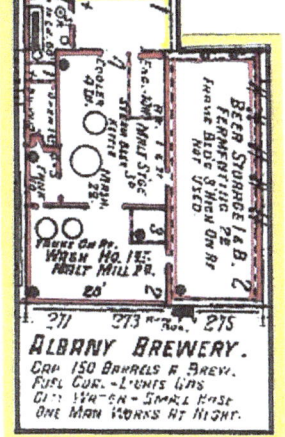

Front: AHRENS BOTTLING CO. / "monogram" / OAKLAND, CAL.

    Quart, Pint and ½ Pint, Tooled Blob Top
    Amber
    Quart, $30.00 - 2002 ABA
    ½ Pint, $40.00 - 2020 GWA
    Scarce in all sizes

    HISTORY: Deitrich N. Ahrens worked for the Oakland Bottling Co. from 1892 thru 1902. In 1903 he formed his own bottling co. at 1565-1567 Linden. He was also an agent for National Lager Beer at this time. This lasted until at least 1907, as there is no directory for 1908. He is listed as a driver in 1909, and in 1910 only his residence is listed. These bottles should date 1903 - 1907.

**ABERDEEN BREWING CO. /
TRADE / "monogram" / MARK /
ABERDEEN, WASH.**

*Quart and Pint, Tooled Blob Top
Amber
Rarity: Scarce in both sizes*

**ABERDEEN BR'W'G CO. /
TRADE / "monogram" / MARK /
ABERDEEN, WASH.**

*Quart, Tooled Crown Top
Amber
Rarity: Scarce*

**ABERDEEN BR'W'G CO. /
TRADE / "monogram" / MARK
ABERDEEN, WASH.
(in round plate)**

*Quart, Tooled Crown Top
Amber
Rarity: Scarce*

**ABERDEEN BREWING CO. / "PRIMA" /
ABERDEEN, WASH.**

*Quart and Pint, Tooled Crown Top
Amber
Rarity: Scarce in both sizes*

HISTORY: Alvin Hemrich, son of John Hemrich of the Seattle Brewing and Malting Co., started the brewery in Aberdeen in 1901, raising capitol. The first brew came in 1902. They lasted until 1915, when prohibition in Washington started. Photo circa 1907. History and ads courtesy of Gary Flynn, brewerygems.com.

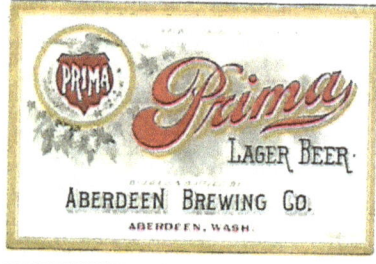

Front: ALBANY BREWING CO / "monogram" / ALBANY, OR.
         (in round plate)

> Quart, Tooled Blob and Crown Top
> Bulge Neck
> Amber
> Rarity: Both style tops are Scarce

Front: ALBANY / BREWING CO. / ALBANY, OR.

> Quart, Tooled Crown Top
> Amber
> Rarity: Scarce

> HISTORY: There were two breweries operating in Albany in the late 1870's – 1880's period. They were the Keifer and the Star. By 1890 they were both out of operation.
> The Albany Brewery commenced operations in the early 1890's and were fully up and running by 1895. They were out of business by 1908, as the map below states. It is circa 1908 with the brewery East 9th St. The bottles listed here would date to this brewery, not the two older ones.
> No further info.

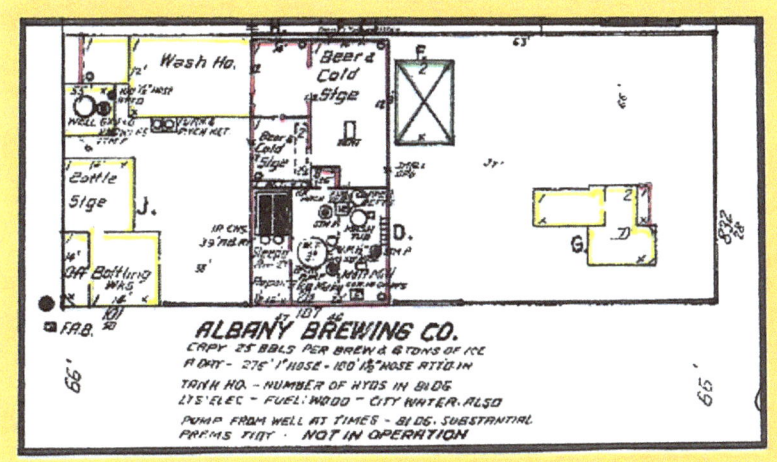

Front: ALBION / BURNELL & CO. / S.F. / BREWERY

> Pint and ½ Pint, Tooled Crown Top
> Amber
> Very Rare

Front: ALBION / BURNELL & CO. / S.F. / BREWERY
         (in round plate)

> ½ Pint, Tooled Crown Top
> Green
> ½ Pint; $650.00 - 2005 ABA
> Ex. Rare

> History: The first listing I could find for the Albion Brewery was in 1878 with Burnell and Simkins as the proprietors, and located at 9th Ave in South San Francisco. In 1879 and 1880 the listing is the same but the address is 9th between G & H.
> From 1885 - 1889 J. H. Brunell and Bro. are listed as the proprietors with the address being Corea, between Santos and Penobscot.
> From 1905 until 1890 the name was listed as the Albion Ale and Brewing Co., with Burnell & Co., props. The address was 9th Ave South.
> In 1906 the address changed to 107-1009 Golden Gate Ave. and this remained the same until 1910 when it changed to 494 O'Farrell St.
> This lasted until 1916, when they moved again to 1491 Mission.
> It was the same in 1917, then to Griffith and Innes in 1918. They incorporated in 1919 with the address now being 877 Innes. No further listings in the brewery business. It is hard to believe that after 40 years in business that the only embossed bottles that they used were these two crown top bottles.

Front: AMERICAN BREWING CO. / "eagle" / WEST BERKELEY, CAL. /
       THIS BOTTLE NOT TO BE SOLD

Quart, Pint and ½ Pint
Tooled Blob and Crown Top
Amber
½ Pint, Blob Top, $220.00 - 2019 ABA
               $50.00 - 2020 GWA
Rarity: Scarce in all sizes with Blob Top
       Rare in all sizes with Crown Top

Front: AMERICAN BREWING CO.
Re: WEST BERKELEY, CAL.

Quart, Tooled Blob Top
Amber
Rarity: Very Rare

HISTORY: In 1894, Joseph Raspiller and John Wohlfrom became partners, and started the American Brewing Co. It was located on San Pablo, corner of Francisco, in West Berkeley. Raspiller became sole proprietor in 1898 when Wohlfrom left the business.
The name was finally changed in 1904, when it became the Raspiller Brewing Co.
The brewery continued until 1910, when Raspiller became involved with the Golden West Brewery.
The ad below is circa 1898.

Front: AMERICAN BREWING CO. / SEATTLE, WASH.
        (embossed vertically)

½ Pint, Tooled Blob and Crown Top
Amber
Rarity: Scarce in both style of tops

HISTORY: Henry West came to Seattle looking for work in the brewing business. He has experience in the trade, coming from a family of brewers in England. Once in Seattle he noticed that none of the locale breweries offered British style porters and ales. By 1899 he found financial backing and started the Britannia Brewery, doing business as West & Co. However his beer was not very good and his company was declared insolvent in 1900. In 1901, West had convinced Joseph May to purchase the brewery from the receiver. It resumed operation as the Seattle Ale & Porter Co. This second attempt lasted only four months and West sold the company to Theodore Krutzer, who resumed operations as the American Brewing Co. This venture failed as well. In 1902 West formed a partnership with the Spellmire Brothers. This lasted until 1905, when West decided to get out of the brewing business, and moved to Oakland, Cal. This bottle should date between 1901 - 1902. Map circa 1905. History courtesy Gary Flynn, brewerygems.com.

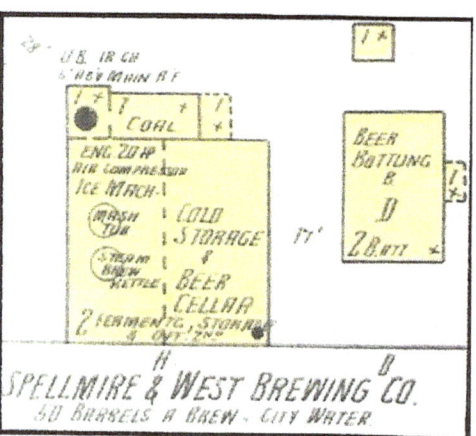

Front: ALABAMA BREWING CO. / "monogram" / SAN FRANCISCO
         (in round plate)

½ Pint, Tooled Blob Top
Amber
Common
Varient: Red Amber, Applied Blob Top
        Rare

Front: ALABAMA BREWING CO. / "monogram" / SAN FRANCISCO

½ Pint, Tooled Blob Top
Amber
½ Pint, $50.00 - 2020 GWA
Common

Front: ALABAMA BREWING CO. / SAN FRANCISCO

½ Pint, Tooled Blob Top
Amber
$50.00 - 2006 ABA
Scarce

Front: ALABAMA BREWING CO. / "monogram" / SAN FRANCISCO

½ Pint, Oversized Applied Blob Top
Green
Ex. Rare

HISTORY: The Alabama Brewing Co. got its start in 1899. The first listing came in 1900 with Weikert & Brondberg listed as the proprietors. The address was the corner of Dolores and 29th. The listings from 1901 until 1905 listed only 1600 Dolores as the address, nothing else. The trade mark drawings for the embossing patterns were applied for in 1899. See below. The map is also in 1899, at 29th and Dolores.

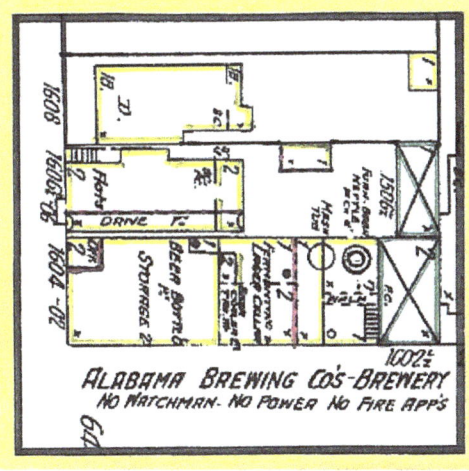

Front: AMERICAN BREWING & C. I. CO. / BAKER CITY, ORE.
(embossed vertically)

Quart, Tooled Crown Top
Amber
Rarity: Rare
Note: Beer glass at right from the American Brewing and Crystal Ice Co. of Baker City, Oregon., 3 ½" tall. Map below left is circa 1903, right circa 1911. Showing the brewery fronting on Dewey Ave.

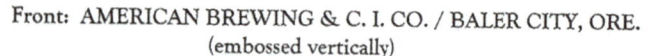

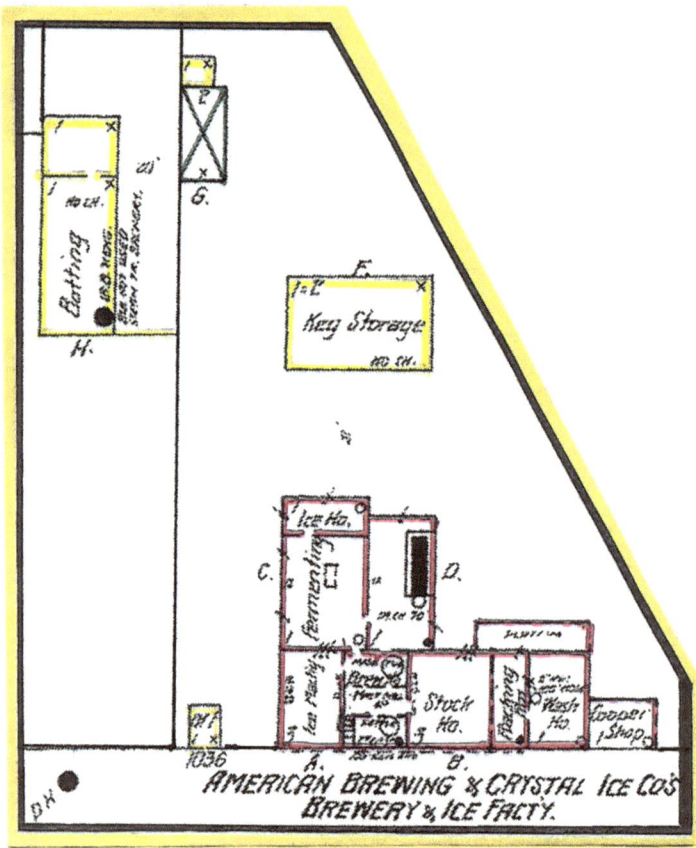

Front: ANCHOR BREWERY / OAKLAND, CAL.

 Quart, Tooled Blob and Crown Top
 Amber
 Rare in both style tops

Front: ANCHOR BREWERY / "anchor" / OAKLAND, CAL.

 Pint, Tooled Blob Top
 Amber
 $300.00 - 2011 ABA
 Rare

HISTORY: The Anchor Brewery was established in 1894 by Charles Kramm. It was located at 49th and Shattuck. In 1903 Augusta Kramm was the proprietor as Charles had passed away. Joseph Kramm was listed as the manager in 1907. The listing stayed the same thru 1912. Joseph Kramm went on to work with the new Golden West Brewing Company. These bottles are very hard to find, and must have been used for a very short time. They probably used paper label bottles only, after the initial order of embossed bottles were used. Map below is circa 1902. Ad circa 1895.

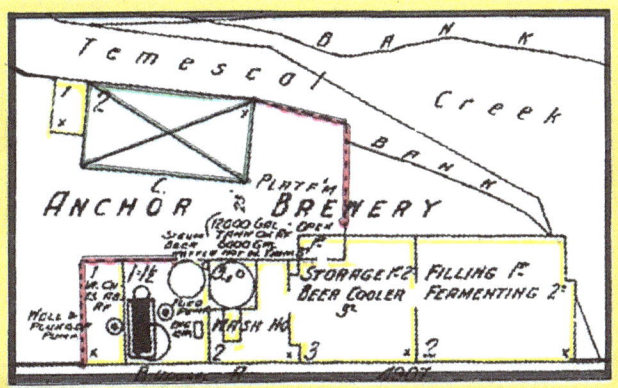

Front: ANDERSON BOTTLING CO. / "monogram" / S. F. CAL.
              (in round plate)
Re: THIS BOTTLE / NEVER SOLD

 ½ Pint, Tooled Blob Top
 Amber, $250.00 - 2017 (chip) ABA
 Rarity: Very Rare

History: The only listing that I could find for an Anderson in the beer business was in 1911. A. Anderson was listed as a bottler at 1105 Golden Gate Ave. The search was for the years 1900 to 1918, the years this style of bottle was likely used.

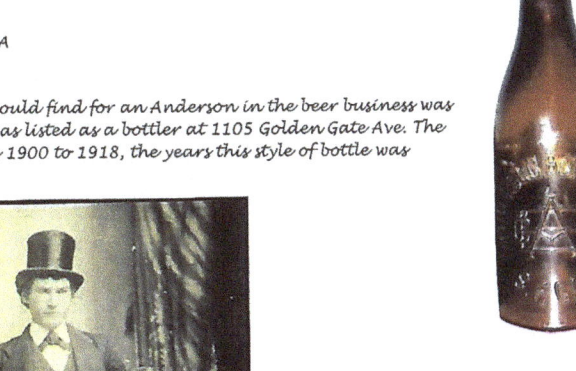

Front: ANGELS BREWERY / AND / SODA WORKS / ERNST HUBLER / PROP.

Quart, Tooled Blob Top, 4 Piece Mold
Amber, $120.00 - 2001 ABA
Rarity: Rare

Front: ANGLES BREWERY / AND / SODA WORKS / E. F. HUBLER / PROP.
(in round plate)

Quart, Tooled Blob Top
Amber, $550.00 - 2001 ABA
Rarity: Very Rare

Front: ANGLES BREWERY / AND / BOTTLING WORKS / ERNST F. HUBLER / PROP.

Quart, Tooled Blob Top
Yellow Amber
Rarity: Rare

HISTORY: From around 1893 to 1912, Ernst Hubler was the proprietor of the Angels Brewery and Soda Works. In 1913 he sold out to A.D. Mentz who ran the brewery until prohibition, but the soda works continued on for a few more years. Crown top and hutchinson style ½ pint soda type bottles exist that may have been used for beer also.
Photo below in around 1900, and the Sanborn map is circa 1908, showing the brewery on South Main St.

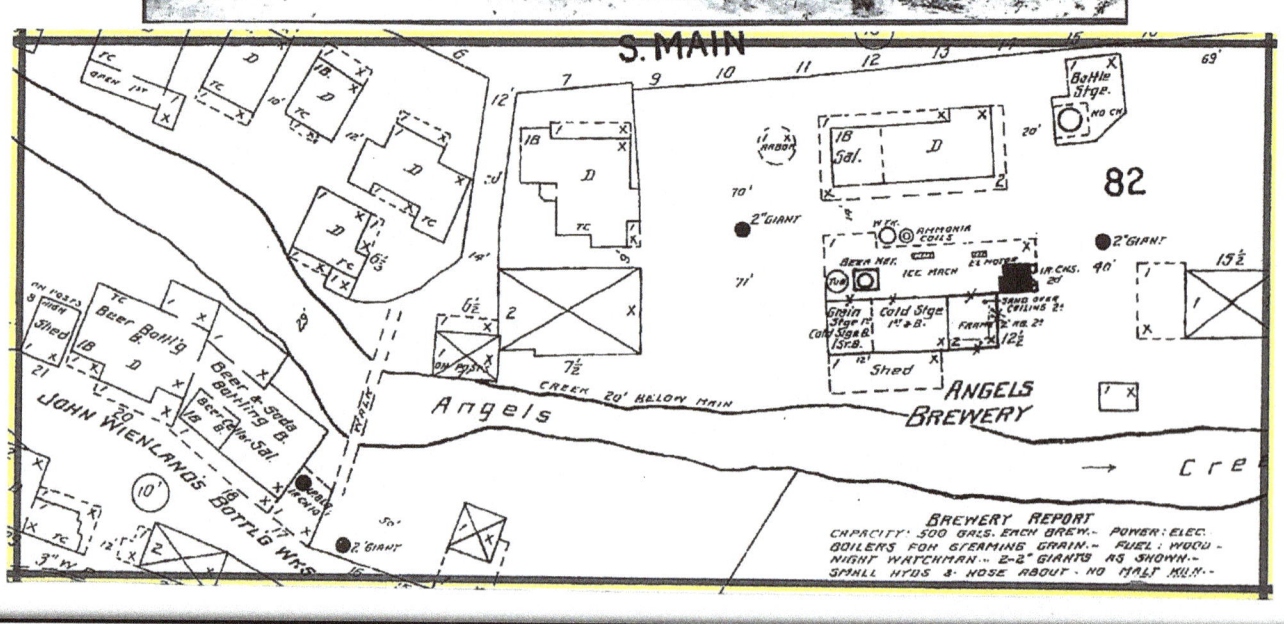

Front: ANHEUSER – BUSCH / BOTTLING WORKS / LOS ANGELES CAL.

½ Pint, Tooled Blob Top
Bulge Neck
Amber, $900.00 - 2013 ABA
Rarity: Ex. Rare

HISTORY: The earliest listing I could find was 1884 - 1885, Asheuser Busch Brewing Association on N. Alameda. No directory for 1886 was available.
1887 - 1890, Bauer & Gollmer were the agents for the bottling department on North Alameda, with the offices at 563 North Spring and 285 North Main.
1891 - 1892 has Charles Bauer, Agent of the Brewing Asso..
Mathie & Theobald were the Proprietors of the Bottling works in 1893.
1894 brings V.H. Theobald as the proprietor, and Charles Bauer again in 1895, at 243 South Spring. This confusing because the listings don't seem to state if it's the brewing or bottling dept. every time
Then in 1896 Theobald & co. is the prop of the bottling works, at 409 N. Alameda, and Bauer is the head of the brewing asso. at 243 S. Spring. This seems to last thru 1898. 1899 has Theobald and F. Scharwitz as props. Of the bottling works.
In 1904 until 1918, F. A. Heim is the agent for the brewing asso. and the bottling works. He was located at 946 - 948 E. 2nd.

Front: THE / ANHEUSER BUSCH / BEER

½ Pint, Tooled Blob Top
Amber, $1000.00 - 2005 ABA
Rarity: Ex. rare
Locale: Unknown at this time

History: No info available

Front: ANHEUSER BUSCH BWG. ASS'N / A with "eagle" / S. F. AGENCY

Quart, Pint, and ½ Pint
Bulge Neck
Applied Export Top
Amber, ½ Pint, $275.00 - 2020 "flake) ABA
       Pint, $800.00 - 2017 ABA
       Quart, $600.00 - 2005 ABA
Rarity: All sizes are Rare

HISTORY: I could find no listings for this company in the San Francisco directories from from the 1870's until the 1890's, the era when this bottle should have been in use.
In 1879 thru 1883 Bach, Meese & Co. were the agents for C. Conrad & Co. the western agents for Budweiser. They were located at 321 Montgomery. They may have used the bottle, but I doubt it.

Front: BARNER & RIEBE / BOTTLERS / REDDING, CAL.
(in round plate)

Quart, Pint, and ½ Pint
Tooled Crown Top
Amber
Rarity: Common in all sizes

HISTORY: No info at this time. Map below is circa 1904.

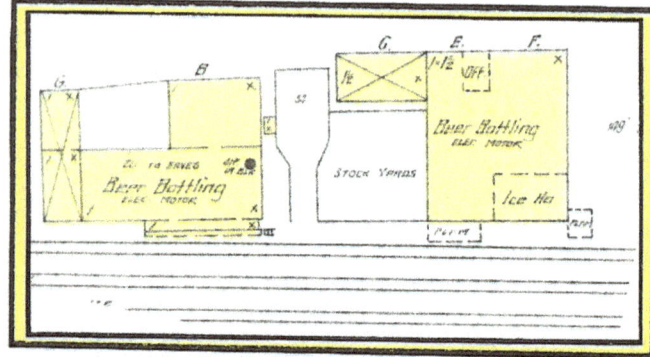

Front: THE BAY / BOTTLING CO. / SAN FRANCISCO / CAL.

Quart, Pint and ½ Pint
Tooled Blob Top
Amber, Quart, $80.00 - 2000 ABA
½ Pint, $80.00 - 2020 GWA
Rarity: Rare in Quart and Pint size
Ex. Rare in the ½ Pint size

HISTORY: I could find no listings for this company in the San Francisco Directories from 1895 - 1918. This bottle should have been in use in the 1900 to 1910 period.

Front: BARNOLD'S / B / SEATTLE, WASH.

½ Pint, Tooled Blob Top
Some have a Bulge Neck
Amber, $40.00 - 2020 GWA
Rarity: Scarce

HISTORY: Here is what little I have found on the beer. Charles Barold was in Spokane from 1889 thru 1893, when he moved to Seattle. He became the bottler for the Hemrich Bro's brewery. See label below.
At some point, he probably owned a saloon or store, and issued this token, a common practice at the time.
He passed away in 1942. No further info.

Front: BAY VIEW / BREWING CO. / SEATTLE, WASH.
(in round plate)
Re: NOT TO BE SOLD

Quart, Pint and ½ Pint
Applied Blob Top
Pint and Quart have Bulge Necks
Green, Quart, $375.00 - 2017 ABA
   Pint, $600.00 - 2000 ABA
Rarity: Very Rare in all sizes

Front: BAY VIEW BOTTLING / WORKS / SEATTLE, WASH. (in round plate)

Quart, Pint and ½ Pint
Tooled Crown Top
Amber
Rarity: All sizes are Rare

HISTORY: In 1883, Andrew Hemrich and partner John Kopp established a small brewery south of downtown Seattle. It was located on the corner of 9th Ave. and Hanford St.
In 1884, Andrew's father joined the company by purchasing Kopps share. The business was now as Hemrich & Company's Bay View Brewery. In 1887, a new inlarged plant went into production, this is when the Brewery started using the green German made bottles. In 1893, Bay View joined forces with breweries of Albert Braun and Claussen-Sweeney to form the Seattle Brewing & Malting Company. The Bay View plant continued to operate, and in 1906, they added a bottling plant. Brewing ceased in 1913, with all production shifting to the Sweeney plant in Georgetown Wash. With the coming of prohibition they decided to sell the Bay View plant. Photos are circa 1896 and 1898. Thanks to Gary Flynn brewergems.com, for the photos, and ads.

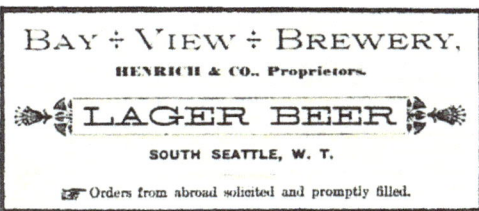

Front: BELLINGHAM BAY / "anchor, monogram" / BREWERY / WHATCOM, WASH.

½ Pint, Tooled Crown Top
Bulge Neck
Amber
Rarity: Very Rare

Front: BELLINGHAM BREWERY / 3 B BEER / SAN FRANCISCO, CAL. (embossed vertically)

Quart, Tooled Blob Top
Amber
Rarity: Rare

HISTORY: The history of the Bellingham Bay Brewery started when Leopold Schmidt, the president of the Capitol Brewing Co. of Tumwater, chose the site for his new brewery. The 3 B trade mark was registered in 1902.
Work on the new brewery started on Jan. 10, 1902, and was completed on Nov. 28, 1902. It stood on North Elk St. in Whatcom. The ½ Pint bottle that says Whatcom instead of Bellingham, must have been ordered before the city changed its name. They would date from 1903 to about Oct. 1904.
The brewery shipped its beer to major markets on the west coast, with D. Meinke being the agent in San Francisco in 1906. The 1905 directory has Joseph Cuneo as the agent, both at the 20th St. location.
In 1910, Schmidt announced that he had leased the brewery and ice plant to Pierre Andrae and Edward Stowe. The name was changed soon after, and the final blow came when prohibition took effect in 1916. Map circa 1904. History and breweriana courtesy of Gary Flynn, brewerygems.com.

BELLINGHAM BAY BREWERY, COLD STORAGE AND REFRIGERATING PLANT
WHATCOM, WASHINGTON.

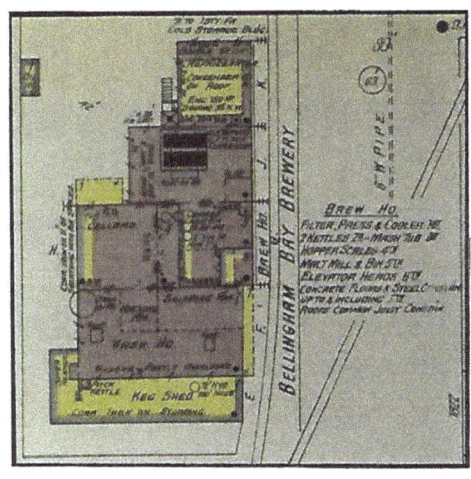

Front: BENICIA BREWERY / G / BENICIA, CAL.
(in round plate)
Re: THIS BOTTLE / NOT TO / BE SOLD

½ Pint, Tooled Blob Top
Clear, $40.00 - 2020
Scarce

Front: G. GNAUCK / G / BENICIA, CAL.

Quart, Tooled Blob Top
Amber
Very Rare

Front: GUSTAVE GNAUCK / BENICIA
BREWERY / BENICIA, CAL.

Pint and ½ Pint, Tooled Blob Top
Amber
Ex. Rare in the Pint size
Scarce in the ½ Pint size

History: The Brewery was started in 1855 when Major Cooper sold the California House Hotel to John Rueger. Rueger came to Benicia from Marysville where he had operated a brewery there. The California House was one of the oldest buildings in Benicia, built in 1847. The first floor was adobe with wood frame rooms above. In 1875 Gustave Gnauck was hired by Rueger to brew beeer for the growing businesss. Sometime in 1879 Gnauck took on Richard Massle as a partner and they purchased the brewery from John Rueger. They inlarged the plant, and turned the original adobe part of the building into a saloon. This can be seen on the 1899 Sanborn Map, next page, at the lower left of the map. The buildings faced West H St., just off of First St.

An interesting side note to the Rueger ownership of the brewery, the Home Mutual Insurance Company paid out a $200.00 loss to John Rueger in the 1860's. This was for horses, wagons and hay destroyed by fire. It was the first loss paid by the company in Benicia. Fred P. Weinman was the agent, and his son later became a prominent druggist in town.

By 1879 Gnauck had bought out Massle and was the sole owner. He married the widow of John Rueger around this same time. He hired his step son Theodore to help at the brerwey, and was there until 1911 when he left to start a hardware store.

In the 1890's, Gus Gnauck started a soda works to go along with the brewery business. It was located across H St. from the brewery property. The Hutchinson style bottles from this business are rare and the crown cap style are common.

In the early 1900's Gus Gnauck became an agent for the El Dorado Brewery of Stockton, Fredericksburg and Enterprise Brewery of San Francisco. It is this authors opinion that Gus reused the other companies vessels to bottle his own beer, when they were returned. This may be the reason the Gnauck bottles are so rare. Many more of the bottles from other companys have been dug in Benicia than his own. The operation continued until prohibition, and the soda works until the late 1920's. The picture below is circa 1908, with the original adobe section behind the first wagon, ground level, framed rooms above.

ADS BELOW ARE CIRCA 1900- 1915 from the BENICIA NEW ERA and BENICIA HERALD

BENICIA BREWING & SODA WORKS
GUSTAV GNAUCK, Proprietor
Distributors of Blue and Gold, Valley Brew and Fredericksburg Lager, Red Lion Porter.
Domestic Peerless Steam Beer
Pure Mountain Spring Water, 50 Cents, in Tilting Demijohn
We manufacture all kinds of Carbonated Beverages. Selzer Water in Siphons
Distributors of Bartlett, Cook's and Napa Soda
MINERAL WATERS

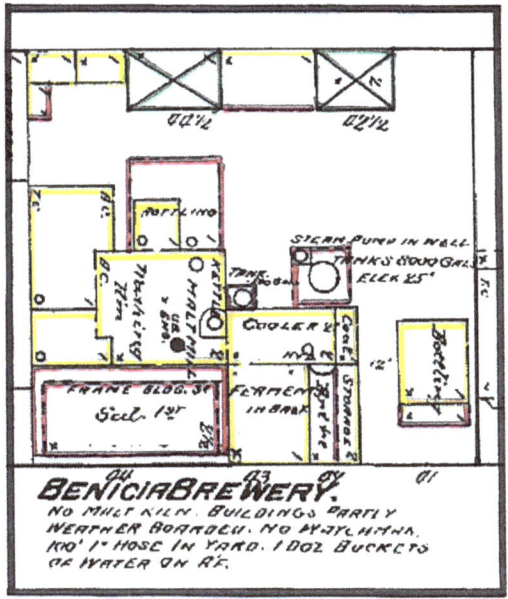

Benicia Brewery
GUSTAV GNAUCK, Proprietor
This long and well-known establishment manufactures the
Best Lager Beer in the County.
Beer on Draught at the Brewery.

Benicia Soda Works
GUS. GNAUCK, Prop.
Manufactures
ALL KINDS OF
CARBONATED DRINKS
SELZER WATER IN SIPHONS

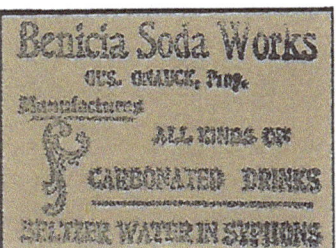

Front: C. BECK / SANTA CRUZ

Quart, Tooled Blob Top
Amber, $300.00 - 2017 ABA
$170.00 - 2020
Rarity: Rare

HISTORY: Charles Beck came to Santa Cruz in 1884, and was employed by the Bausch Brewery. Then in 1894 he decided to go into the brewing business for himself, and built the Big Trees Brewery, fronting on Market St.
In 1906, after the earthquake, he took on some partners and moved to a new brewery on Blackburn St. He called this the Santa Cruz Brewery. This lasted until 1917, as prohibition was soon coming. This bottle should date from the late 1890 - 1905 period. Map at right is circa 1905.

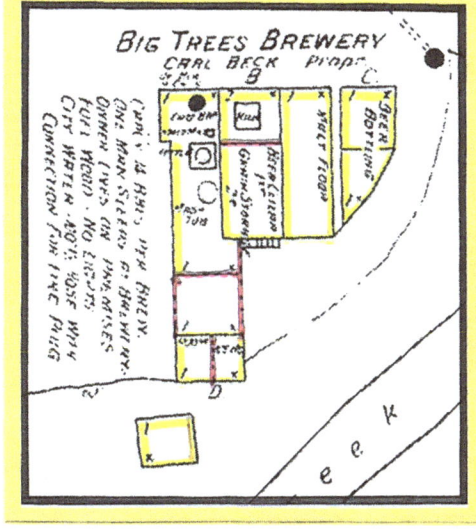

Front: BORELLO & PORTER / B & P / MADERA

Quart, Tooled Blob Top
Amber, $200.00 - 2017 ABA
Rarity: Very Rare

HISTORY: Frank Borello and Grant Porter bottled soda water and beer together from the late 1890's until 1907. At that point, Borello moved to Fresno and became the manager of the Las Palmas Winery. Grant Porter continued to run the soda works with no mention of beer bottling operation. Crown top soda type bottles exist from this company and are rare. This bottle here should date pre 1907. Map below is circa 1898.

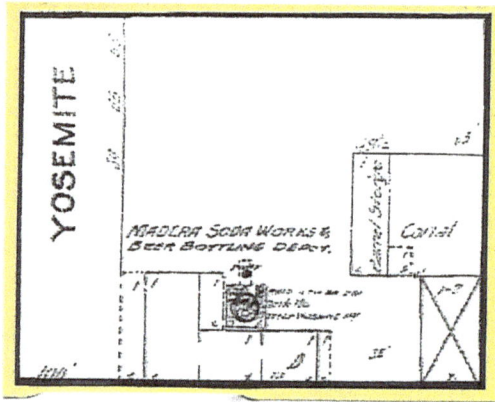

Front: VAL BLATZ / BREWING CO. / DENVER, CO.
             (in round plate)
Re: BOTTLE / NOT TO / BE SOLD

Quart, Pint and ½ Pint
Tooled Blob Top
Aqua
Varient: Re: "BOTTLE IS / NEVER SOLD"
Rarity: Common in all sizes and varients

HISTORY: Val Blatz is a Milwaukee Brand and came to Denver in 1881. The distributors were as follows.
  1881 - 1887, Brasher Brothers are the first agent in Denver, 351-353 Holladay St.
  1888 - 1889, F. Wich, 1215 - 1217 20th St.
  1890 - 1892, Max Kauffmann, 1513 - 1523 10th St.
  1893 - 1897, William Jung, 1519 - 1523 10th St.
  1897 - 1900, Fred Alcock, 1519 - 1523 10th St.
  1900 - 1904, Joeseph Patterson, 1517 - 1523 10th St.
  1905 - 1910, Henry Clodius, 1517 - 1523 10th St.
The bottles here were probably used by Alcock or Patterson.

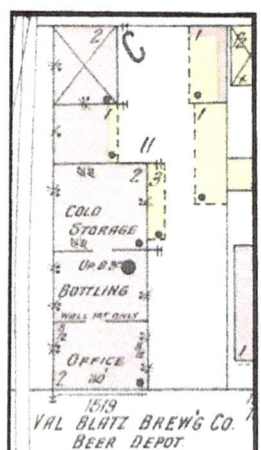

Front: BOCA / BOB / BEER
Re: blank plate

Quart, Applied Double Collar Top
Amber with plate, $400.00 - 2017 ABA
Varient: no plate on reverse
Scarce with plate
Common without plate

History: The town of Boca was located about 10 miles downriver from Truckee, Cal., where the Little Truckee River joins the Truckee River. A lumber mill was started in 1866 and an ice works shortly after that.

The Boca Brewing Co. was formed in 1875, and work commenced on the brewery in August 1876 and completed in July 1876. By 1880 there were 80 men employed at the brewery. Stockholders were L. Doan, H. Bacon and C. Thompson of Boca, A. Dibble of Grass Valley, and J. Fargo of San Francisco. The first brewer was Leonard Frierichs and compacity of the plant was 100 barrels a day. Boca was the first brewery on the West Coast to produce lager beer. Bisiness was booming and they opened an office and warehouse in San Francisco in 1877.

In the 1880's new beers were being introduced to the market. Bohemian Beer in 1885 and Weiner Beer in 1884. At this time the company was second in beer production on the West Coast with 25,000 to 30,000 barrels annually. Then in January of 1893 the brewery burned to the ground, a total loss. The business was never rebuilt.

The quart bottles were the first embossed quarts made and distributed in the west. Mostly found in the Boca, Truckee and Reno area, with some coming from mining and lumber camps in the Sierras. Pictures are the Brewery in 1878, box car and workers 1880, trade card front and back circa 1883 and an ad circa 1886.

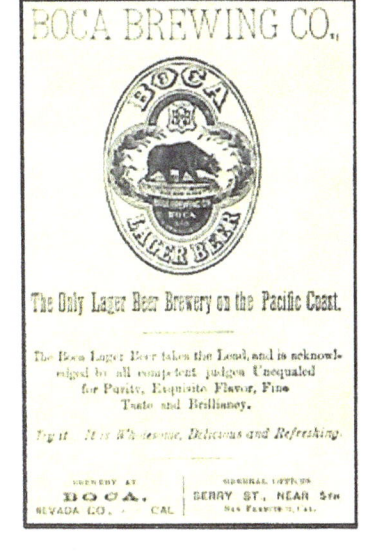

Front: B. & J. / OAKLAND

   ½ Pint, Tooled Blob Top
   Amber
   $70.00 - 2020 ABA
   Scarce
   Note; this is a Brenckenfelder & Jochem bottle

Front: BRENCKENFELDER / & / JOCHEM / OAKLAND, CAL.

   Quart, Pint, Tooled Blob and Crown Top
   Amber
   Quart size with Blob Top is Common
   Pint, with Blob Top is Scarce
   Crown Tops are Scarce

Front: BRENCKENFELDER & JOCHEM / OAKLAND, CAL.
            (around shoulder)

   Quart, Pint, Tooled Blob Top
   Amber
   Common in all sizes

   HISTORY: Brenckenfelder and Jochem were first listed in the beer business in 1906. They were agents for Valley Brew Beer from the El Dorado Brewery in Stockton. In 1907-1908 the listing was unchanged. In 1909 the partnership dissolved, and Wm. Brenckenfelder is listed as a Brewers Agent at 858 Adeline. No further listings. Billhead below is circa 1908.

Front: FRANK BUCHER / REDDING, CAL.

   Quart, Pint and ½ Pint, Tooled Crown Top
   Amber and Aqua
   Rarity: Common in Amber, all sizes
          Rare in Aqua, all sizes

   HISTORY: Frank Bucher operated the Redding Brewery From 1902 to 1909. At that point, he sold the brewery to Joseph Hoefer. Bucher was an agent for John Wieland products and Rainier Beer in the Redding area. Map below is circa 1904.

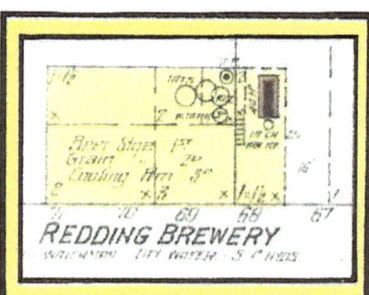

Front: F. O. BRANDT / HEALDSBURG / CAL.

   Quart, Pint and ½ Pint, Tooled Blob Top
   Amber, Quart, $100.00 - 2005 ABA
          ½ Pint, $50.00 - 2020 ABA
   Rarity: all are Scarce
   Varient: ½ Pint with Bulge Neck, Rare

Front: F. O. BRANDT / HEALDSBURG
Base: S.F. & P.G.W.

   Quart, Tooled Blob Top
   Bulge Neck
   Amber
   Rarity, Rare

Front: F. O. BRANDT / HEALDSBURG / CAL. / BOTTLE NOT TO BE SOLD

   Quart, Pint, Tooled Crown Top
   Amber
   Rarity: Rare

HISTORY: In the mid to late 1880's, Frederick Brandt started the F. O. Brandt Bottling Works in Healdsburg. It was located on University St. between Matheson and North Sts. His specialty was bottling beer from the bigger breweries far away. They came in in kegs by railroad. Buffalo Beer from Sacramento, National Brewery and Enterprise Brewery from San Francisco. In 1910 he also added Valley Brew from Stockton to his growing business. Plus he became a major northern distributor of Grace Brothers Beer from Santa Rosa. Steam Beer was his specialty, and he was in full operation by 1895. He also bottled soda water and Hutchinson and crown top bottles exist from his company.
Frederick Otto Brandt passed away in 1918, and prohibition closed the plant shortly after. Ad below is circa 1911.

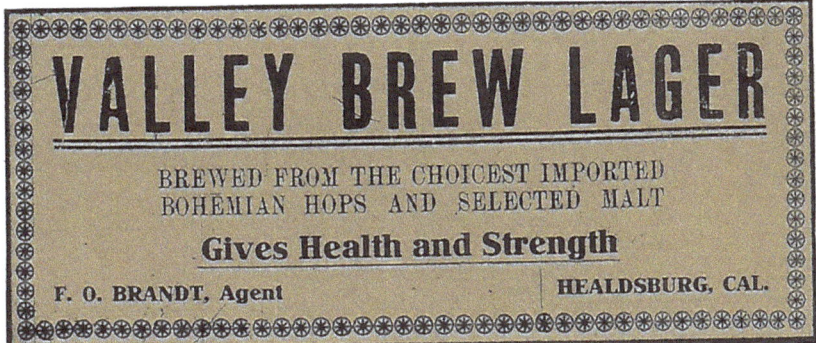

Front: CELEBRATED / B & S / LAGER BEER

   ½ Pint, Applied Blob Top
   Aqua, $250.00 - 2017 ABA
   Rarity: Very Rare

HISTORY: No info on this company. It is a soda type bottle that should date from the mid 1870's to the mid 1880's. Looks to be western blown.

Front: GEO. BRAUN BOTTLER / "monogram in shield" /
        2219 PINE ST. S.F.

    Quart, Applied Blob Top
    Red Amber
    Rarity: Ex. Rare

Front: GEO. BRAUN BOTTLER / "monogram in shield" /
        2219 PINE ST. S.F.
        (all in round plate)

    Quart, Pint, ½ Pint
    Tooled Blob and Crown Top
    Amber and Clear
    Rarity: ½ Pint, Blob Top, Amber, $40.00 - 2020 ABA
        Amber Blob Tops are Scarce
        Clear with Blob Top is Ex. Rare
        All Crown Tops are Rare

HISTORY: The first directory listing for George Braun was in 1893. He was listed as a beer bottler at 2219 Pine. He would stay at this address his entire time as a bottler.
He is listed thru 1905, There is no listing in 1906 and 1907, after the quake.
Then in 1908 he is a Soda Water Mfg. at the same address. 1909, no listing, and the from 1911 - 1921, he is again listed as a beer bottler. No Further mention of Braun in the bottling business.
Embossing pattern at was trade marked in 1900, by George Braun.

Front: HENRY BRAUN / BEER BOTTLER / OAKLAND CAL.

½ Pint, Tooled Blob Top
Amber
$275.00- 2020 ABA
Ex. Rare

History: John Wendler states the Henry Braun was an agent for Boca Beer from 1881 - 1883, and the ad below supports that. I could find no listing for that in the directories.
Henry Braun was first listed in 1884-85 as a beer bottler at 406 Ninth in Oakland. The next listing was in 1887. At that time he was the proprietor of the U.S Bottling Co. at the corner Webster and 8TH. This remained the same until 1893-93 when he was the General Agent for the Buffalo Brewing and Beer Bottling Co. at 870 Webster Cor. 8TH.
There were no directories from 1893 - 1902.
According to the ad below he was an agent for Pabst Brewing in 1894.
The bottle listed here would probably date in the late 1890's to early 1990's range.
I found no proof that the Henry Braun listed in Los Angeles is the same man. His first listing down south was in 1896, most likely before the Oakland bottle was made.
Pabst ad below in 1894, Boca ad circa 1882, Buffalo ad circa 1891.

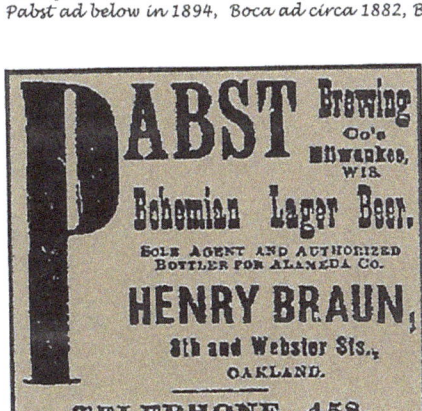

Front: HENRY BRAUN / "monogram" / LOS ANGLES, CAL.

Quart, Pint and ½ Pint, Tooled Crown Top
Amber
Aqua
Quarts and Pints are Scarce
½ Pints are Rare

HISTORY: Henry Braun's first appearance in the Los Angeles directory was in 1896, as an agent for Buffalo Beer at E. 7th and Santa Fe. In 1897 his address changed to 1044 N. Alameda.
In 1898 he is an agent for Buffalo and Pabst Beer at 1044 N. Alameda. Than in 1899 He adds Jackson's Napa Soda to his agency, at the same address.
In 1900 he is listed as a bottler only, at the Alameda St. address.
Then from 1901 to 1904 his inventory expanded to include being an agent for Jackson's Napa Soda, Bartlett Mineral Water, Buffalo Beer, Ruhstaller's Gilt Edge Beer, Rainer Beer, and Pabst Beer, all at the 1044 N. Alameda address.
No further listings.

Front: JOHN J. BUCK / P. B. / SAN FRANCISCO
            (in round plate) /
        THIS BOTTLE IS NEVER SOLD

Quart, Applied Blob Top
Amber
Rarity: Ex. Rare

HISTORY: John J. Buck was listed in the Grocery & Liquor business in 1882 to 1884. His location was 231 2ND.
Then in 1885, Bottler of Philadelphia Beer was added to his listing., at 231-233 Second St. All further listings has him in the grocery business only.
Now we know why this in one of the rarest western beers. He probably only bottled it for less than a year.

Front: BUFFALO / BREWING CO. / SACRAMENTO / CAL.

   Quart, Tooled Blob and Crown Top
   Bulge Neck
   Amber
   Rarity: Scarce in both styles of tops

Front: BUFFALO BR'G CO. / SAC. CAL.
      (embossed vertically in rect. plate)

   ½ Pint, Tooled Blob Top
   Bulge Neck
   Amber
   Rarity: Rare

Front: THIS BOTTLE / B.B. CO. / NOT TO BE SOLD

   Quart and Pint, Applied Blob Top
   Clear
   Quart, $375.00 - 2009 ABA
   Quart and Pint, $500.00 - 2018 ABA
   Rarity: Rare in both sizes
   Note: Thought to be the first Buffalo Beer.

Front: BUFFALO BREWING CO. /"horseshoe, buffalo" /
        SACRAMENTO, CAL.

   Quart, Tooled Blob Top
   Bulge Neck
   Aqua, $325.00 - 2009
   Rarity: Rare

Front: BUFFALO BREWING CO. / "horseshoe, buffalo" / SACRAMENTO, CAL.

Quart, Tooled Crown Top
Aqua
Rarity: Rare

Front: BUFFALO BREWING CO. / "horseshoe, buffalo" / SACRAMENTO, CAL.

Quart, Pint and Tooled Blob and Crown Top
Amber
Rarity: Common in all varients

Front: THIS BOTTLE / BUFFALO BR'G CO. / SACRAMENTO / NOT TO BE SOLD

Quart and ½ Pint, Applied and Tooled Top
Amber, ½ Pint, Tooled Top, $800.00- 2020 (chip) ABA
Red Amber, Applied Top, Qt., $100.00- 2005 ABA
Olive Amber, Applied Top, Qt., $50.00- 2017 ABA
Raruty: Quarts with the Applied Top is Scarce
Quarts with Tooled Top are Rare
½ Pints are Ex. Rare

Buffalo Brewing Co. Lager Beer label above trade marked in 1891 by the Sacramento Brewing Co. Buffalo Lager Beer label below was trade marked in 1890 by the Buffalo Brewing Co.

Bottle embossing patterns below were trade marked in 1891 by the Sacramento Brewing Co.

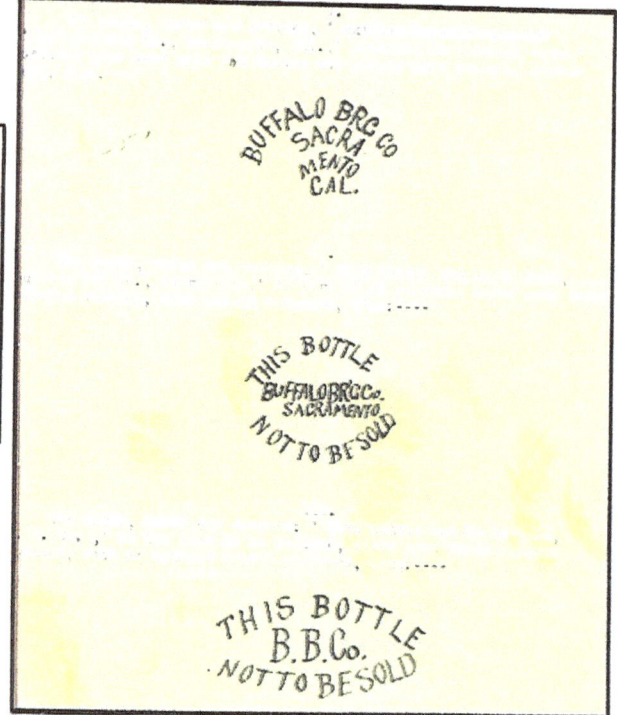

Front: BUFFALO BOTTLING WORKS /
         S.L.O. / BUFFALO LAGER BEER
         (embossed in circle)

Quart, Tooled Blob Top
Amber, $250.00 - 2013
Rarity: Very Rare

Front: BUFFALO BREWING CO. / "monogram" /
         S.F. AGENCY (in round plate)

Quart, Pint, and ½ Pint
Tooled and Applied Export Top
Amber, ½ Pint, Tooled Top, $50.00 - 1999 GWA
      Quart, Tooled Top, $30.00 - 1999 GWA
Green,, Pint, Applied Top, $500.00 - 2018 GWA
      Quart, Applied Top, $400.00 - 2018 GWA
Rarity: Ambers are Common
        Greens are Rare

Front: BUFFALO BREWING CO. / "monogram" /
         S.F. AGENCY (in round plate)

Quart, Pint, Tooled Crown Top
Aqua and Amber
Rarity: Common in Amber
        Rare in Aqua

Front: BUFFALO BREWING CO. / "monogram" /
         S. F. AGENCY (in round plate)

Pint and ½ Pint, Tooled Blob Top
Clear, $160.00 - 2005 ABA
Amber, $60.00 - 2005 ABA
Rarity: Scarce in Amber
        Rare in Clear

Front: BUFFALO BREWING CO. / "monogram" /
         S. F. AGENCY (in round plate)
Re: BOTTLE NEVER SOLD

½ Pint, Tooled Blob Top
Clear, $70.00 - 2020 (chip) GWA
Rarity: Very Rare

HISTORY: A. H. Lochbaum & Co. were the first agents in San Francisco for Buffalo Beer. In 1891 They were at 521 - 525 15th St. By 1898, they had moved to King St. In 1908, they has a new agent in Louis Brandt, at the same King St. address. This remained the same until 1915, when they moved to 132 - 136 Bluxome. They were still listed there in 1918, when research ended. Lochbaum trade marked the label below in 1893. Map is circa 1899.

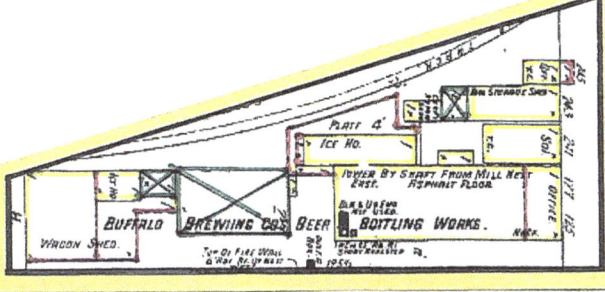

Front: BUFFALO BREWING CO. / "monogram" / S. F. AGENCY

Pint, Tooled Blob Top
Bulge Neck
Amber, $120.00 - 2020 ABA
Rarity: Very Rare

Advertising Sign

4" Tall Beer Glass

Pilsener Label on Quart Buffalo Brewing Bottle

Matchsafe, 2 ¾" X 1 ½" Reverse Side on the Left

Bohemian Buffalo Beer Label on a Hansen & Kohler Oakland Quart Bottle

Matchsafe, 2 ¾" x 1 ½" Very Rare Reverse Side on the Left

3 ¾" Tall Beer Glass

Buffalo Brewing Co. Bottle Label

Stopper Tops for Decanters

I believe this to be a very early view of the Buffalo Brewery in Sacramento

Front: CAL. BOTTLING CO. / JOHN WIELAND'S / EXPORT BEER / S.F. (embossed vertically)

Quart, Pint and ½ Pint, Applied and Tooled Blob Top
Red Amber
Green, Applied Top, Pint, $450.00 - 2009 ABA
Variant: minus "S.F.", Pint, Red Amber, A.T.
Variant: S.F.& P.G.W. on base, ½ Pint, $90.00 - 2020 GWA
Rarity: Red Amber Quart with Applied Top is Rare
Common in all sizes with Tooled Top

Front: CAL. BOTTLING CO. / EXPORT BEER / S.F. (embossed vertically)

Quart, Pint and ½ Pint, Applied and Tooled Blob Top, and Tooled Crown Top
Amber, Red Amber
Rarity: Common in all sizes with a Tooled Top in Amber
Rare in Red Amber with Applied Top
Common with a Crown Top in all sizes

Front: CALIFORNIA / BOTTLING CO. / S.F. (embossed vertically)

Quart, Tooled Blob Top
Amber and Aqua
Rarity: Common in Amber
Rare in Aqua

Front: CAL. BOTTLING CO. / JOHN WIELAND / EXTRA PALE / SAC. (embossed vertically)

Pint and ½ Pint, Tooled Blob Top, Bulge Neck
Amber
Rarity: Rare in both sizes

Front: CAL. BOTTLING CO. / JOHN WIELAND'S / EXPORT BEER / S.F. (embossed vertically)

Quart, Pint and ½ Pint, Tooled Crown Top
Bulge Neck
Amber, Quart, $130.00 - 2013 ABA
Rarity: all sizes are Scarce

Front: CAL. BOTTLING CO. / EXPORT BEER / S.F. (embossed vertically)

½ Pint, Tooled Crown Top, Bulge Neck
Amber
Rarity: Common

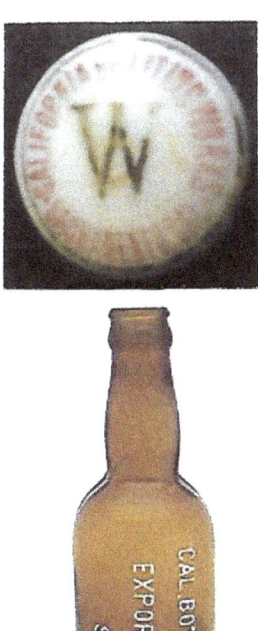

Wieland's Extra Pale Label on a Cal. Bottling S.F. Quart Bottle

Wieland's Tivoli label. Trade marked in 1900 by the California Bottling Co. S.F.

Extra Pale Lager label, John Wieland Brewery. Trade marked in 1897 by the Cal. Bottling Co. S.F.

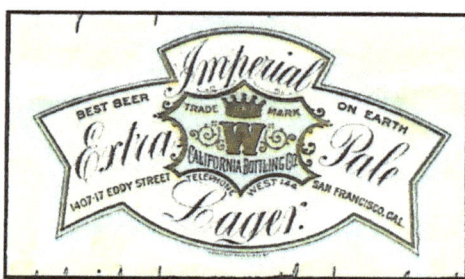

Imperial Extra Pale Lager label, trade marked in 1893 by the California Bottling Co. S.F.

Little Pop John Wieland's Extra Pale. Label trade marked in 1893 by the California Bottling Co. S.F.

Special Brew Jas. P. Dunne & Co. Lager Beer. Trade marked in 1893 by the California Bottling Co. S.F. Special Brew labeled for a Rest., Saloon, Hotel or private customer.

John Wieland's Lager Beer label. Trade marked in 1888 by the California Bottling Co. S.F.

Gold Seal Lager Beer label. Trade marked in 1894 by the California Bottling Co. S.F.

Big Pop The Popular Brew. John Wieland's Extra Pale label. Trade marked in 1897 by the California Bottling Co. S.F.

The following 32 labels were trade marked in 1893 by the California Bottling Co. S.F. They were probably Used for private customers such as Saloons, Hotels, Resteraunts, ect.

Bottom label courtesy of Bob Welch.

Extra Pale Lager label on a Cal. Bottling ½ pint bottle.

Weinhard California Bottling Co. label on a Gambrinus S.F. pint bottle.

Stopper pattern trade marked in 1899, by the California Bottling Co. S.F.

Imperial Extra Pale Lager label trade marked in 1893 by the California Bottling Co. S.F.

John Wieland's Standard label trade marked in 1892 by the California Bottling Co. S.F.

HISTORY: 1889 was the first listing for the California Bottling Works. John Buck was the president, and they were located at 1407 - 1417 Eddy. They were sole bottlers of John Wieland's Lager.
This remained unchanged thru 1891. In 1892, Robert Wieland became president of the firm. He remained until 1895, when Edward Kalben assumed the position, all the time at the same address. In 1904, the company moved to 1265 Harrison, until they closed the doors in 1908.

Front: CALIFOTNIA / BOTTLING WORKS / T. BLAUTH /
407 K ST. / SACRAMENTO

Quart, Tooled Blob and Crown Top
Amber
Rarity: Scarce

Front: CAL. BOTTLING WORKS / T. BLAUTH
SAN CO. / SACRAMENTO, CAL.

Quart, Tooled Blob and Crown Top
Amber
Rarity: Common with both style tops

Front: CALIFORNIA / BOTTLING WORKS /
T. BLAUTH / 407 K STREET /
SACRAMENTO

Quart, Tooled Crown Top
Aqua
Rarity: Scarce

Front: CALIFORNIA / BOTTLING WORKS /
THEO. BLAUTH SONS CO. / 407 K
STREET / SACRAMENTO

Quart, Tooled Crown Top
Amber
Rarity: Scarce

HISTORY: Theo Blauth was an agent for John Wieland's Beer, at 407 K St. from 1891 until 1905. The bottling works also bottled soda water. In 1905, Blauth turned the business over to his sons. The business was known as T.H. Blauth Sons Co. from 1905 - 1912, and as T.H. Blauth & Son from 1913 - 1918. Ad circa 1892.

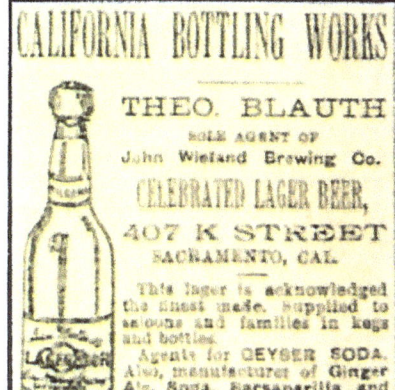

Front: CAPITOL BRG. CO. / CAPITOL
BEER / REGISTERED / THIS
BOTTLE / NEVER SOLD

½ Pint, Tooled Crown Top
Aqua and Clear
Rarity: Common in both colors

HISTORY: No info at this time.

Front: CARDILLO & LAMB / PUEBLO /
COLO.   (in round plate)

Quart and ½ Pint, Tooled Blob Top
Clear, ½ Pint, $30.00 - 2020 GWA
Rarity: Scarce

HISTORY: No ifl at this time.

Front: THE L. CERF CO. / VENTURA / CAL.

Quart, Bulge Neck
Tooled Blob and Crown Top
Amber
Rarity: Rare in all varients

HISTORY: The Louis Cerf Co. was a wholesale liquor dealer and an agent for Fredericksburg Beer in the early 1900's.

35

Front: CAPITOL BOTTLING WORKS / SL / PETALUMA / CAL.

Quart, Pint and ½ Pint
Tooled Blob Top
Amber
Varient: Embossing pattern is smaller
Rarity: Quart and Pint size are Scarce
½ Pint and all varients are Rare

Front: CAPITOL BOTTLING WORKS / JH / PETALUMA / CAL.

Quart, Pint and ½ Pint
Tooled Blob Top
Amber
Varient: misspelled "CAPITAL"
Rarity: Scarce is all sizes
Varient is Rare

HISTORY: Louis Schmidt was the proprietor of the Capitol Bottling Works as early as 1896. In 1906 he was located on the corner of Upham & Stanley Sts. He was an agent for Wunder Lager and the Chicago Brewery of San Francisco.
Sometime in 1906 Schmidt sold the bottling works to Henry Hammerman and John Jarr. This lasted until 1908, when Jarr left the partnership. Hammerman operated the business alone until 1911. History courtesy of John Wendler.

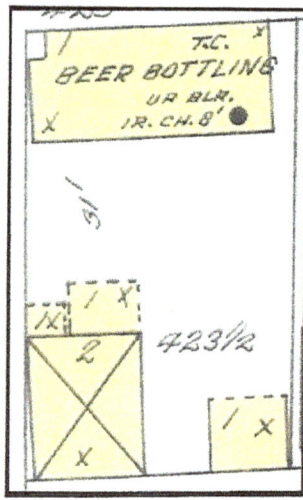

CAPITAL
Soda and Bottling Works
PETALUMA, CAL.
LOUIS C. SCHMIDT, Proprietor.
Agent for Napa Soda, Quiros' Syphon and the Chicago Brewery.

IT'S GOOD!
IT'S FINE!
IT'S GREAT!
WUNDER BEER
It's so exhilarating, so good in taste, so perfect in color. NO WONDER EVERY ONE LIKES IT. Sold under the exclusive agency of . . .
Hammermann & Jarr
Proprietors of
Capitol Bottling Works
Upham, S. W. Cor. Stanley Streets
Petaluma, - California
Telephone Black 1582
. . . . . ALSO AGENTS FOR . . . . .
Jackson's Napa Soda, Mineral Water and Quiros Siphon Seltzer. Also Manufacturers of All Kinds of Soft Drinks. The . . . .
Finest Made in the County

CAPITOL
Bottling Works
H. Hammermann, Prop.
Manufacturer of
ALL KINDS OF
SODA WATER.
Agent for Napa Soda, Quiros Seltzer and Mineral Waters. Bottlers of the celebrated Wunder Lager.
Cor. Upham and Stanley Sts.
Phone Black 1582....Petaluma

Front: CONSOLIDATED / MILWAUKEE BEER / AGENCY / HELENA, MONT.

½ Pint, Tooled Blob Top
Amber
Rarity: Rare

HISTORY: No info at this time.

Front: A. CAPPELLI & CO. / "deer" / TRADE MARK / BOTTLE BEER / S. F. CAL.

Quart, Applied Blob and Ring Top
Amber, Ring Top, $3000.00 - 2017 (repaired) ABA
Rarity: Ex. Rare in both style of tops

HISTORY: The first mention of Antonio Cappelli was in 1883, as a beer bottler. 1884 ha him as an agent, but it does't say for whom. 1885 he is listed as a Bottle Beer Dealer, no address given. This is the final listing for Cappelli.

Front: "monogram" / CASCADE / LAGER / S.F. CAL.

   Quart, Tooled Blob Top
   Amber
   Common

Front: "monogram" / CASCADE / LAGER / S.F. CAL.

   Quart, Pint and ½ Pint, Tooled Crown Top
   Aqua and Amber
   Scarce in Amber, all sizes
   Rare in Aqua
   Note: monogram is for the "UNION BREWING & MALTING CO"

   HISTORY: Cascade Lager is first listed in 1905, bottled by the Union Brewing and Malting Co., at 423-427 Valencia St. In 1906 the address is 18th and Florida. It remained the same thru 1908. No further listings after that.

Front: CASCADE BOTTLING CO. / PEREIRA BROS. / SANTA CLARA, CAL. (embossed vertically)

   Quart, Pint and ½ Pint
   Tooled Blob Top
   Amber
   Rarity: Scarce in the Quart and Pint size
          Rare in the ½ Pint size

   HISTORY: The Pereira Bros. were in the bottling business from the early 1990's to at least 1907. They were located at the corner of Alviso and Liberty in Santa Clara.

Front: M. CASEY / GILROY BREWERY / CAL.

Quart, Applied Blob and Ring Top
Amber, Blob Top, $3500.00 - 2020 GWA
Ex. Rare in either style top

HISTORY: Michael Casey arrived in Gilroy in 1872, and was employed as the manager of Pain's Livery Stable until 1882. He then became involved in the brewing business. The Gilroy Brewery was established in 1868, by Adam Riehl. The business was sold to Adam Herold and Michael Casey purchased a partnership with Herold after that point. Casey bought out Herold after he became involved in politics.

Casey himself served several terms as a city councilman and mayor of Gilroy. He also served as chairman of the board of the Gilroy branch of the Bank of Italy.

Casey sold the brewery in 1906 to a Hoffman and Berg, who then operated it until prohibition came. Sanborn Map below is circa 1892, and shows the brewery on Monterey St. in Gilroy. This bottle is one of the rarest California beers.

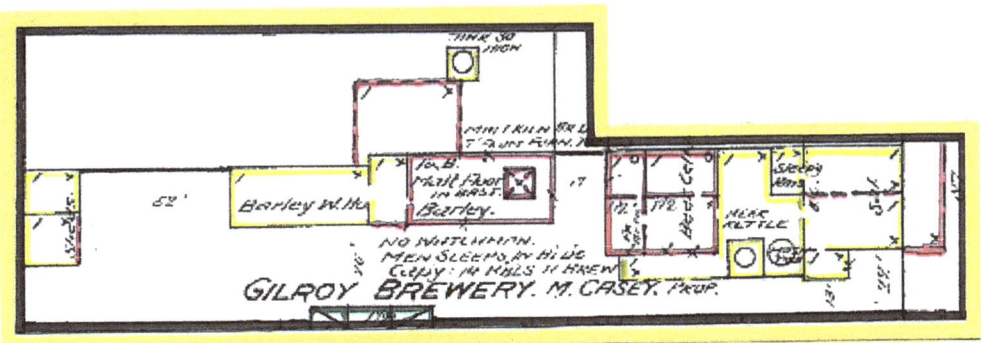

Front: N. CERVELLI / 615 FRANCISCO ST. / S.F.

> Quart and ½ Pint, Tooled Blob Top
> Amber
> ½ Pint, $110.00- 2020 GWA
> Quart, $80.00- 2005 ABA
> Rare in both sizes

Front: N. CERVELLI / "monogram" / 615 FRANCISCO ST. / S.F.

> Quart, Pint and ½ Pint, Tooled Blob Top
> Amber
> ½ Pint, $140.00- 2005 ABA
> Rare in all sizes

> HISTORY: Narcisso Cervelli was first listed in the beer bottling business in 1893, with his place of business being 507 Francisco. There was no listing for 1894, but then it was the same thru 1899. In 1900 the address had changed to 615 Francisco. That address remained constant thru 1905. It should be assumed these bottles were used during this period. There are no directories for 1906 or 1907.
> Then in 1908 his business changed to N. Cervelli & Co. 2527 Greenwich, with Narcisso listed as manager and Nicholas Cervelli as bottler. In 1909 the address remained the same with Rudolph added as a bottler.
> In 1910 the address changed again to 3303 Fillmore with Narcisso only listed with the company. This remained unchanged until 1914 when the address changed again to 1311 Fillmore St. They lasted at this address until prohibition forced them to close the doors in 1919.
> As a side note to the Cervelli family, there was J. Cervelli listed as a bottler at 514 Vallejo St. in 1913, and a D. Cervelli, bottler, at 551 Green St. in 1917. I do not believe they are associated with N. Cervelli.

Front: PROPERTY OF / CHICAGO BREWERY / 1420 – 1434 PINT ST. / SAN FRANCISCO (in round plate)
Base: S. F. & P. G.W.

   Quart, Tooled Blob Top
   Bulge Neck
   Amber
   Rarity: Very Rare

Front: CHICAGO (block letters) / TRADE "monogram" MARK / LAGER BEER / CHICAGO BREWING CO. / S.F.

   Quart, Applied Blob Top
   Amber
   Rarity: Rare

Front: CHICAGO BOTTLING WORKS / SAN FRANCISCO / D. MEINKE, PROP.

   Quart and ½ Pint
   Applied and Tooled Blob Top
   Amber and Green
   Quart, Amber, Tooled Top, $30.00 - 2000 ABA
   ½ Pint, Amber, Tooled Top, $120.00 - 2020 GWA
   Rarity: Rare in the ½ Pint size
        Quarts with a Tooled Top are Scarce
        Green Quart with Applied Top is Ex. Rare

Front: CHICAGO BOTTLING WORKS / SAN FRANCISCO / D. MEINCKE, PROP.

   ½ Pint, Tooled Blob Top
   Amber, $210.00 - 2020 GWA
   Rarity: Ex. Rare

Front: CHICAGO BOTTLING WORKS / "monogram" / SAN FRANCISCO / D. MEINCKE, PROP.

   ½ Pint, Tooled Blob Top
   Amber, $325.00 - 2010 (bruise) GWA
   Rarity: Ex. Rare

HISTORY: 1873 was the first year for the Chicago Brewing Co. Nibbe & Co. were listed as the proprietors, with the place of business being 1408 - 1410 Polk. It remained the same in 1874, but in 1875, they had moved to 1428 Pine.
1876 - 1878, just listed it as the Chicago Brewing Co.
1879 - 1880, They were listed as the Chicago Brewing and Bottling Co., with Alexander Aronsohn the agent at 1507 Folsom.
1881 - 1882, Chicago Brewing Co. only with Henry Ahrens & Co., proprietors.
1883 - 1884 has Theodore Vorborstel as President at 1420 - 1434 Pine St.
1885 - 1890, has N. Olandt as prop. at the Pint St. address. The bottling plant is at 8th and Brannan.
From 1891 - 1897, no bottling plant was listed. 1895 has the bottling works at 615 Howard.
1902 has the bottling works at 925 Florida, with the Brewery remaining at 1420 - 1424 Pine thru 1905.
1906 has the Brewery moving to 240 2nd St. and remaing there until 1908, when business ceased.
The ad on the next page is circa 1888.

Front: CELERY BEER / KELLER / CANDY COMPANY / DISTRIBUTERS / OAKLAND / CAL.
        (in round plate) /
REGESTERED (near base)

Quart, Tooled Blob Top
Amber, $100.00 - 2010 ABA
Rarity: Rare

HISTORY: The Keller Candy was first listed in 1905, with Edward M. Keller as the president. They were located at 475 - 477 7th St.
In 1906 there was not listed, probably due to the earthquake.
1907 found them at 372 12th St, with Edward still running things.
There was no directory in 1908, but in 1909 they had moved to 407 12th St.
1910 - 1911, Keller is listed as a salesman, no more listings for the candy company.

Front: CITY BOTTLING CO. / SAN FRANCISCO / CAL.
        (embossed vertically)

Quart and ½ Pint
Tooled Blob Top
Amber
Quart, $230.00 - 2011 ABA
Rarity: Rare in the Quart size
       Very Rare in the ½ Pint size

HISTORY: The City Bottling Company was listed for one year only.
In 1904, they were located at 219 Point Lobos Ave.
No further listings or info.

Front: CLAUSSEN BREW'G ASS'N / SEATTLE, WASH.
(embossed vertically)

Quart, Pint and ½ Pint
Tooled Crown Top
Bulge Neck
Amber
Rarity: Common in all sizes

HISTORY: Han Claussen established his new brewery in 1901. In 1891, he had sold his interest in the Claussen - Sweeney Brewery and left to pursue other interests. He, along with Charles Crane and George Sackett, formed the Diamond Ice and Storage Company.
Then in 1901, he had raised enough stock to start the Claussen Brewing Association. Claussen's group bought a new brewery that had been built by the Standard Brewing Co.. It was called the Interbay Brewery. It was almost immediately deemed to small, and pland were made to enlarge it.
The new brewery was called Tannhaeeser, after their flagship beer. With the coming of prohibition in Wash. in 1915, the brewery was closed near the end of 1914, and Claussen retired. History ads, and brewiana courtesy of Gary Flynn, brewerygems.com

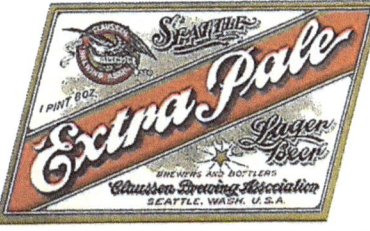

43

Front: CLAUSSEN – SWEENEY / BREWING CO. / SEATTLE, WASH.   (in round plate)

Quart, and ½ Pint,   Applied Blob Top
Green and Aqua
Rarity: Very Rare

HISTORY: In 1884, the Puget Sound Brewery became the property of E.F. Sweeney., after his partner W. Rule retired. By 1888, the plant was more commonly known as the Sweeney Brewery.
The later in 1888, a new corporation was formed when Hans Claussen, the brewmaster, joined Sweeney to establish the Claussen-Sweeney Brewing Co.
The two men had worked together previously at the Fredericksburg Brewery in San Jose, Cal. In 1890, Sweeney Claussen established an ice plant and bottling Plant on Grant St., just north of the brewery. See picture.
In 1891, Hans Claussen sold his interest in the brewery to George Gund. Sweeney continued on and in 1893, joined with Albert Braun and Hemrich's Bay View Brewing to form the Seattle Brewing and Malting Co.
Maps are circa 1893.
History and photos courtesy of Gary Flynn, brewerygems.com

Front: COLUMBIA / BREWING CO. / TACOMA, WASH.
(in round plate) / THIS BOTTLE IS
NEVER SOLD

½ Pint, Tooled Blob Top
Amber, $70.00 - 2020 GWA
Rarity: Rare

HISTORY: Emil Kliese came from Germany in 1883. After working in St. Louis, he made his way to Washington. He found a job with the Capitol Brewing Co. But he wanted to operate his own brewery, so he along with William Klitz, raised enough capitol to open the Columbia Brewery in 1900.
The brewey's start up was aided by the Pacific Brewing & Malting Co., who was a major shareholder. By 1906, it controlled Columbia, but allowed it to operate on its own. The plant was at 2120-2132 South C St. in Tacoma. Prohibtion put an end to the beer brewing, but they continues to make non alcoholic drinks.
History, ads and brewiana courtesy of Gary Flynn, brewerygems.com. Map circa 1912.

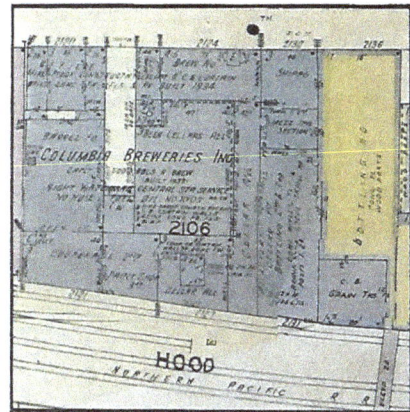

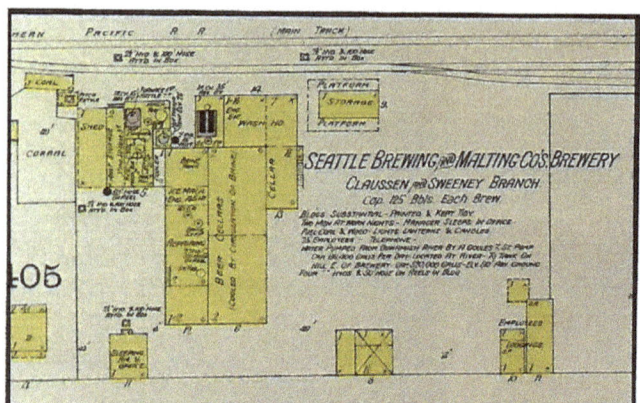
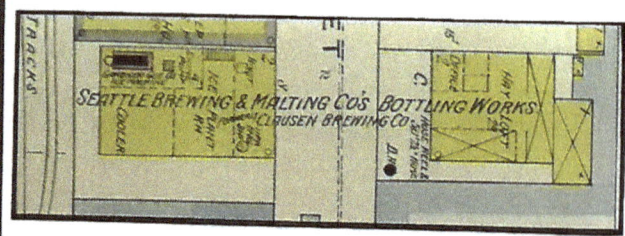

Front: CONSUMERS BOTTLING CO. / "monogram" / REDWOOD, CAL.

    Quart, Pint and ½ Pint
    Tooled Blob Top
    Amber
    Rarity: all sizes are Rare

    HISTORY: No info at this time.

Front: CONSUMERS / "monogram" / BOTTLING CO. / S.F. CAL.

    Quart, Pint and ½ Pint
    Tooled Blob Top
    Amber, ½ Pint, $70.00 - 2020 GWA
            Quart, $350.00 - 2005 ABA
    Rarity: Scarce in ½ Pint size
           Rare in the Quart size

    History: The first listing for the Consumers Brewing Co. was in 1902. They were located at 40 Ellis. There was no listing for them in 1903.
    1904 finds them at 3070 23rd, with Carl Tornberg as the proprietor. The listing stated them as Beer Bottlers
    In 1905, it was Consumers Brewery and Bottling Co., with Tornberg as the prop. at the 3070 23rd St. address.
    There was no listing in 1906.
    In 1907, the listing was the same as 1905, all the way to 1920, when they were no longer in business.

Front: C. CONRAD & CO. / ORIGINAL /
　　　　BUDWEISER / US PATENT
　　　NO 6376

Quart and Pint
Applied Double Collar Top
Aqua, Quart, $120.00- 2009 ABA
Amber and Green
Rarity: Common in Aqua
　　　　Very Rare in Amber and Green

Front: ORIGINAL / BUDWEISER
Re:　 THIS BOTTLE / NOT TO / BE SOLD
Base:　U S T 6376

½ Pint, Applied Blob Top
Aqua
Rarity: Ex. Rare

HISTORY: Carl Conrad was a friend of Adolphus Busch and he contracted Busch to brew and bottle his beer in 1876. A series of glass factories made the bottles and Busch filled them. Conrad was very successful at first and soon his beer was being sold nationwide.
But in the early 1880's business took a down turn and forced Conrad to declare bankruptcy in 1883.
To pay off Conrad's debt's, the Anheuser Busch Brewing Asso. took control of Conrad's company in 1886. He was given a lifetime job with Anheuser Busch.
Budweiser was being sold in the west as early as 1876, with an ad Being in the Oakland Tribune on 10/19/76. The bottles with his name date from 1878 - 1883. Bach, Meese & Co. of San Francisco, were the northern California agents in the early 1880's.

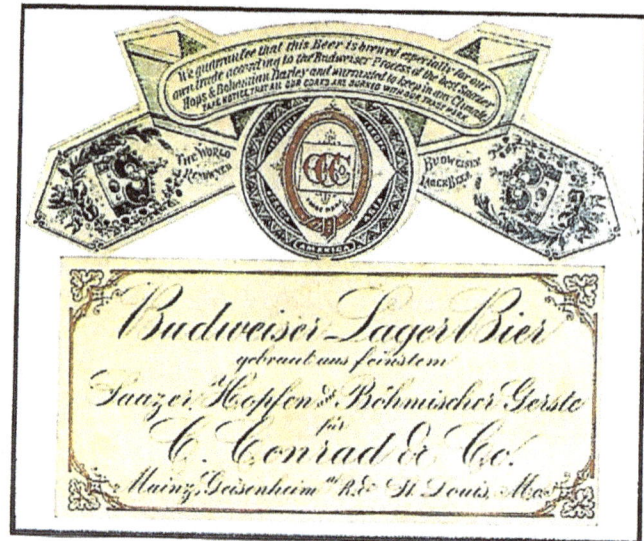

Front: COORS GOLDEN BEER / C "monogram" /
GEO. JACKSON AGT. / PUEBLO, COLO.
(in round plate)

Quart and ½ Pint, Tooled Blob Top
Aqua
Rarity: Scarce

Front: COORS GOLDEN BEER / P.B.R. /
PUEBLO, COLO. (in round plate)

Quart, Tooled Blob Top
Aqua
Rarity: Rare

Front: THE STANDARD / BOTTLING CO. /
DENVER, COLO. (in round plate)
Re: COORS / "mountain" / TRADE MARK /
GOLDEN BEER (in round plate) /
THIS BOTTLE NOT TO BE SOLD

Quart and Pint
Tooled Blob Top
Aqua
Rarity: Scarce

HISTORY: In 1873, two German immigrants, Jacob Shueler and Adolph Coors, founded the Brewery in Golden, Colorado. Coors invested $2000.00 and Schueler $18,000.00.
By 1880, Coors had bought out his partner, and now owned the brewery in total. The name was changed to Adolph Coors Golden Brewery. The business lasted until prohibition, and then made other non alcoholic products to keep going during the ban. After prohibition they resumed brewing beer and became one of the largest selling beers in the world. Picture of delivery truck is circa 1910.

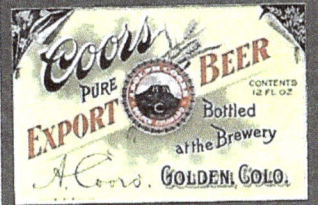

49

Ads circa 1880 and 1886, center picture is 1883, bottom picture is 1900

Front CRIPPLE CREEK / REGISTERED / BOTTLE / BOTTLING WORKS
(in round plate)

½ Pint, Tooled Blob Top
Amber, $60.00 - 2020 (chip) GWA
Rarity: Rare

HISTORY: No info available.

Front: CRYSTAL SPRINGS / BREWING / AND ICE CO. / BOULDER, COLO.

Quart and ½ Pint, Tooled Crown Top
Amber and Aqua
Rarity, Rare in both colors.

HISTORY: The first brewery in then what was called Boulder City was founded in 1875. In 1897, Samuel Pell purchased the brewery and changed the name to the Cyrstal Springs Brewing and Ice Co. He was in business until 1911, at 954 Arapahoe St.

Front: J. B. CUNEO / SAN FRANCISCO (embossed vertically)

    Pint, Tooled Blob Top
    Amber
    $190.00 - 2005 ABA
    Rarity: Rare

    HISTORY: The first listing for J. B. Cuneo that is not connected to the United States Beer Bottling Co. was in 1903. He was listed at 2194 Folsom, than at 3109 20th the next two years. There is no listing for 1906, due to the earthquake.
    In 1907 he is again listed as a bottler, now at 3129 20th. In 1908 finds him moving again, this time to 118 Conneticut St. No further listings.

Front: DELANEY & YOUNG / "monogram" / EUREKA, CAL.

    Quart, Pint and ½ Pint
    Tooled Blob and Crown Top
    Amber, Quart, $40.00 - 2001 ABA
           ½ Pint, $40.00 - 2020 GWA
    Rarity: All Crown Tops are Rare
           Scarce in the Quart and Pint size with a Blob Top
           Rare in the ½ Pint size with a Blob Top

    HISTORY: Peter Delaney and Clarence Young became partners in the bottling business in 1903. They were a wholesale liquor distributor previously. I am assuming that they bottled beer from the large breweries in San Francisco and probably the Grace Bros. in Santa Rosa also.

Front: DEL NORTE / CRESENT CITY / CAL. / BOTTLING WORKS

    Quart and ½ Pint
    Tooled Blob Top
    Amber, ½ Pint, $160.00 - 2020 (flake) GWA
    Rarity: Ex. Rare in the Quart size
           Very Rare in the ½ Pint size

    HISTORY: Herman Kubler operated a brewery in Cresent City from 1897 - 1906. He built his business in front of the old Mahoffer's brewery, which was closed in 1890. Even though these bottles say "DEL NORTE BOTTLING", these are the ones that Kubler most likely used. He was the only brewery operating at the time in Cresent City. Map at right is circa 1903.

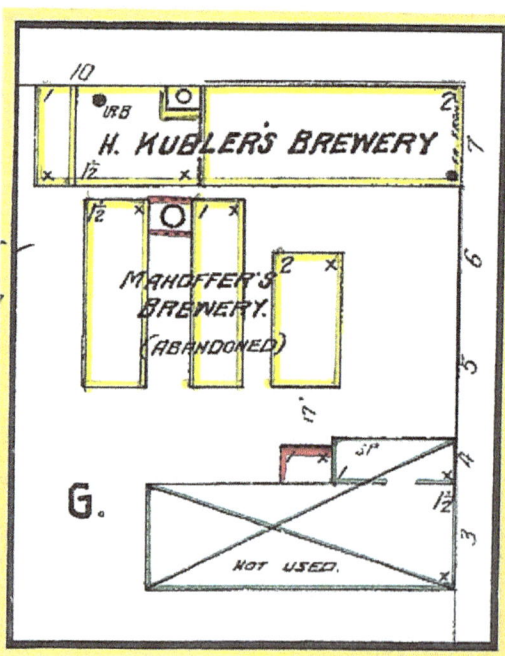

Front: DEUCHER & KALBEN / S. "monogram" F.
 (in round plate) /
 THIS BOTTLE / NOT TO BE SOLD

Quart, Applied Blob Top
Amber
Rarity: Ex. Rare

HISTORY: 1882 - 1886 finds Edward Kalben listed as Beer Bottler at 101 Tehema St. 1183 has Gottried Deucher also as a Beer Bottler at 243 Second. In 1886 they were listed together, as the Philadelphia Beer Bottling Co., at 245 Second.
This remains the same in 1887 and 1888, with the address now being 108 - 110 Jackson.
In 1888 Gottried Deucher was a salesman for the Cal. Bottling Co. and Edward Kalben was a secretary for the same. Company. This bottle should date from 1886 - 1888, the years they were listed together.

Front: DENVER. ALE. BREWING CO. / DENVER.

Squat Pint, Applied Double Collar Top
Amber
Rarity: Ex. Rare

Front: DENVER ALE BREWING CO. / DENVER

Pint, with Bulge Neck
Applied Double Collar Top
Amber
Rarity: Ex. Rare

HISTORY: The Denver Ale Brewing Co. was located at 6th and Cheyenne Sts., from 1869 - 1874. No further info.

Front: JACOB DENZLER / "3 drinking bears" / SAN
 FRANCISCO (in round plate) /
 THIS BOTTLE / NOT TO BE SOLD

Quart, Applied Blob Top
Amber, $550.00 - 2020 (repaired) GWA
Rarity: Ex. Rare

HISTORY: The first listing for Jacob Denzler was in 1867. He was employed by the Philadelphia Brewery Co. This lasted until 1882. He started his own business at that point, and is listed as a beer bottler. He still worked for the Philadelphia Brewery, but now as the bottler.
1886 has him as a milk carrier, with no more listings in the beer business. This bottle must have been used from around 1882 to 1885.
The label at right was trade marked by Denzler in 1881. Notice it is almost identical as the bottle embossing.

Front: F. A. DOHRMANN / SAN FRANCISCO / CAL. /
     BOTTLE NOT TO BE SOLD

Quart and ½ Pint, Tooled Blob Top
½ Pint has a Bulge Neck
Amber
½ Pint, $375.00 - 2020 GWA
Quart, $300.00 - 2017 ABA
Very Rare in both sizes

History. The earliest listing I found was for F.A. Dohrmann listed him as being in the liquor business at 310 O'Farrell St from 1893 to 1895. 1896 finds him as a driver for the National Bottling Company. He is still listed as a driver in 1897, but does not mention who his employer was.
1898 finds him as the proprietor of the Bavarian Bottling Company, at the corner of Montgomery Ave. and Chestnut St. He must have used these bottles at this time. He was in a partnership with George J. Kerth as beer bottlers in 1899, and 1900 finds him as the proprietor of the Western Bottling Company at 409 8th St. No further listings.

At some point Dohrmann must have sold his unused bottles to John Kroger of the Wunder Brewery as they have been found with Wunder labels on them.

Front: THOS. DOWNING / HANFORD / CAL. / NOT TO BE SOLD

½ Pint, Tooled Crown Top
Amber
Rarity: Rare
Note: Quarts and Pints probably exist from this bottler.

HISTORY: Thomas Downing started a bottling business in Hanford in 1891. He was joined in this venture in 1899, by Joseph Schnerger. They were the local agency for Wieland's and Rainier Beer. They prospered and lasted until they were closed by prohibition in 1918.

Front: "eagle" on shield" / EAGLE / BREWING CO.
SAN FRANCISCO

Quart, Pint and ½ Pint
Tooled Blob Top
Amber, ½ Pint, $200.00 - 2020 GWA
Varient: Embossing is lower on body.
Rarity: Rare in all sizes and varients.

Front: EAGLE BREWERY / SAN FRANCISCO CAL.
(embossed vertically) /
BOTTLES NEVER SOLD

Quart and Pint
Tooled Blob Top
Amber, Quart, $70.00 - 2009 ABA
Rarity: Scarce in both sizes

HISTORY: This version of the Eagle Brewery was started in 1900. There was an earlier brewery with the same name. They were located at 1329 Guerrero, with Carl Thornburg as the proprietor. Things remained the same in 1901.
The address is the same in 1902, but does not mention Carl Thornburg. 1903 - 1909 the listing changes to Eagle Brewery Co., Mfg. of Steam Beer & Porter, 2213 Harrison. This remains the same until J.H. Claasen is added as the proprietor in 1910 - 1911, with the address still on Harrison.
1912 brings an address change to 5050 Mission St. They remain here thru 1918, when prohibition forces them to close the doors in 1919.

Front: J. F. G. EGGERS / SAN FRANCISCO

Quart, Applied Ring Top
Amber
Rarity: Ex. Rare, Possibly Unique

HISTORY: Listings were sparse for J.F.G. Eggers. He was a saloon owner from 1878 to 1885 at 533 California St. In 1882 he was in a partnership with Henri Deters on another saloon, this one at 327-329 Bush. By 1886 he was listed as a bartender. No further listing. This style of bottle dates from the early to mid 1880's, so he must have had a sideline of bottling beer in his saloon. The bottle shown was found in Washington state, and is unique at this time.

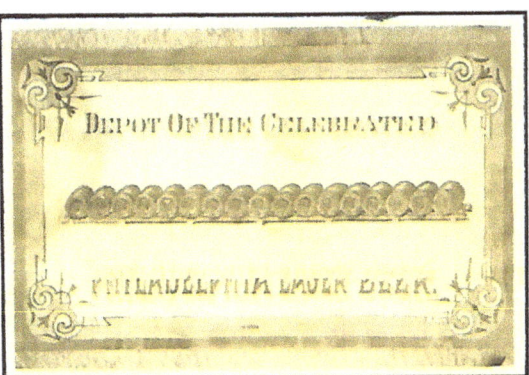

DEPOT of the CELEBRATED PHILADELPHIA LAGER BEER. LABEL TRADE MARKED in 1881 by J.F.G. EGGERS, S.F.

Front: ETNA BREWERY / ETNA MILLS

½ Pint, Tooled Blob and Crown Top
Amber, Blob Top, $20.00 - 2001 ABA
Rarity: Common with Blob Top
  Scarce with a Crown Top

Front: CHAS. KAPPLER / ETNA BREWERY / ETNA, CAL. (in round plate)

Quart, Pint, Tooled Crown Top
Amber and Aqua
Rarity: Quart size is rare
  Aqua Pint is very Rare

HISTORY: P. A. Heartstrand has started a brewery on the outskirts of Etna sometime before 1868. In 1872, Charles Kappler purchased it, and moved it to the town of Etna. The brewery itself was destroyed by fire in 1875, but the business survived and soon Kappler had built a new and larger plant. The brewery lasted until prohibition, and Kappler died shortly after. History courtesy of John Wendler.
Map of the Etna Brewery and Bottling Works is circa 1908.

Circa 1900 view of the Etna Brewey & Ice. Co.

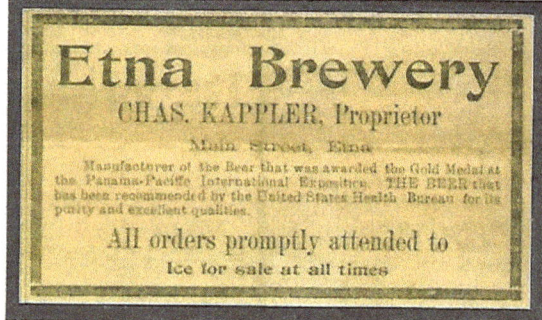
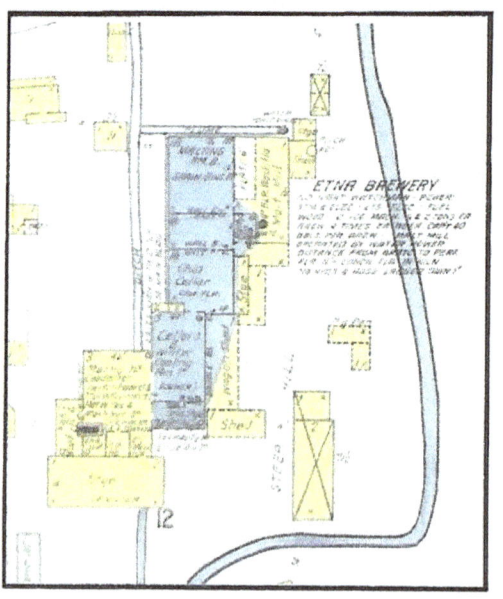
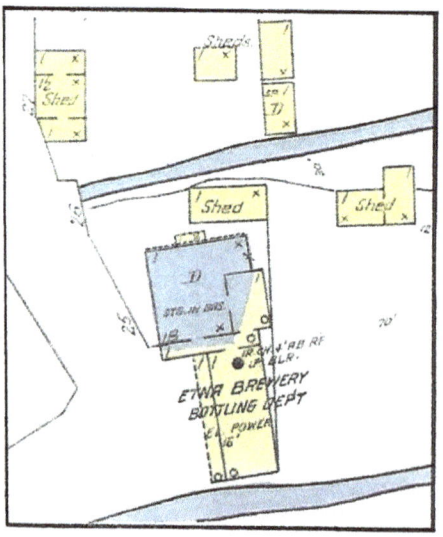

Beer Glass 3 ½"

Beer Glass 4 ¼"

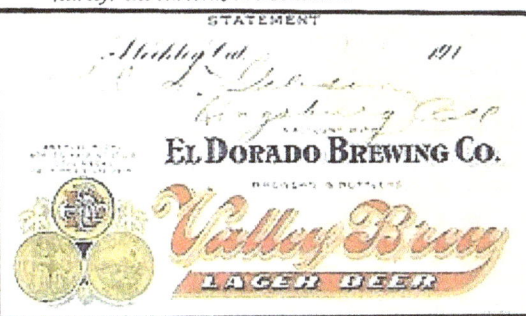
1893 View of the El Dorado Brewery

Front: EL DORADO BREWING CO. /
"monogram" / STOCKTON, CAL.

Quart, Pint and ½ Pint
Tooled Blob and Crown Top
Amber and Aqua
Rarity: all varients are Common

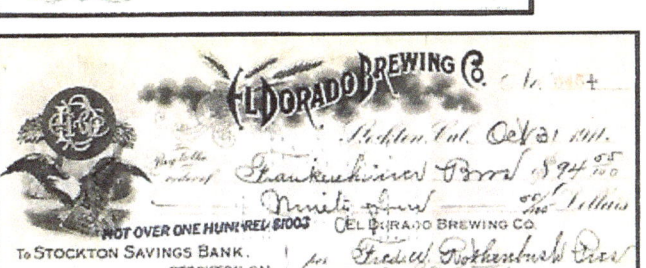

57

Front: EL DORADO / BREWING CO. /
STOCKTON, CAL.
(embossed vertically)

Quart, Pint and ½ Pint
Tooled Blob and Crown Top
Amber, $70.00 - 2020 GWA
Rarity: All varients are Common

HISTORY: In 1859, Peter Rothenbush purchased an existing brewery in Stockton, started in 1855, by Busch & Denacker. Then in 1860, Peter's brother Daniel bought out control of the brewery from the elder brother. When Daniel padded away, his son Fred took over, and built the brewery up to be one of the largest in the central valley. The Valley Brew Lager Beer brand was introduced in 1902. They has depots in many towns in northern Cal. The picture of the depot on the right is circa 1905, and the map is circa 1895.

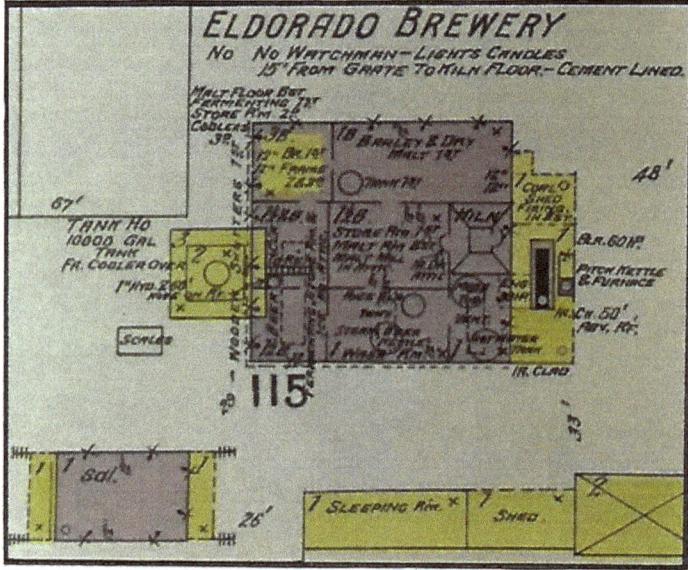

Below we have two early beer labels courtesy of Bob Welch.

XXX Porter Label on a ½ Pint
Enterprise Bottle

17" x 13" Enamel on
Steel Sign

Yosemite Lager Label on a Pint
Enterprise Bottle

Front: ENTERPRISE BREWING CO. /
KERN, CAL.
½ Pint, Tooled Crown Top
Amber
Rarity: Rare
HISTORY: no info at this time

Front: ENTERPRISE / BREWING CO. /
S.F. CAL. (embossed vertically)
½ Pint, Tooled Blob Top
Clear, $150.00 - 2009 ABA
Rarity: Rare

Front: ENTERPRISE / BREWING CO. /
S.F. CAL (embossed vertically)
Quart, Pint and ½ Pint
Tooled Blob and Crown Top
Amber
Rarity: Common in all varients

Front: ENTERPRISE BREWING CO. /
"monogram" / SAN FRANCISCO
(in round plate)
Quart and ½ Pint, Bulge Neck
Applied Blob Top
Red Amber, ½ Pint, $140.00 - 2017 ABA
Rarity: Rare in both sizes

Front: ENTERPRISE BREWING CO. /
S.F. CAL. (embossed vertically)
Quart, Applied Blob Top
Red Amber, $170.00 - 2017 ABA
Rarity: Very Rare

Front: ENTERPRISE BREWING CO. /
"monogram" / S.F. CAL.
(in round plate)
Quart, ½ Pint, Tooled Blob Top
Amber, ½ Pint, $40.00 - 2020 GWA
Rarity: Scarce in both sizes

Front: ENTERPRISE / "monogram" / BREWING CO. S.F.
Quart, Applied Blob Top
Amber
Rarity: Scarce

Front: ENTERPRISE / "monogram" / BREWING CO. S. F.

Quart and Pint
Tooled Blob and Crown Top
Amber
Rarity: Common in all varients

HISTORY: The Enterprise Brewing Co. was founded in 1874, by F. Hildebrandt & Co. They were located at 2015 - 2019 Folsom their entire history.
This listing was unchanged until 1891, when Ulrich Remensperger was listed as president. This also remained unchanged to at least prohibition when research was stopped. Embossing pattern was trade marked in 1893, see drawing. Map is circa 1900/

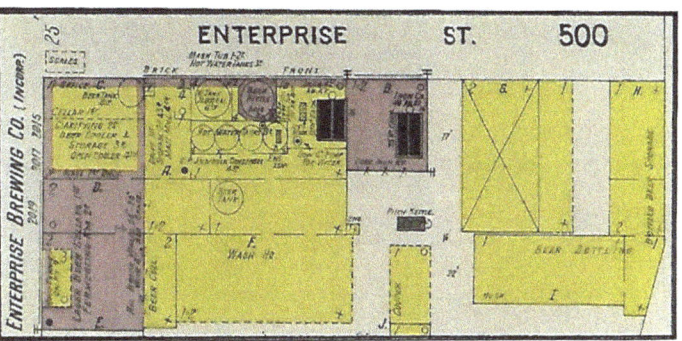

ENTERPRISE BREWERY, 2015-2023 FOLSOM STREET

Extra Pale Lager label, trade marked in 1892 by the Enterprise Brewing Co. S.F.

Enterprise Standard Beer label, trade marked in 1898 by the Enterprise Brewing Co. S.F.

Frisco's Best label, trade marked in 1896 by the Enterprise Bottling Co. S.F.

E.B.C. Bohemian Lager label, trade marked in 1898 by the Enterprise Brewing Co. S.F.

Milwaukee Pilsener Export Lager label, trade marked in 1891 by the Enterprise Brewery, F. Hillebrandt & Co. S.F.

Enterprise Bohemian Lager label, trade marked in 1898 by the Enterprise Brewing co. S.F.

Lowen Brau Export Lager, label trade marked in 1895 by the Enterprise Brewing Co. S.F.

Front: EUREKA GINGER BEER CO. / "monogram" / S. F. CAL.
½ Pint, Tooled Blob Top
Amber
Rarity: Very Rare

HISTORY: In searching thru the San Francisco directories from 1890 - 1918, the year this bottle should have been in use, I could find nothing on the S.F. Ginger Beer Co.

Front: FRANKS BROS. / SAN FRANCISCO

    Quart, Pint and ½ Pint
    Tooled Blob Top
    Amber and Clear and Aqua
    Varient: Bulge Neck Quart
    ½ Pint, Amber, $90.00 - 2020 (chip) GWA
    ½ Pint, Clear, $70.00 - 2020 (chip) GWA
    Rarity: Scarce in the Quart size
           Rare in Amber in the Pint sizes and ½ Pint size
           Ex. Rare in Clear and Aqua, ½ Pints
           Bulge Neck Quart is Rare

HISTORY: The first listing in the bottling business states, James Franks, Jr. located at Fillmore and Herman. In 1896 its Joseph, James and Edward Franks at the same address. This remained the same until 1902, when Joseph left the firm.
By 1905 the address had changed to 98 Fillmore. No listings in 1906.
Then from 1907 - 1910, they were listed as Franks Bros, E & J, Beer Bottlers at 98 Fillmore. No further listings in the beer business.

Front: FRESNO BREWING CO. / FRESNO / CAL. (in round plate)

    Quart, Tooled Crown Top
    Amber
    Rarity: Scarce

HISTORY: The Fresno Brewing Co. was in business from 1900 until 1920, located on E. Heaton Ave. Earnst Eilert and Son were the proprietors. Beer glass is from 1903, bottle label is 1907. Map circa 1906.

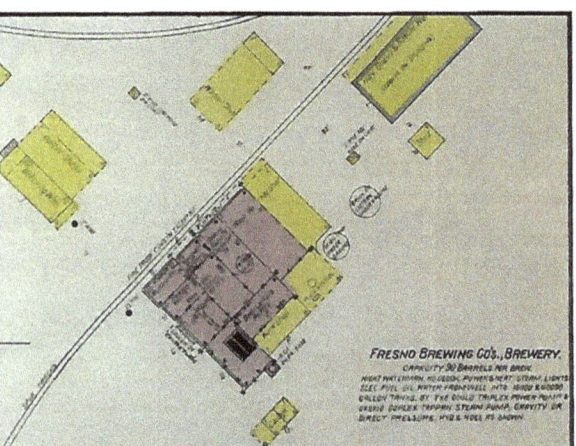

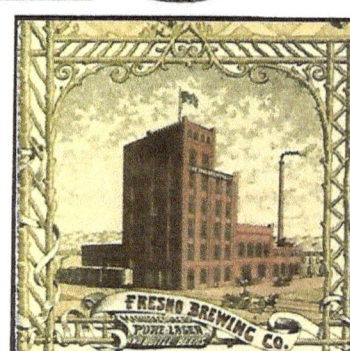

Front: CHRIS FELDMAN & CO. / 14, 16 AND 18 / GEARY ST. / SAN FRANCISCO

    Pint, Tooled Blob Top
    Aqua, $325.00 - 2017 ABA
    Rarity: Ex. rare

HISTORY: I could find nothing on this bottle in the San Francisco directories, in the 1890 - 1918 time frame. It should have been used during this time.

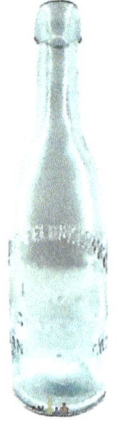

Front: FINK & MUGLER / BOTTLERS / KESWICK, CAL.
            (in round plate)

Quart, Pint and ½ Pint
Tooled Blob and Crown Top
Bulge Neck
Amber, ½ Pint, $275.00 - 2020 GWA
Rarity: Quart is Very Rare
            Pint and ½ Pint are Rare

HISTORY: No doubt an offshoot of the Mugler Brewery of Sisson. The bottling
              plant in Keswick was operating from the early 1890's to about
              1909. Henry Watson bought out Fink at that point. No other info.

Front: PROPERTY / OF / FREY & CO. / SAN RAFAEL

Quart, Pint and ½ Pint
Tooled Blob and Crown Top
Amber
Rarity: all sizes and varients are Rare

HISTORY: The Lang Brothers of San Francisco were likely the fisrt distributers
              of Fredericksburg Beer in Marin Co. They were succeeded by Frey &
              Lenz as early as 1897. They were located at the corner of 4TH and
              D St. John Lenz left the partnership later in 1897 and Franz Frey
              became the sole proprietor of the wholesale liquor business.
              These bottles were used after Frey became the sole Prop. and would
              date from around 1900 until he closed the business. No other info.
              On the 1907 map, you can see the liquor store equipped for bottling
              beer. This was the Frey & Co. location as early as 1894.

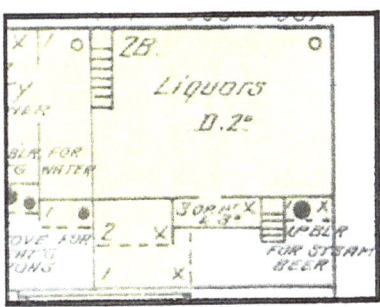

Front: FREDERICKSBURG / BOTTLING COMPANY /
            "monogram in shield" / LAGER BEER / S. F.
            (all in rect. plate)

1/2 Pint, Tooled Blob Top
Amber, Clear and Amethyst
Clear, $40.00 - 2020 GWA
Rarity: Scarce in Clear and Amethyst
            Rare in Amber

Front: FREDERICKSBURG / "monogram in shield" /
            BOTTLING CO. S. F.

5 ½ Sample, Tooled Blob Top
Yellow Amber, $90.00 - 2020 GWA
Rarity: Rare

Front: FREDERICKSBURG / "monogram
in shield" / BOTTLING CO. S.F.
(in round plate) /
THIS BOTTLE NOT / TO
BE SOLD

Quart, Pint, Applied Blob Top
Green, Quart, $60.00 - 2009 ABA
Pint, $140.00 - 2014 ABA
Rarity: Common in both sizes

Front: FREDERICKSBURG /
"monogram in shield" /
BOTTLING CO. S.F.
(in round plate) /
THIS BOTTLE NOT /
TO BE SOLD

Quart, Pint, Applied Blob Top
Red Amber, Quart, $150.00 - 2017 ABA
Rarity: Scarce in both sizes

Front: FREDERICKSBURG /
"monogram in shield" /
BOTTLING CO. S.F.
(in round plate) /
THIS BOTTLE NOT /
TO BE SOLD

Quart, Tooled Blob Top
Yellow Olive
Rarity: Scarce

Front: PROPERTY OF / FREDERICKSBURG /
BREWERY / SAN JOSE, CAL.
(in round plate)

Quart, Applied and Tooled Blob Top
Bulge Neck
Red Amber
Regular Amber
Varient: has S.F. & P.G.W. on base,
Tooled Top, regular Amber
Rarity: Rare in all varients and colors

HISTORY: Will follow at the end of the Fredericksburg
listings.

Front: FREDERICKSBURG / "monogram in shield" / BOTTLING CO. S.F. (in round plate) / THIS BOTTLE NOT / TO BE SOLD

Quart, Tooled Blob and Crown Top
Amber
Rarity: Common with a Blob Top
Scarce with a Crown Top

Front: FREDERICKSBURG / "monogram in shield" / BOTTLING CO. S.F. (in round plate)

Pint, ½ Pint, Tooled Blob and Crown Top
Amber, ½ Pint, $30.00 - 2020 GWA
Rarity: Clear Pint is Ex. Rare, 1 Damaged Specimen
Common in Amber, both sizes

Front: FREDERICKSBURG BREWING CO. / L. CERF & SON / VENTURA, CAL.

Pint, ½ Pint, Tooled Blob Top
Amber, ½ Pint, $550.00 - 2020 GWA
Pint, $180.00 - 2002 ABA
Rarity: Rare in both Sizes

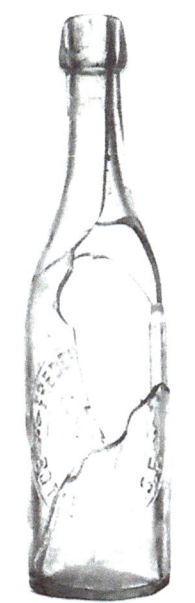

Front: FREDERICKSBURG BEER / C.E. ROOS AGT. / SEATTLE, WASH.

Quart, ½ Pint, Tooled Blob Top
Amber
Variant: S.F. & P.G.W. on base of Quart
Rarity: all varients are Rare

Front: FREDERICKSBURG / "monogram in shield" / BOTTLING CO. S.F. (in round plate) / THIS BOTTLE NOT TO BE SOLD

Quart, Tooled Blob and Crown Top
Amber and Aqua
Rarity: Common in Amber
Rare in Aqua
Rare with a Crown Top

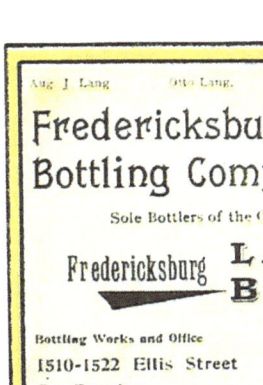

Front: FREDERICKSBURG / "monogram in shield" /
        BOTTLING CO. S.F. (in round plate)
Base: S.F. & P.G.W.
    Quart, Bulge Neck, Tooled Blob Top
    Amber
    Rarity: Rare

Extra Pale label on a Fredericksburg pint bottle   4 ½" Beer Glass

Early view of the Fredericksburg Brewery in San Jose

HISTORY: The Fredericksburg Brewery was established in 1869, by Fred Kranhenberg, on Cinnabar & Alameda in San Jose. In 1870, Alfred Recard joined as a partner, continuing business in the original building. Then in 1872, Recard sold his interest to Schramm & Schnabel, and the name of the firm became Kranhenberg & Co. Also in 1872, the new company erected many new buildings on the site, while production had increased to between four and five thousand barrels a year.

In 1876, Kranhenberg sold his stock to Schramm & Schabel. In 1880, E.A. Denicke bought out Schramm's share of the business, with the partnership becoming Schnabel and Denicke.

The period of 1881 thru 1888 saw great growth and expansion, with Fredericksburg agencies and bottling depots being established in many western states and cities. The brewery produced lager beer from the start and brewed many different styles. Genuine Salvator, Pilsner, Extra Pale, Pschorr, Culmbacher and Bavaria Lager Beer were the names in 1894.

As early as 1878, the brewery established an agency in San Francisco at 621 Brannan St. but its not clear who did the bottling. Then in 1880 they moved to 539 California St.

The brewery established a bottling depot in Los Angeles in 1886. E.C. Schnabel was the proprietor, son of co-owner Ernst Schnabel. Also in 1886 Arnold and Rudolph Postel, and the Lang Bros, were used as local bottlers. By 1887, the Lang Bros. were the sole bottlers of Fredericksburg beer in San Francisco. This began a long term business partnership, and the forming of the Fredericksburg Bottling Co.

Ernst Schnabel managed the brewery in San Jose, while his partner managed the bottling and outside interests from San Francisco. The company had become one of the most important commercial institutions of the state.

The bottling works handled the bottling of beer for export to other countries, and for local markets. Beer distributed for other west coast areas was sent in kegs to local agents, who either bottled the beer or sent it out to be bottled by a local bottler. Some of the west coast bottlers were: Charles Maurer, in San Jose, Oakland Bottling Co. in Oakland, J. Luttrell & Son, San Diego, H. Loose in Lovelock, Nevada, C.E. Roos, Seattle, Wash, Hoefer & Mevius in Redding, H.C. Heidtmann in Reno, C. Schneer, Sacramento and an agency in Klamath Falls, Oregon.

In 1890, controlling interest in the company was purchased by San Francisco Breweries, Ltd. It was a British syndicate that especially formed to acquire breweries in the San Francisco bay area. They consisted of Fredericksburg and Pacific breweries of San Jose, Hofburg Brewery of West Berkeley, the Oakland Brewery and Brooklyn Brewery of Oakland, the United States Brewery, Chicago Brewery, South San Francisco Brewery and the Willows Brewery, all of San Francisco.

By 1899, four of the breweries had been sold. Of the remaining six, the 1906 earthquake destroyed three more. Only the John Wieland, the Brooklyn and the Fredericksburg Brewing Co. remained.

In May of 1912, the Fredericksburg Brewing Co. announced that their beer was now "bottled by the brewery, not at the brewery, which would indicate that they were now the owners of the Fredericksburg Bottling Co. as well. The company continued to operate as the Fredericksburg Bottling Co. until 1918. At that point the brewery and bottling co. were both closed by prohibition.

History, photos and ads, courtesy of Gary Flynn, brewerygems.com

Pattern for the Fredericksburg bottle stopper. Trade marked in 1899 by the Fredericksburg Bottling Co. S.F.

Fredericksburg Lager Beer label. Trade marked by the Fredericksburg Bottlin Co. S.F. in 1893.

Fredericksburg Extra Pale label. Trade marked in 1893 by the Fredericksburg Bottling Co. S.F.

Fredericksruhe Lager Beer label. Trade marked in 1892 by John Kroger S.F.

Fredericksburg Lager Beer, bottle and neck label. Trade marked in 1893 by Abramson Hennisch & Co. San Jose.

Fredericksburg Bottling Co. ca.1905

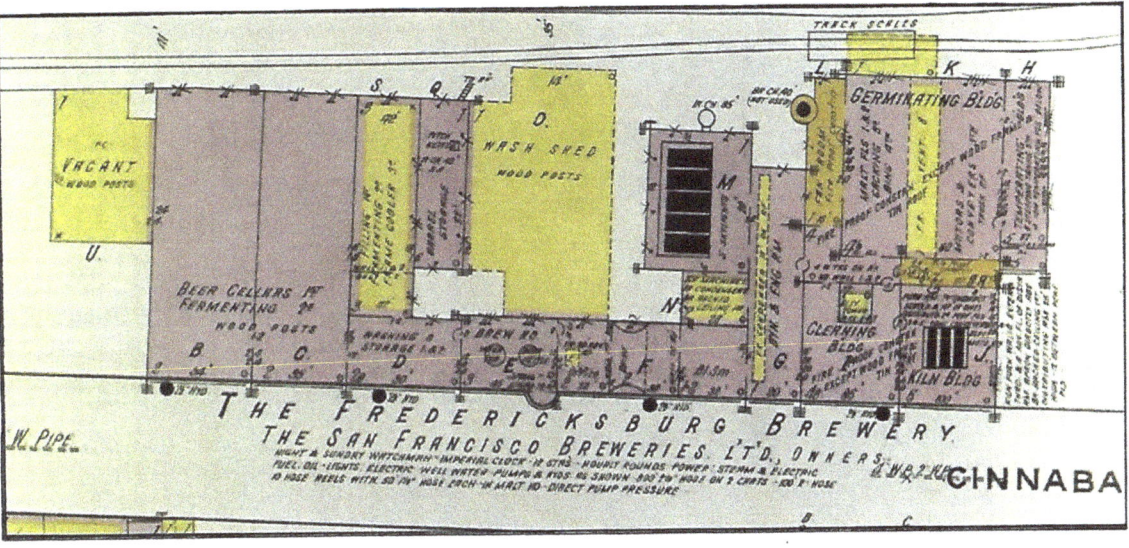

Front: GAMBRINUS BREWING CO. / "monogram" /
PORTLAND, OR. (in round plate)
Re: THIS BOTTLE IS NEVER SOLD

   Quart, Pint and ½ Pint
   Tooled Blob Top
   Amber
   Varient: some have a Bulge Neck
   Rarity: Scarce in the Quart and Pint size
            Rare in the ½ Pint size

Front: GAMBRINUS BREWING CO. / "monogram" /
PORTLAND, OR. (in round plate)

   Quart, Pint, Bulge Neck
   Tooled Blob and Crown Top
   Amber and Aqua
   Varient: "GAMBRINUG" is misspelled on the pint
   Rarity: Scarce in Amber
            Aqua is Rare

Front: GAMBRINUS BREWING CO. /
PORTLAND / ORE.
   (in round plate)

   ½ Pint, Tooled Crown Top
   Amber
   Rarity: Scarce

   HISTORY: Louis Feurer was the founder in 1875. Located on 22nd. St. from 1892 to 1916 the brewery was at 24th and Washington. Louis Feurer ad is circa 1884, and the map is circa 1889. No other info.

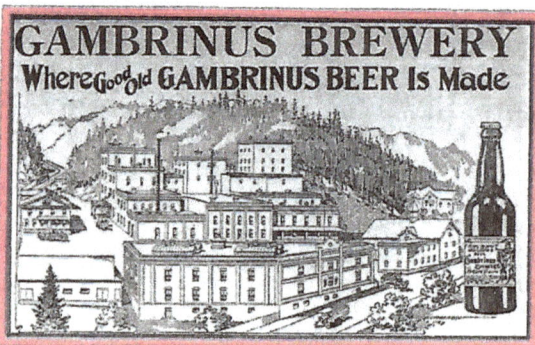

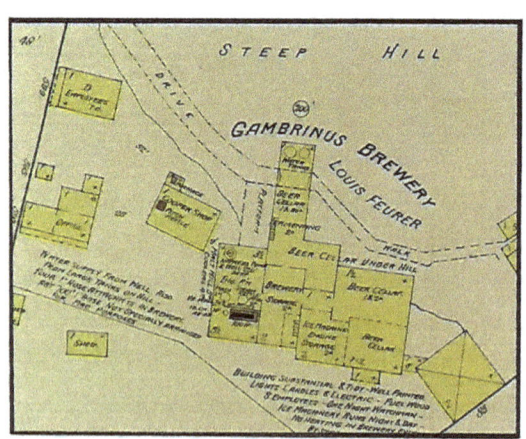

Front: GAMBRINUS BOTTLING CO. / "monogram" /
SAN FRANCISCO, CAL. (in round plate) /
REGISTERED

Pint, Bulge Neck
Tooled Blob Top
Amber, $50.00 - 2005 ABA
Rarity: Scarce

Front: GAMBRINUS BOTTLING CO. / "monogram" /
SAN FRANCISCO, CAL. (in round plate) /
REGISTERED

Pint, 10 Sided Mug Base
Bulge Neck
Tooled Blob Top
Amber
Rarity: Rare

Front: GAMBRINUS BOTTLING CO. / "monogram" /
SAN FRANCISCO, CAL. / THIS
BOTTLE IS NOT SOLD

Quart, Pint and ½ Pint
Tooled Blob Top
Amber and Clear
½ Pint, Amber, $30.00 - 2020 GWA
Rarity: ½ Pint in Clear is Ex. Rare
½ Pint in Amber is Scarce
Quart and Pint are Common

Front: GAMBRINIS BOTTLING CO. / "monogram" /
SAN FRANCISCO, CA; / THIS
BOTTLE IS NOT SOLD
Base: S. F. & P.G.W.

Quart and Pint
Bulge Neck
Tooled Blob Top
Amber, Quart, $50.00 - 2006 ABA
Rarity: Both sizes are Scarce

HISTORY: 1887 is the first listing for the Gambrinus Bottling Co.
Louis Mohlfeldt and Gustave Liebold were the proprietors. Address was, 25 27 Stockton, for 1887 - 1891, with the same props.
They were not listed between 1892 and 1897.
Gambrinus Bottling Co. is again listed in 1898 - 1904, with Gustave Liebold as the proprietor at 316 10th. In 1906, they are at 160 13th. No further listings.

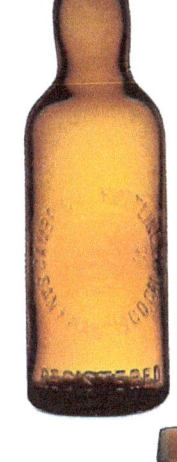

Front: D. GERMANUS / 228 / MORRISON ST. / PORTLAND /
OR. / HONEST MEASURE STORE / RETURN
THIS BOTTLE AND GET 10 CENTS
(in round plate)

½ Gallon Picnic Beer
Tooled Blob Top
Aqua, $375.00 - 1999 (chip) ABA
Rarity: Very Rare

History: The Germanus Co. was a wholesale liquor house. He was in business in Portland from 1893 until 1925. Even though this looks like an over sized beer, I believe it contained wine.

Front: GARDEN CITY BOTTLING WORKS / GERDTS BROS. / SAN JOSE, CAL.

Quart, Pint and ½ Pint
Tooled Crown Top
Amber, ½ Pint, $40.00 - 2020 (chip) GWA
Rarity: Scarce is all szies

HISTORY: The Garden City Brewery was started by Dominick and George Geoffroy in 1884. In 1897 the Business moved to the corner of San Pedro and Bassett Sts. The Gerdts Bros. were agents until the doors were closed in 1918 due to prohibition. Map below circa 1915.

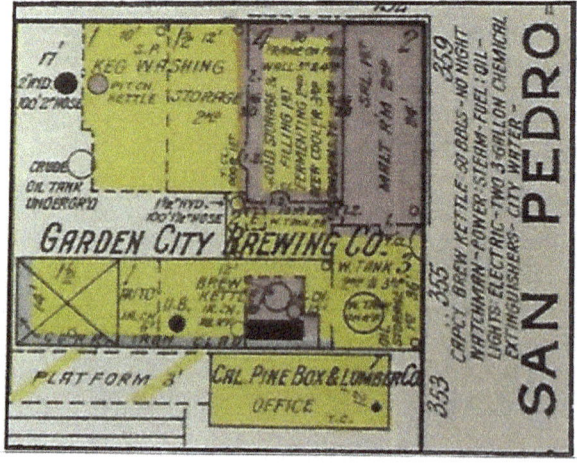

Front: BEER STEAM BOTTLING CO. / W G & SON / WM. GOEPPERT
        & SON / SAN FRANCISCO

   Quart, Applied Ring Top
   Aqua
   Rarity: Very Rare

Front: BEER STEAM BOTTLING CO. / W G & SON / WM. GOEPPERT
        & SON / SAN FRANCISCO   (in round plate)

   Quart, Applied Blob Top
   Amber
   Rarity: Ex. Rare

HISTORY: 1882 was the first listing for William Goeppert. He was a bottler of Felson Beer, at 2208 Taylor. This stayed the same thru 1884. In 1885 George Goeppert joined the listing and it only states they are beer bottlers at 519 Chestnut. There is no mention of Beer Steam Bottling Co. in the directories, but I would guess that the bottles were used in the 1882 - 1885 period.
1886 has George I. Goeppert and William Goeppert Jr., plus Frederick Haussler at the 519 Chestnut St. address, as beer bottlers.
1887 - 1888 has John Rapp joining George Goeppert in the bottling business at NE Cor. of McAllister and Franklin Sts.
William Goeppert surfaces again in 1889 thru 1891 as a bottling forman for the Chicago Bottling Co.
In 1892 thru 1898 he is working the same job for the John Wieland Brewing Co. No further listings.

Note: In 1889 George Goeppert is shown on the map below to be the proprietor of the Yolo Brewery in Woodland. There are no embossed bottles from this brewery. George must be William's brother. The author dug one of the William Goeppert bottles in Woodland and heard of two others being dug there as well. Seems that George used them at the Woodland Brewery, when he was the proprietor there.

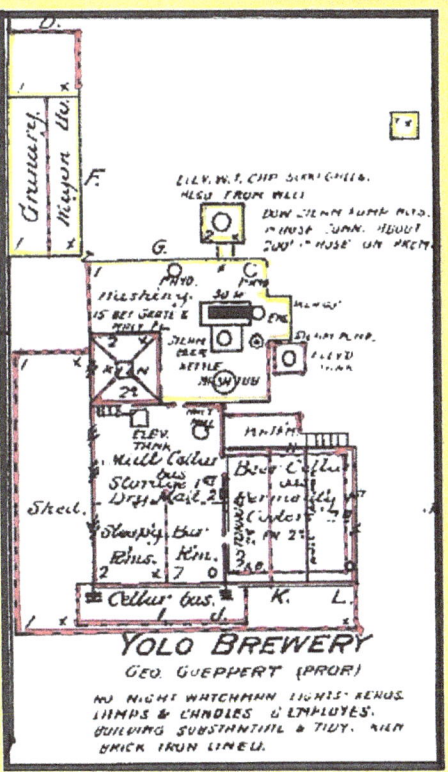

Front: THEO GIER CO. OAKLAND /
       & / SAN FRANCISCO /
       RETURN BOTTLE / AND
       GET 10 CENTS
          (in round plate)

   ½ Gallon Picnic Beer
   Tooled Blob Top
   Amber
   Rarity: Rare

HISTORY: The Theo Gier Co. was a wholesale liquor distributor from the 1890's until prohibition. This bottle probably contained wine, even though it is considered to be a beer.

Front: GOLD EDGE BOTTLING WORKS / J. F. DEININGER / VALLEJO

Quart, Pint and ½ Pint
Tooled Blob and Crown Top
Amber and Aqua
½ Pint, Amber, $40.00 - 2020 GWA
½ Pint, Aqua, $30.00 - 2020 GWA
Rarity: ½ Pint in Aqua is Scarce
 All other varients are commom.

Front: GOLD EDGE BOTTLING WORKS / J. F. DEININGER / VALLEJO
Base: S. F. & P.G.W.

Quart, Bulge Neck
Tooled Blob Top
Amber
Varient: Base is plain
Rarity: Scarce

HISTORY: *Fred Deininger started the Philadelphia Brewery in South Vallejo in 1870. It was then on Chestnut, which is now Sonoma Blvd.*
His son Jacob bought half interest in 1885, and became proprietor in 1891. Their Gold Edge Beer was the popular brand.
The Gold Edge Bottling Works and the Philadelphia Brewery bottled Wieland's Extra Pale, and Lohengren Beer from the Chicago Brewery in S.F., as well as their own brands. J. F. deininger's stayed involved until 1909, when left for health reasons. He died in 1916. History courtesy of John Wendler. Map is circa 1901, as is the Gold Edge ad. Philadelphia Brewery ad is circa 1881.

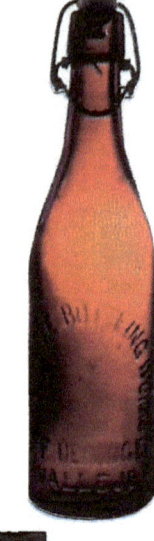

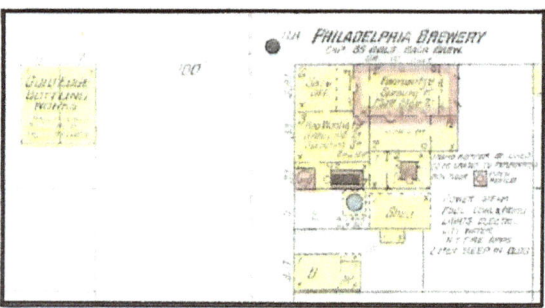

Front: GOLDEN GATE BOTTLING WORKS / CHAS. ROSCHMANN / SAN FRANCISCO
Re: TRADE "bear" MARK / THIS BOTTLE NEVER SOLD

½ Pint, Tooled Blob Top
Amber, $220.00 - 2020 GWA
Yellow, $600.00 - 2020 GWA
Varient: without "THIS BOTTLE NEVER SOLD"
Rarity: All varients are Rare

Front: GOLDEN GATE BOTTLING WORKS / TRADE "bear" MARK / SAN FRANCISCO

Quart, Pint and ½ Pint
Tooled Blob Top
Amber, ½ Pint, $110.00 - 2020 GWA
Rarity: Scarce in all sizes

Front: GOLDEN GATE BOTTLING WORKS / CHAS. ROSCHMANN / SAN FRANCISCO / THIS BOTTLE IS NEVER SOLD

Quart, Pint and ½ Pint
Tooled Blob Top
Amber, ½ Pint, $170.00 - 2020 GWA
Rarity: All sizes are Rare

Front: GOLDEN GATE BOTTLING WORKS / TRADE "bear" MARK / CHAS. ROSCHMANN / SAN FRANCISCO / THIS BOTTLE IS NEVER SOLD

Quart, Pint and ½ Pint
Tooled Blob Top
Amber
Rarity: Rare in all Sizes

Front: GOLDEN GATE BOTTLING WORKS / TRADE "bear" MARK / McGRATH & MAHONEY / SAN FRANCISCO

Quart, Pint and ½ Pint
Amber
Varient: "ZIMMERMAN" is the agent
Rarity: Very Rare in all sizes

HISTORY: The first listing for the Golden gate Bottling Works was in 1897. Charles Roschmann was the Prop. at 120 Shotwell. He is first listed as far back as 1884 as a bottler at the same address. In 1898 there was no listing.
Then from 1899 until 1902 it is still listed at 120 Shotwell, with Roschmann as the agent.
McGrath and Mahoney are listed for the first and only time in 1903, but no occupation is listed.
In 1904 and 1905, the botting works is still on Shotwell, with only McGrath listed. No listing in 1906.
Then from 1907 to 1910, the bottling works is on Valley. This is all very confusing for sure. It seems that McGrath & Mahoney were only with the firm in 1903, Roschmann from 1896 to 1899.
The embossing pattern was trade marked by Roschmann in 1896.

Front: GRACE BROS. BREWING CO. / "monogram" /
SANTA ROSA, CAL. / THIS BOTTLE
NOT TO BE SOLD

   Quart, Pint and ½ Pint
   Tooled Blob Top
   Amber, ½ Pint, $20.00 - 2020 GWA
   Rarity: Common in all sizes

Front: GRACE BROS. BREWING CO. / "monogram" /
SANTA ROSA, CAL. / THIS BOTTLE
IS NEVER SOLD
Base: S. F. & P.G.W.

   Quart, Pint and ½ Pint
   Tooled Blob Top
   Bulge Neck
   Amber
   Varient: Base is blank
   Varient: without "BOTTLE IS NEVER SOLD"
   Rarity: Scarce
          Varients are Rare

Front: GRACE BROS. BREWING CO. / "monogram" /
SANTA ROSA, CAL. / THIS BOTTLE
NOT TO BE SOLD

   Quart and Pint, Tooled Crown Top
   Bulge Neck
   Amber
   Rarity: Scarce in both sizes

Front: GRACE BROS. / BREWING CO. /
"monogram" / SANTA ROSA, CAL. /
BOTTLE NOT TO BE SOLD

   Quart, Tooled Blob and Crown Top
   Amber
   Rarity: Common with Blob Top
          Scarce with Crown Top

HISTORY: Frank and Joseph Grace purchased the Santa Rosa Steam Brewery from the Haltinner family after Jacob Haltinner passed away. This was in February of 1897. Then in May of the same year, the brewery burned down. It was a complete loss. The brothers rebuilt the business and it was open again in July of 1897.
The brewery grew to one of the largest north of San Francisco. It even survived the 1906 earthquake, which devastated Santa Rosa. After prohibition the company acquired several other brewing companys and added to their empire. The company was finally put to rest in 1970, as the buildings were torn down.
Large bottle label courtesy of Bob Welch. Photos are circa early 1900's, and the map circa 1904.

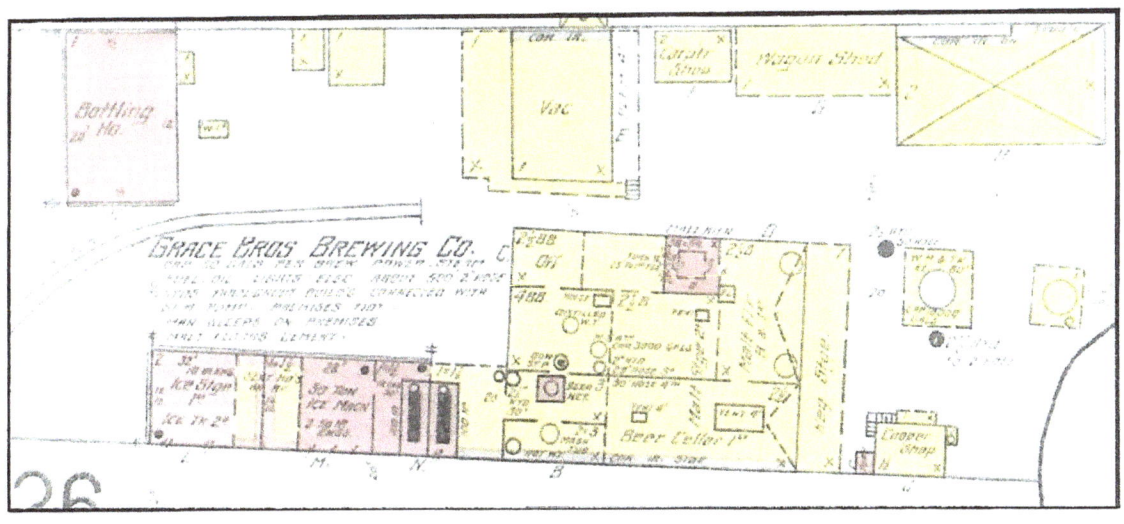

Front: GOLD MEDAL AGENCY / C. MAURER PROP. /
SAN JOSE, CAL. (embossed vertically)

Quart, Pint and ½ Pint
Applied and Tooled Blob Top
Bulge Neck
Red Amber, ½ Pint, $30.00 - 2020 (flake) GWA
    Pint, $130.00 - 2006 ABA
Rarity: All Red Amber varients are Scarce with applied Tops
   All Tooled Tops are Common in Amber

HISTORY: No info at this time. Maurer must have owned this
    company before the San Jose Bottling Works.

Front: THE A. GOUX CO. / BOTTLERS / SANTA BARBARA

Quart, Tooled Crown Top
Amber
Rarity: Rare

HISTORY: The Goux family owned a winery and olive
    orchard in the 1905 - 1915 period. This
    bottle may have contained olive oil.
    No further info at this time.

Front: PROPERTY OF / JOS. HAMMER / EXPORT BEER /
VISALIA, CAL.

½ Pint, Bulge Neck
Tooled Blob Top
Amber, $600.00 - 2020 GWA
Rarity: Ex. Rare

HISTORY: In 1895, Andrew Hammer and his brother Joseph acquired the John Wieland
    distribution plant from Davis and Knupp. It was at 330 N. Stevenson. They
    bottled beer together until 1899 when Andrew passed away. Joseph ran the
    business alone until he passed in 1903. This bottle should date from 1900 to
    1903. Picture below in the same era.

Front: HANFORD ICE CO. / HANFORD / CAL.

Quart, Bulge Neck
Tooled Blob Top
Amber
Rarity: Rare

Front: HANFORD / ICE / COMPANY
        (in round plate)

Quart, Bulge Neck
Tooled Blob Top
Amber
Rarity: Scarce

Front: HANFORD / ICE / COMPANY

½ Pint, Tooled Blob Top
Amber
Rarity: Very Rare

HISTORY: The Hanford Ice Co. was incorporated in 1903, with George Aydelott as the manager. They were located on West 6th St. They were also bottling soda water as well as beer, as hutchinson, crown top and seltzer water type bottles exist from this company. They were still in business after prohibition due to the soda water trade. Picture is circa 1903. History notes courtesy of Peck Markota. Map is circa 1913.

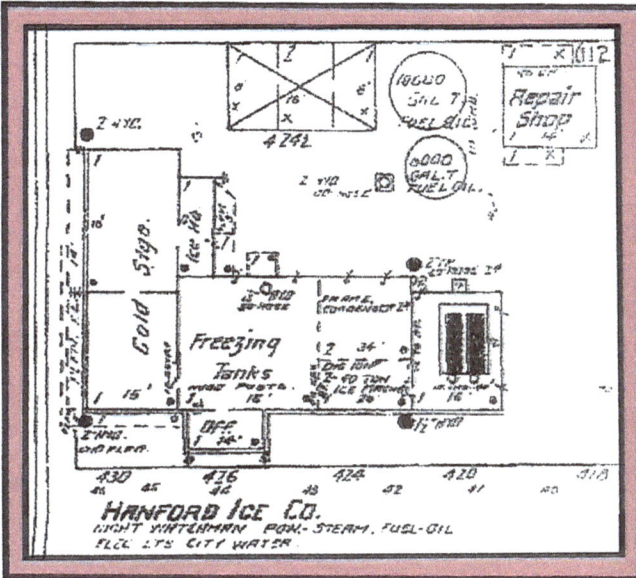

Front: HANSEN & KAHLER OAKLAND, CAL.
(embossed around shoulder)

Quart, Pint and ½ Pint
Tooled Blob and Crown Top
Amber, ½ Pint, Blob Top, $50.00 - 2020 GWA
Rarity: ½ Pint Blob Top is Rare
All other Varients are Common

Front: HANSEN & KAHLER / H & K / OAKLAND, CAL.

Quart, Tooled Blob Top
Amber
Rarity: Common

Front: HANSEN & KAHLER / H & K / COR 8TH AND / WEBSTER STS. / OAKLAND

Quart, Tooled Blob Top
Bulge Neck
Amber
Rarity: Very Rare

HISTORY: In 1897, Peter Hansen and Charles Kahler took over the Buffalo Lager Beer agency from Henry Braun. They were located at the 8th and Webster St. address, and they remained there until 1907. After that their new location was at 870 Webster. They went out of business in 1908. They advertised heavily in the local papers at the time, and were very successful. The ads are circa 1896 to 1907.
Some of the history notes courtesy of John Wendler.

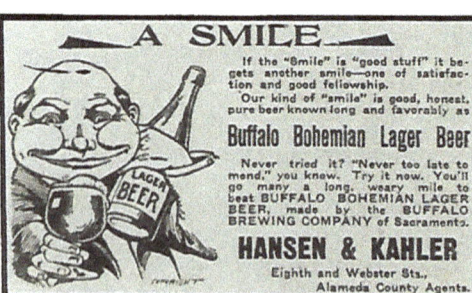

Front: HOEFER & MEVIUS / BOTTLERS / REDDING, CAL.
(embossed vertically)

Quart, Tooled Crown Top
Bulge Neck
Amber
Varient: smaller embossing
Rarity: Common

HISTORY: Mr. Mevius took over for Burgbacher when he left the company. They bottled Wieland Beer products as well as Fredericksburg Beer until sometime in 1903.

Front: FERD HEIM / BREWING CO. / BEER / BOTTLED BY / HYMAN LEVIN / PUEBLO (in round plate)
Re: THIS BOTTLE / NOT TO BE SOLD

Quart and Pint, Tooled Blob Top
Amber
Rarity: Both sizes are Scarce

HISTORY: No info at this time.

Front: HENRY HOCK / 224 TURK ST. / S.F.

Pint, Tooled Blob Top
Amber
Rarity: Very Rare

History: This name on this bottle is somewhat of a mystery. There were a few Henry Hocks in the directories, but none were listed in the beer bottling business. The only Hock that was, his name was listed as Nicholas Hock, Bottler in 1907 until 1910, no address given. In 1911, he was listed as brewer. No other info.

Front: HONOLULU BREWING & MALTING CO. LTD. / HONOLULU, T.H. (embossed vertically)

Quart, and Pint, Tooled Crown Top
Bulge Neck
Aqua
Rarity: Common

Front: HONOLULU / BREWING CO. / HONOLULU, H.T.

Quart, Tooled Blob Top
Bulge Neck
Aqua
Rarity: Scarce

HISTORY: The Brewery construction was started in 1899, and the first brew was in 1901. Located at 547 Queen St. It lasted until prohibition in 1918. Map is circa 1914.

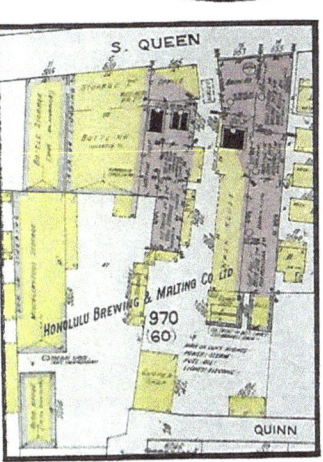

Front: JOHN HAUB / "monogram" / SACRAMENTO, CAL.

Quart and Pint, Bulge Neck
Tooled Blob and Crown Top
Amber
Rarity: Scarce in both style of tops

HISTORY: John Haub came from Nevada where he had operated restaurant. He arrived in Sacramento in 1885 and bought the restaurant of the Fisher Co.. In 1900 haub decided to go into the bottling business as well as his restaurant and other businesses. He had acquired the Rainier Beer agency and the Sacramento directory shows him at 1013 - 1015 6th St., along with the Pabst Café. He was no longer listed after 1905, and George Ticoulet took over the Rainier business. History courtesy of John Wendler.

Front: F. A. HEIMS / BOTTLING WORKS / LOS ANGELES, CAL.
(in round plate)

Quart, Tooled Crown Top
Bulge Neck
Amber
Rarity: Very Rare

HISTORY: Ferdinand Heim came to Los Angeles in 1891. He took an inheritance and started a bottling business at 401 Ramirez. This was most likely in 1895.
In 1901 he expanded the company to include brewing. To accommodate this he moved to 1834-1868 North Main. In 1903 he sold out to the Los Angeles Brewing Co. of Edward Mathie. Heim died in 1941.

Front: HERMES VINTAGES / WILL REFUND / 10 cents UPON RETURN / OF THIS BOTTLE / 128-130 SPRING ST. / L. A. / GOODMAN & CO. (in round plate)

½ Gallon Picnic Beer,
Tooled Blob Top
Aqua
Rarity: Rare

HISTORY: The Goodman Co. was no doubt a wholesale liquor concern, and this botte probably held wine.

Front: MARSTON HIGGINS & CO. / MILWAUKEE BEER / DENVER, COL.
Re: THIS / BOTTLE / NOT TO BE / SOLD

Pint, Tooled Blob Top
Aqua
Rarity: Scarce

HISTORY: Marston Higgins was the agent in Denver for Milwaukee Lager Beer as early as 1878. This bottle probably dates to the 1890's. Ad circa 1878.

Front: HOEFER & BRUGBACHER / BOTTLERS / REDDING, CAL.

Quart, Tooled Crown Top
Bulge Neck
Amber
Rarity: Very Rare

HISTORY: Joseph Hoefer succeeded Joseph Kahny at the Redding Beer Bottling Works. The partnership lasted only six months though. Jan. 1901 to May 1901.

MARSTON, HIGGINS & CO.
Wholesale Dealers and
Bottlers of Milwaukee Lager Beer.
Particular Attention Given to Bottling for Family Use.
All Goods Cash on Delivery.

Front: HUMBOLDT / BREWING CO. / EUREKA, CAL. /
THIS BOTTLE / IS NOT FOR SALE

Quart, Pint and ½ Pint, Tooled Crown Top
Amber
Rarity: Scarce in all sizes

Front: HUMBOLDT / BOTTLING / CO.

Quart, Pint and ½ Pint, Tooled Blob Top
Amber
½ Pint, $30.00 - 2020 GWA
Scarce in Quart and Pint size
Rare in the ½ Pint size.

HISTORY: P. McAllen owned the Eureka Brewery in 1889. It was located on First St. By 1895 John Haltinner had acquired it. Then in 1904 a new brewery was built on Broadway with the assistance of Palmtag and Cressman. I believe the name was changed to the Humboldt Brewing Co. at this time.
The partners eventually sold out to Max Kuehnrich of Los Angeles. He incorporated in 1905 and took control of the plant.
In 1907, when the Zobeleins acquired the Los Angeles Brewery they also gained the Humboldt Brewery in the deal. In 1911 John Hagen was sent north to take over the plant. The output doubled in volume in a short time and lasted until closed by prohibition in 1918.
I do not know the relationship of the Humboldt Bottling Co. and the Brewery discussed here. The bottles diffently predate the crown top style. No further info at this time.
Map of the Eureka Brewery is 1889, Humboldt Brewery, 1920, after it had ceased operations. Some of the history courtesy of John Wendler.

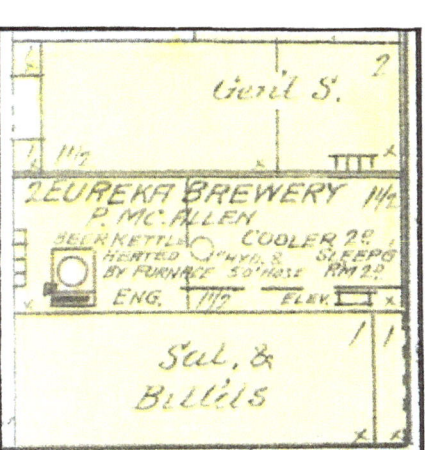
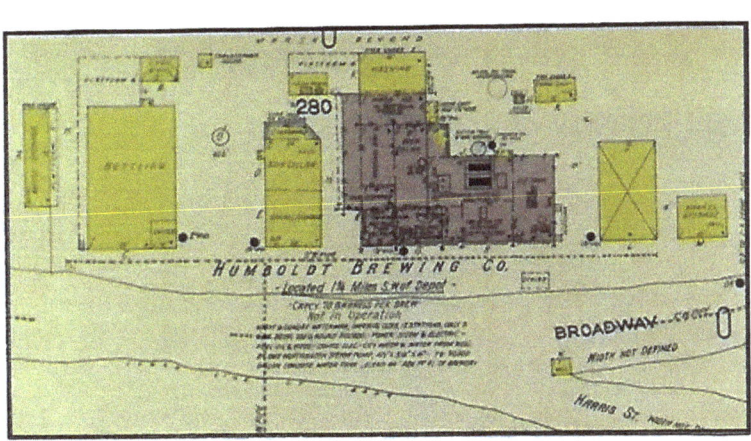

Front: INDEPENDENT BREWING CO. / "monogram" / SEATTLE, U.S.A.
           (in round plate)

Quart and Pint, Tooled Crown Top
Amber
Rarity: Scarce in both sizes

HISTORY: Samuel Loeb came to Seattle in 1902. Brewing commenced in late 1902, despite an arson attempt to burn down the new building. IN 1904, Loeb incorporated the company with himslf as President,, brother in law, Albert Weinberg as Vice President, and Benjamin Moyses as sec./treasurer. The brewery was located at 4202 8th Ave. The photo below was taken in 1902, shortly after it was finished. They continued production until prohibition.

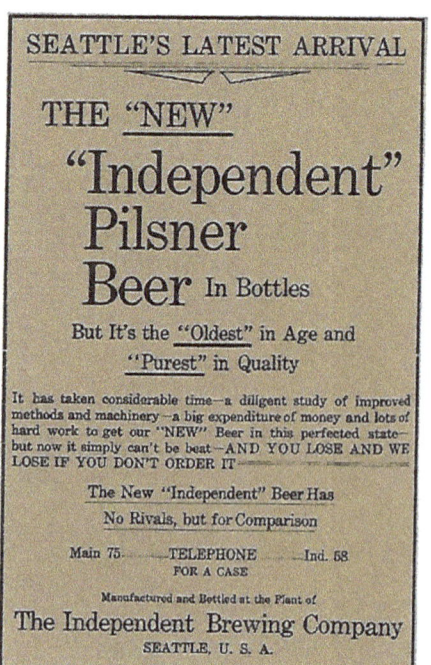

Front: JAPAN BREWING CO. / "Japanese figures" / S. F. CAL.

    Quart, Tooled Double Collar Top
    Aqua, $70.00 - 2005 ABA
    Rarity: Scarce

    HISTORY: The first listing in the San Francisco Directories was in 1902. H. Soejima was the President, and they were located at 317 Mason with the brewery itself being in West Berkeley. It was located on San Pablo and Addison Sts. Map below is circa 1902. This remained unchanged until 1905. They were not listed after that so I assume the earthquake in 1906 put them out of business.

Front: JAPAN BREWING COMPANY LIMITED / YOKAHAMA

    Quart, Applied Double Collar Top
    Yellow Amber, $475.00 - 2006 ABA
    Rarity: Rare

    HISTORY: There is no reference to this company in the S.F. directories. They may have been bottled in Japan for the western market, as they have been found in San Francisco bay area. No other info.

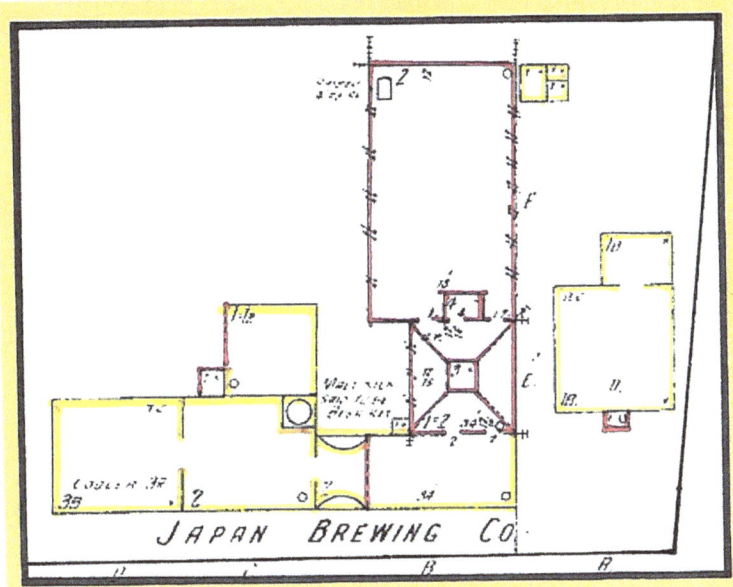

Front: JACKSON / "monogram" / BREWING CO. / S. F. CAL.

    Quart, Tooled Blob Top
    Amber
    Rarity: Common

    History: The Jackson Brewing Company was in business for many years. Starting in 1867, with Frederick & Behrens as the proprietors at 235 First St.
    In 1868 the listing remained the same.
    From 1869 thru 1877, W.A. Frederick is listed as the sole prop. at the 235 First St. address.
    Then from 1894 to 1878 the address was 1428 Mission St., with Frederick still the proprietor.
    They remained at the Mission St. address until 1909 when they moved to 351 11th St..
    In 1919 they were noe at 11th and Folsom, then at 1489 Folsom. W.A. Frederick was the proprietor this entire time. Research ended at this time. This is the only embossed bottle produced by this company for the long period they were in business.

Front: V. JONES / "monogram" / SAN DIEGO, CAL.
   (in round plate)

Pint, Tooled Blob Top
Amber
Rarity: Very Rare

HISTORY: Victor Jones came to San Diego from Santa
   Rosa in 1885. He started a wholesale wine
   and liquor business at 619 5th St.
   He must have bottled beer as a side line.
   No further info.

Front: KAHNY & BURGBACHER / BOTTLERS /
   REDDING, CAL. (embossed vertically)

Quart, Pint and ½ Pint
Tooled Blob and Crown Top
Amber, ½ Pint, Blob Top, $30.00 - 2020 GWA
Rarity: Common in all varients

HISTORY: The partnership was founded in 1890.
   They were agents for Wieland's Beer. This lasted
   until the early 1900's, when Joseph Kahny
   retired and Joseph Hoefer replaced him.
   Ad circa 1895, courtesy of John Wendler.

Front: A. W. KENISON CO. / AUBURN / CAL.

Quart, Pint and ½ Pint
Tooled Blob and Crown Top
Bulge Neck
Aqua and Amber
½ Pint, Amber, Blob Top, $210.00 - 2020 GWA
Rarity: all Aqua varients are Rare
   ½ Pint in Amber in Very Rare
   Quart in Amber is Common
   Pints in either color are Rare

HISTORY: Albert Kenison was in business with a
   Mr. Roll up until 1894, when he was then listed
   as Kenison and Johnson. Kenison died in 1904,
   and his family kept the business operating until
   1918. He was an agent for Buffalo Beer and
   Ruhstaller's Lager. It is believed that he also
   bottled the local brew from the Auburn Brewery.

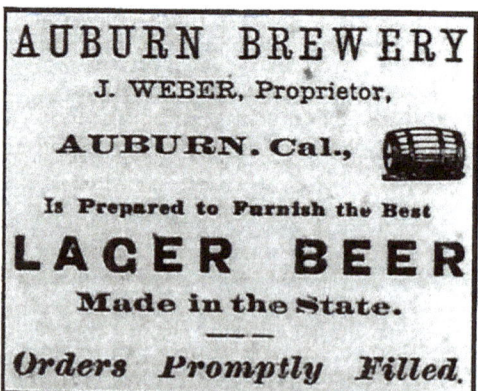

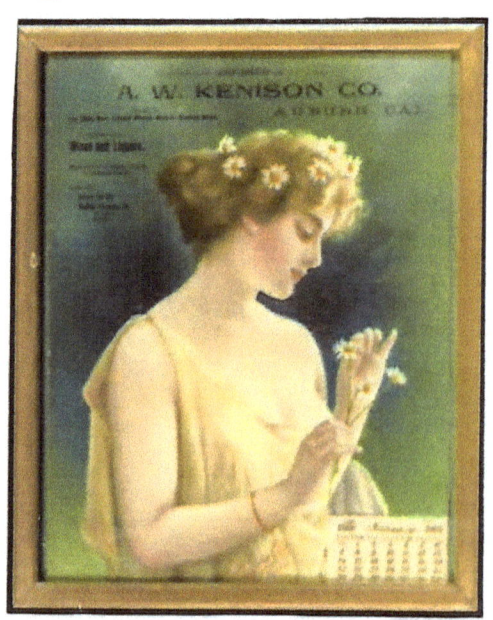

Front: T. KAGAWA CO. / "japanese figures" / SAN FRANCISCO

Quart, Tooled Double Collar Top
Amber, $40.00 - 2003 (chip) ABA
Rarity: Very Rare

History: There was only one listing for Mr. Kagawa in the San Francisco directories. That was in 1912, he was the president of the Pacific Trading Co. No address given.

Front: KALISPELL MALTING / AND / BREWING CO. / KALISPELL / MONT. (in round plate)

Quart and Pint, Tooled Crown Top
Amber and Aqua
Rarity: Scarce in both sizes and colors

HISTORY: *The Kalispell Malting and Brewing Co. was established in 1894 by Gust Gamer, and his partners Henry and Charles Lindlahr. They purchased block 50 on the west side of Kalispell. Their brewery prospered until 1898, when Lindlahr passed away. Lindlahr's share of the business was purchased by Frederick Pabst, of Pabst Blue Ribbon Beer. The brewery did well right up until prohibition, when they started to make soda, cider and near beer, to keep the doors open. This bottle should date from the early 1900's.*

Front: KAMM / S. L. O.

Quart, Tooled Crown Top
Amber
Rarity: Common

HISTORY: *I could not find much on Mr. Kamm. He was in business in the early 1900's, in San Luis Obispo. He sold his operation to the Maier Brewing Co. of Los Angeles in 1913. No other info.*

Front: KERN COUNTY / BAKERSFIELD CAL. / BOTTLING WORKS

Quart, Tooled Crown Top
Amber, $50.00 - 2013 ABA
Rarity: Rare

HISTORY: *The bottling works was started by Fred Gunther in 1903. He was located at 32nd and M St. until 1915. Then he relocated to 703 20th St. He was an agent for Buffalo Beer until he was shut down by prohibition.*

Re: THIS BOTTLE / NOT TO / BE SOLD (in round plate)

Pint, Tooled Blob Top
Amber
Rarity: Rare

Front: KESSLER / BREWING CO. / HELENA, MONT.
Re: THIS BOTTLE / NOT TO / BE SOLD

½ Pint, Tooled Crown Top
Amber
Rarity: Scarce

HISTORY: The Kessler Brewing Co. was originally founded by Charles Breeher in 1865. It was called the Ten Mile Brewery. Nick Kessler bought out Breeher in 1868 for $345.00 in gold. The original brewery was enlarged between 1868 and 1874, with bricks from a brick plant that Kesssler had started. It had the first carbonic ice machine west of the Mississippi. Nick Kessler died in 1901, and the brewery was passed on to his two sons.

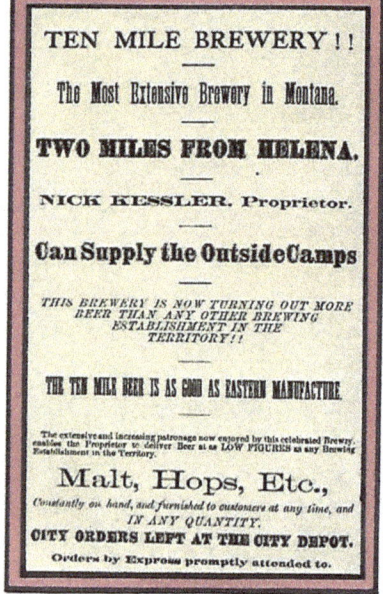

Front: KIRCHNER & MANTI OAKLAND CAL.
(embossed around shoulder)

Quart and Pint
Tooled Blob and Crown Top
Amber and Aqua
Rarity: Common in Amber, both top styles
   Rare in Aqua, Crown Top

Front: K & M (block letters) / OAKLAND

½ Pint, Tooled Blob and Crown Top
Amber, Blob Top, $50.00- 2001 ABA
Rarity: Scarce

Front: NATIONAL BOTTLING CO. / "eagle" / TRADE MARK / OAKLAND, CAL.

½ Pint, Tooled Blob Top
Amber, $130.00- 2020 (stain) GWA
Rarity: Very Rare

HISTORY: George Kirchner came to San Francisco from Germany in 1882. He worked for the Lang Bros. for two years, and then for other bottling establishments. In 1888 he moved to Oakland and went to work for the Buffalo Bottling Co. of Oakland. Then in 1893, with partner Herman Boek, they started their own bottling business, the National Bottling Co. of Oakland. In 1897 Ferdinand Mante joined in a partnership with Kirchner and there is no further mention of Herman Boek, or the Oakland National Bottling Co. Adolph Lang took the National Bottling name in San Francisco in 1899 and started his famous company. Kirchner and Manti were very successful and were agents for the Seattle Brewing and Malting Co. and bottlers of Rainier Beer until prohibition. Ad below for the National Bottling Co. is circa 1895, Rainier circa 1904. The Rainier label shown is on a quart Kirchner & Manti bottle.

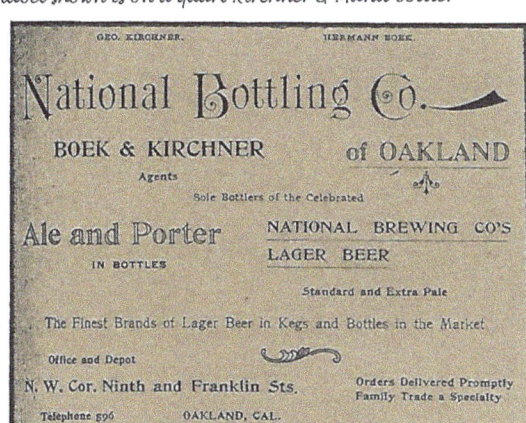

Front: M. KREISS / "goat" / REDWOOD CITY / THIS BOTTLE / NOT TO BE SOLD

Quart, Applied Blob Top
Amber
Rarity: Ex. Rare

HISTORY: Michael Kreiss founded the Pioneer Brewery in 1873. It was located at Willow and El Camino in Redwood City. He was listed as the proprietor thru 1881, then in 1882 - 1884, Diercks & Co. were the owners. Kreiss regained ownership from 1889 - 1894. Julies Faron was listed as the prop. in 1894, then Kreiss again from 1894 until 1906. This bottle should date from the 1889 - 1894 Kreiss ownership. One of the rarest and most desirable of the western beers.

Front: FRED KOSTERING / "monogram" / SAN FRANCISCO

Quart, Pint and ½ Pint, Tooled Blob Top
Amber
Very Rare in all sizes
Note: Even though this bottle comes in three sizes I could not locate one to photograph.

HISTORY: The earliest mention of Frederick Kostering was in 1894 when he was in the employ of Charles Kostering, who was in the grocery and liquor business at 1788 Folsom.
Then in 1895 and 1896 he was listed as a bottler for the Fredericksburg Brewing Co. at 1014 Pierce. These bottles must have been used at this time.
His next listing in the beer business was in 1902 when he was the manager of the Los Angeles Bottling Co. at 10th and Brannan Sts. in San Francisco. He is not listed in 1903, then in 1904 he is again working for the Los Angeles Bottling Co. as an agent, with the address as 1329 Guerrero St. No further mention of him being in any beer related business.

Front: GEO. S. LADD & CO. / LIQUOR / DEALER / 19 SO. HUNTER ST. / STOCKTON / RETURN THIS BOTTLE AND GET 5 CENTS
(in round plate)

½ Gallon Picnic Beer
Tooled Blob Top
Amber
Rarity: Rare

HISTORY: George Ladd owned a wholesale liquor business from the mid 1890's to around 1910. This bottle is considered to be a beer because of its shape and stopper type. But it probably held wine, being that most were used by wholesale liquor merchants.

Front: JOHN LAGOMARSINO / "monogram" / VENTURA CAL.

Quart, Tooled Crown Top
Amber and Clear
Varient: in oval slug plate
Rarity: Both varients are Rare

HISTORY: John Lagomarsino was an agent for Maier and Zobelein Beer in Ventura Co. Their address was on B St. in Oxnard. He was also an agent for Jesse Moore Whiskey and John Wieland beer products. This bottle should date from the 1900 – 1915.

Front: LAGOMARSINO PARMA CO. / SANTA BARBARA (in round plate)

Quart, Tooled Crown Top
Amber and Aqua
Rarity: Rare in Aqua
Very Rare in Amber

HISTORY: I believe the Lagomarsino Parma Co. was a wholesale grocery company. They were incorporated in 1903. No further info at this time.

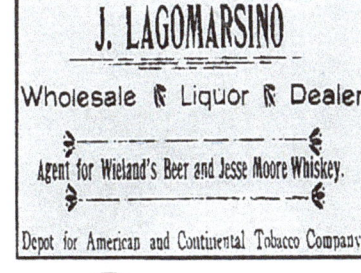

Front: C. A. LAMMERS / DENVER / COLORADO
(in round plate)

Quart, Pint and ½ Pint
Tooled Blob Top
Amber and Aqua
Rarity: Scarce

History: No info at this time, bottle seems to be 1895-1910 era.

Front: AUG. J. LANG / SAN FRANCISCO / CALIFORNIA /
"monogram in shield" / LAGER BEER
(all in square plate)

½ Pint, Tooled Crown Top
Amber
Rarity: Rare

Front: AUG. J. LANG / "monogram" / SAN
FRANCISCO CAL.

5 ¼" Sample Size
Tooled Blob Top
Amber, $550.00 - 2020 GWA
Rarity: Ex. Rare

Front: LANG BROS. / "monogram" /
SAN FRANCISCO / BOTTLE
NOT TO BE SOLD

Quart, Tooled Blob Top
Bulge Neck
Amber
Rarity: Rare

Front: LANG BROS. / 1318 / SCOTT ST. /
SAN FRANCISCO / THIS
BOTTLE / NOT TO BE SOLD

Pint, Applied Blob Top
Amber
Raruty: Ex. Rare
Note: This is the earliest Lang bottle

Front: AUG. LANG & CO. / S. F. /
LAGER BEER

½ Pint, Tooled Crown Top
Clear / Amethyst
Rarity: Rare

Front: AUG. LANG & CO. / S. F. CAL.
Re: "monogram in sunburst"

Quart and Pint
Tooled Blob and Crown Top
Amber
Rarity: Common in all varients

Front: AUG. LANG BREWING ASS'N /
S. F. / LAGER BEER

Pint and ½ Pint
Tooled Crown Top
Clear / Amethyst
Rarity: Very Rare

Note: Beer glass above right is 3 ¾" tall;
      Ad to right is circa 1908

HISTORY: The Lang family came from Gamburg, Germany. They had immigrated a few members at a time. George Lang and his brother Louis came to the San Francisco bay area in the mid 1850's. George's brother Peter remained in Germany, but sent five of his six sons to the bay area also. Louis and George welcomed their nephews and helped them get started in business.

By 1869, George and Louis had established a wine and liquor import business called Lang & Co., and the nephews found employment there.

In the early 1880's, Otto Lang and his brother Adolph, started a business called Lang Bros. They stated that they were importers of Philadelphia Beer, but in reality were bottling beer from John Wieland's Philadelphia Brewery. This business was located at 1406 Polk St.

Then in 1882, another brother, August arrived in San Francisco, and went to work for his Uncle George. He began as a bottler with Lang & Co., then in 1888, he went to work for Lang Bros. Leonard arrived next and joined the firm in 1887.

The Lang family businesses underwent many splits and mergers over the years, with brothers leaving and then rejoining at a later date.

In 1890, the brothers formed the Fredericksburg Bottling Co., located at 1510-12 Ellis St. Otto was the president, Adolph, Vice President, Leonard the Forman and August the Manager. Over the years they rotated titles and duties several times.

By 1892, brother Wilhelm had arrived and became the manager of the Lang's Oakland branch. He later left the family business, and became manager of the Pioneer Soda Water Co. in Oakland.

Then in 1899, Adolph left the company and started his own firm. This was the National Bottling Company. He owned and operated this for the rest of his career.

Lang Bros. moved many times in the 1880's, from the Polk St. location to 1318 Scott St. 1883. Then in 1890 to 1510-12 Ellis St. They remained here until 1906. After the earthquake of 1906, August bought out Otto and Leonard, and formed the August Lang & Co. firm, which owned and operated the Fredericksburg Bottling Co. He then moved the bottling plant to 18th and Alabama Sts, with a branch at Geary and Baker. The branch was established in 1911, when they took control of the Red Lion Ale and Porter Brewing Co.

The Fredericksburg Bottling Co. was sold to S.F. Breweries, Inc. in 1912. They were the owners of the Fredericksburg Brewery in San Jose. That closed in 1918 due to prohibition.

August had married Mary Decker in 1887. Their two sons followed their father in the beer business. By 1911, Guss was the manager of the Red Lion Ale and Brewing Co.. In 1912, Rudy and brother Guss, joined their father in the August J. Lang Brewing Association. But this did not last very long, as the Lang Co. realized the beer business as they knew it was fading fast. In 1913, August Lang started the Lang Realty Company.

1913 was the end of the Lang family involvement in the beer industry. The real estate business was very successful and continues to this day. August Lang died at 90, in 1955.

Front: PHILADELPHIA BOTTLING / CO. / "eagle" / LAGER BEER / LANG BROS' / PROPS' / DEPOT / 1318 S. F. SCOTT

Quart, Applied Blob Top
Amber, $1200.00 - 2005 (crack) ABA
Rarity: Ex. Rare

Front: PHILADELPHIA BOTTLING / CO. / "eagle" / LAGER BEER / LANG BROS' PROPS' / S.F.

Quart, Applied Blob and Ring Top
Amber, Ring Top, $1700.00 - 2017 (repaired) ABA
Rarity: Ex. Rare
Note: Label below was trade marked in 1891 by Otto Offerman & Co. of the Philadelphia Bottling Co. This must have been after the Lang Bros. involvement with this brand.

A Selection of August Lang Tivoli Beer Steins

This one above is 5" Tall

4 ½" Tall   3" Tall

5" Tall

Front: I. F. LAWSON / S.F. (in round plate)

    Quart, Tooled Blob Top
    Amber
    Rare

Front: I. F. LAWSON / S.F. CAL

    Quart, Pint and ½ Pint, Tooled Blob Top
    Amber
    ½ Pint, $450.00 - 2020 GWA
    Rare in all sizes

    HISTORY: *Ivan F. Lawson was first listed as a clerk in 1879. Then he moved on to become a laborer for the California Sugar Refinery from 1880 to 1884. From 1885 thru 1888 he was listed as a newspaper carrier. Then in 1889 is the first listing of any kind of involvement with the liquor industry. He is listed with John Perry as a bottler for S. Lachman & Co. the proprietors of the California Wine Vaults.*

    His first listing as a beer bottler appears in 1891 and continues thru 1895. He seemed to move his residence as often as he changed jobs, as he has a new address almost every year. He was a clerk for Stevenson & Co., a dealer in fancy goods in 1896, than back to being a beer bottler from 1897 to 1903, with no listing for 1900.

    Residence is the only listing for 1904. In 1905 he appears to be out of the beer bottling business as he is listed as a dealer in cigars at 1073 Market St. Again no listing in 1906, the quake year. No address was given for his bottling business in any of the years listed. His final listing was in 1907 with a John Matthews, but no mention of what the business was.

    The bottles with his name are rare and should date from the early 1900's. They are much to rare to have been used for more than a year or two.

Front: LEMP'S BOTTLING WORKS / S. F.
    (embossed at an angle)

  Quart and Pint, Tooled Blob Top
  Amber
  Rarity: Rare in both sizes

  HISTORY: *Emil Lemps was only listed in 1908. He was a bottler with no address given. Another rare beer used for probably less than a year.*

Front: LEMPS / S. L. MUEHLAUSEN / C. C. DIST. / ST. LOUIS BEER
    (in round plate)

  Pint and ½ Pint, Tooled Crown Top
  Aqua
  Rarity: Scarce

  HISTORY: *Muehlausen was the Cripple Creek agent for Lemps beer in 1905. No further info.*

Front: LEMPS / ST. LOUIS / LAGER BEER (in round plate)
Re: THIS BOTTLE / BELONGS TO / A. FRIEDMAN & CO. / DENVER, COLRADO / AND MUST BE RETURNED

  Pint, Tooled Blob Top
  Aqua
  Rarity: Scarce

  HISTORY: *Friedman was the Lemps agent in Denver in 1885. No other info at this time.*

Front: T. W. WRIGHT & CO. / PUEBLO / AGENTS FOR / LEMPS ST. LOUIS BEER (in round plate)

  Pint, Tooled Blob Top
  Aqua
  Rarity: Scarce

  HISTORY: *T.W. Wright was located at 126 Oneida St. in 1885, when he was an agent for Lemps St. Louis Beer.*

Front: I. F. LAWSON / S.F. (in round plate)

Quart, Tooled Blob Top
Amber
Rare

Front: I. F. LAWSON / S.F. CAL

Quart, Pint and ½ Pint, Tooled Blob Top
Amber
½ Pint, $450.00 - 2020 GWA
Rare in all sizes

HISTORY: Ivan F. Lawson was first listed as a clerk in 1879. Then he moved on to become a laborer for the California Sugar Refinery from 1880 to 1884. From 1885 thru 1888 he was listed as a newspaper carrier. Then in 1889 is the first listing of any kind of involvement with the liquor industry. He is listed with John Perry as a bottler for S. Lachman & Co. the proprietors of the California Wine Vaults.

His first listing as a beer bottler appears in 1891 and continues thru 1895. He seemed to move his residence as often as he changed jobs, as he has a new address almost every year. He was a clerk for Stevenson & Co., a dealer in fancy goods in 1896, than back to being a beer bottler from 1897 to 1903, with no listing for 1900.

Residence is the only listing for 1904. In 1905 he appears to be out of the beer bottling business as he is listed as a dealer in cigars at 1073 Market St. Again no listing in 1906, the quake year. No address was given for his bottling business in any of the years listed. His final listing was in 1907 with a John Matthews, but no mention of what the business was.

The bottles with his name are rare and should date from the early 1900's. They are much to rare to have been used for more than a year or two.

Front: LEMP'S BOTTLING WORKS / S. F.
         (embossed at an angle)

Quart and Pint, Tooled Blob Top
Amber
Rarity: Rare in both sizes

HISTORY: Emil Lemps was only listed in 1908. He was a bottler with no address given. Another rare beer used for probably less than a year.

Front: LEMPS / S. L. MUEHLAUSEN / C. C. DIST. / ST. LOUIS BEER
               (in round plate)

Pint and ½ Pint, Tooled Crown Top
Aqua
Rarity: Scarce

HISTORY: Muehlausen was the Cripple Creek agent for Lemps beer in 1905. No further info.

Front: LEMPS / ST. LOUIS / LAGER BEER (in round plate)
Re: THIS BOTTLE / BELONGS TO / A. FRIEDMAN & CO. /
       DENVER, COLRADO / AND MUST BE RETURNED

Pint, Tooled Blob Top
Aqua
Rarity: Scarce

HISTORY: Friedman was the Lemps agent in Denver in 1885. No other info at this time.

Front: T. W. WRIGHT & CO. / PUEBLO / AGENTS FOR /
       LEMPS ST. LOUIS BEER (in round plate)

Pint, Tooled Blob Top
Aqua
Rarity: Scarce

HISTORY: T.W. Wright was located at 126 Oneida St. in 1885, when he was an agent for Lemps St. Louis Beer.

Front: LIVERMORE BREWERY / D. F. BERNAL /
         LIVERMORE, CALIF.

Quart, Tooled Blob Top
Amber, $850.00 - 2011 ABA
Rarity: Very Rare

HISTORY: Charles Schwerin owned the brewery in early 1870's. It was sold to Wendell Jordan later in 1875. It was located on First St. between J and K Sts. Jordan also purchased the saloon next door to his brewery in 1875. He operated both until 1897, when he closed the saloon to tend to the growing beer business. He was an agent for Fredericksburg, John Wieland and United States Beer. He died in 1901 in an accident at the brewery. His widow then sold the business to Dennis Bernal later in 1901. In 1908 the brewery burnt down and was not rebuilt.
Map below is circa 1907, and is fronting First St. The notes on the drawing state that it is not in operation. It probably burnt shortly after it was mapped.

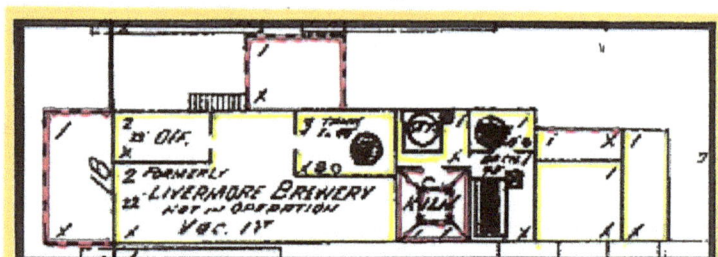

Front: CARL A. LIND OAKLAND, CAL. (embossed near shoulder)

Quart and Pint, Tooled Blob and Crown Top
Amber
Rare in all Varients

History: The first mention of Carl Lind was in 1905, when he was in business with H. Mann in Emeryville, Cal. It does say what the business was, but were located at the corner of Park and Holden Sts. No listing for 1906. In 1907 he is the manager of the Tacoma Beer Co. S.F. No listings for 1908 or 1909. Then in 1910 he has a saloon at 4301 E. 14th St. in Oakland.
His last listing in the beer business was in 1911, when he was a salesman for the Buffalo Bottling Co.

Front: M. LEONARDINI / "monogram" / McCLOUD, CAL.
             (in round plate)

Quart, Tooled Crown Top
Amber
Varient: without the slug plate
Rarity: Ex. Rare in both varients

HISTORY: No info available.

Front: LOS ANGELES BOTTLING CO. / "monogram" /
SAN FRANCISCO

Quart, Tooled Blob Top
Amber
Rarity: Very Rare

HISTORY: The Los Angeles Bottling Co. of San Francisco was
in business for only two years.
1904 - 1905 with the F. Kostering Co. as the prop.
They were located at 1329 Guerrero.

Front: "eagle" / LOS ANGELES BREWING CO.
(all in shield)

½ Pint, Tooled Crown Top
Bulge Neck
Amber, $20.00 - 2020 GWA
Rarity: Rare

Front: LOS ANGELES / "eagle on shield" / BREWING CO.

Quart and Pint, Tooled Crown Top
Bulge Neck
Amber and Aqua
Rarity: Scarce in Aqua
Rare in Amber

Front: "eagle on shield" / LOS ANGELES BREWING CO.
(in round plate)

Quart, Pint and ½ Pint
Tooled Blob and Crown Top
Bulge Neck
Amber and Aqua
Rarity: Common in all varients

HISTORY: George Zobelein purchased the Los Angeles Brewery
in 1907. He called it the East Side Brewery, being
that it was on the east side of the Los Angeles river.
It was located on N. Main and lasted until 1920.
Saloon pic is circa 1900, and map circa 1906.

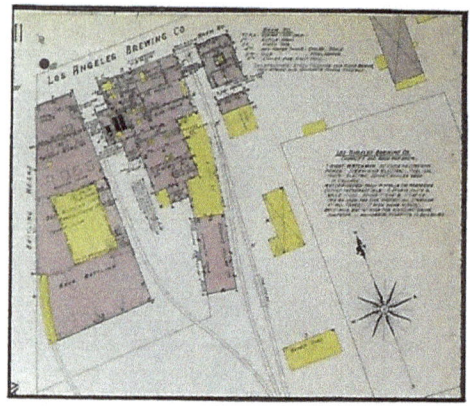

Front: THEODORE LUTGE & CO. / THIS BOTTLE / NOT TO BE
SOLD / SAN JOSE, CAL. (in round plate)

Quart, Applied and Tooled Blob Top
Amber and Green
Green, Applied Top, $250.00 - 2020 GWA
Rarity: Rare in Amber with Tooled Top
Very Rare in Green with Applied Top

HISTORY: No info available at this time.

Front: MACFARLAND & CO. / HONOLULU / HI

Quart, Applied Double Collar Top
Amber, $375.00 - 2008 ABA
Rarity: Very Rare
Note: this bottle closely resembles the Boca Beer.

HISTORY: The Macfarland Co. was a wholesale liquor
dealer in Hawaii, established in 1879. By
1899, they were agents for Schlitz Beer on
the islands.

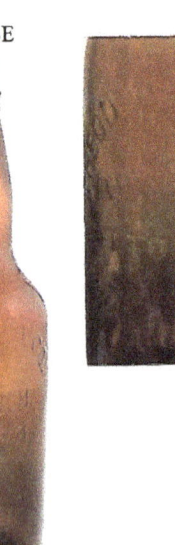

Front: MAIER & ZOBELEIN BREWERY / TRADE / MARK (in hop leaf) / LOS ANGELES, CAL.

5 ¼" Sample, Tooled Blob Top
Amber
Rarity: Very Rare

Front: MAIER & ZOBELEIN / BREWERY / LOS ANGELES, CAL / THIS BOTTLE / IS NEVER SOLD

Quart, Pint and ½ Pint
Tooled Crown Top
Aqua and Amber
Rarity: Scarce in all sizes in Amber
    Rare in Aqua

Front: MAIER & ZOBELEIN / BREWERY / "hops" / LOS ANGELES
    (in round plate)

Pint and ½ Pint, Tooled Blob Top
Amber and Clear
Rarity: Both sizes and colors are Rare

Front: MAIER & ZOBELEIN / BREWERY / LOS ANGELES / CAL.
Re: THIS BOTTLE / IS NEVER SOLD

Pint, Short Tooled Blob Top
Amber and Aqua
Rarity: Rare in both colors

History: The original name of the Maier & Zobelein brewery was the Philadelphia Brewery of Wattelet and Vagel. It was on the corner of Sansevain and Aliso. It went thru a parade of different owners until Joseph Maier and George Zobelein acquired it in 1882. It was then at 440 Aliso, and they operated it until 1907.
At that point Zobelein left the partnership and bought controlling interest in the Los Angeles Brewery. The Maier family continued on until the company was sold to General Brewing Co. in 1971.
Map in circa 1894.

PHILADELPHIA BREWERY.

WE ARE NOW READY TO SUPply the public with the very best kind of

LAGER BEER!

Orders left at CASWELL & ELLIS', or the BREWERY, will be promptly attended to.
jan25 3m   WATTELET & VOGEL.

No Room on Top For More Quality

for better quality beer than the Maier & Zobelein brand would wear out a case of shoes in the search for it. Maier & Zobelein beer is a dear beer to brew, an acme beer to buy because it costs no more for your purchasing than inferior goods. We deliver case lots right at your door free of extra cost.

CIRCA 1900 LITHO, VIEW of the MAIER & ZOBELEIN BREWERY

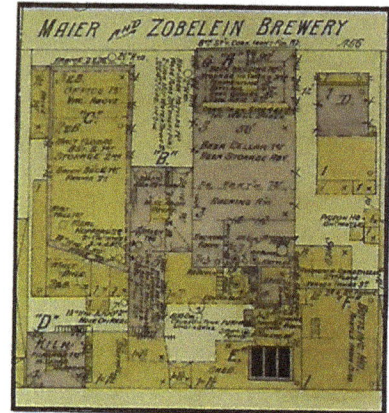

Front: MAJESTIC / "monogram" / BOTTLING CO. (in script) /
       SAN FRANCISCO

Quart, Tooled Crown Top
Amber
Rarity: Very Rare

HISTORY: The Majestic Bottling Co. was listed as a Mfg. of Soda Water in 1906, to at least 1920. No research was done after that. They were located at 20 Biedman near Ellis the entire time they were in business. John Goetz was the president. They may have had beer bottling as a side business as this bottle is considered a beer in most cases. Crown Top and Hutchinson style bottles exist that were no doubt for soda water.

Front: MILWAUKEE / BOTTLING WORKS /
       TACOMA / WASH.

Quart, Tooled Blob Top
Aqua, $375.00 - 2013 ABA
Rarity: Very Rare

HISTORY: The Milwaukee Brewery was in business from 1891 until 1897. They were bought out by the Pacific Brewing and Malting Co.

Front: MOKELUMNE HILL / BREWERY /
       E. LARGOMARSINO
            (in round plate)

Quart, Tooled Blob Top
Amber, $150.00 - 2001 ABA
Rarity: Very Rare

HISTORY: Even though a few different owners operated the Mokelumne Hill Brewery over the years, I could not find anything on E. Largomarsino.

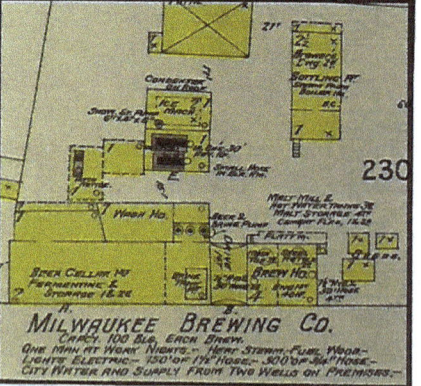

Front: THE MATHIE BREWING CO. / MEANS / QUALITY / LOS ANGELES, CAL.

Quart, Tooled Blob Top
Amber and Aqua
Rarity: Scarce in both colors

Front: THE MATHIE BREWING CO. / MEANS / QUALITY / LOS ANGELES, CAL. (in round plate)

Quart, Pint and ½ Pint
Tooled Blob and Crown Top
Aqua and Amber
½ Pint, Amber, $130.00 - 2020 GWA
Rarity: Scarce in all varients

HISTORY: The Mathie Brewing Company got its start in 1903, when it purchased the Ferd. Heim Brewery. They were located at 1834 - 1836 N. Main. The company lasted until probibtion forced them to shut the doors in 1920. Map below in circa 1906.

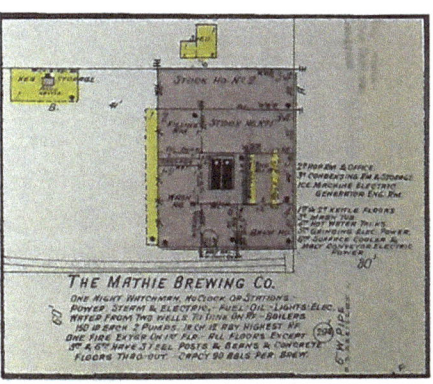
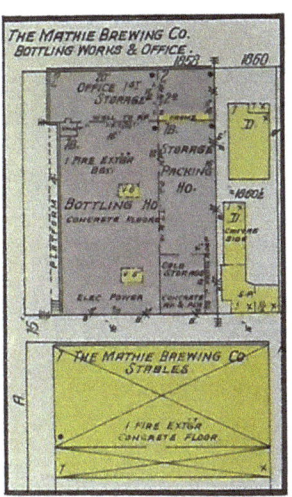

Front: MARYSVILLE BOTTLING WORKS / "monogram" / MARYSVILLE, CAL.
(in round plate)

Quart, Pint and ½ Pint, Tooled Blob Top
Amber
Rarity: Quart and Pint sizes are Rare
½ Pint is Ex. Rare

HISTORY: In 1909 it was located between 8th and 9th along the railroad tracks. No other info.

Front: MARTIN BROS. / ANGELS

Quart, Tooled Blob Top
Amber, $180.00 - 2001 ABA
Rarity: Rare

HISTORY: No info available at this time.

Front: McCAFFREY BRO'S / S.L.O.

Quart, Tooled Blob and Crown Top
Amber
Rarity: Scarce in both varienta

HISTORY: The company was originally a liquor business started by James McCaffery in 1899. Son William was also involved. His brother Hugh joined the firm in 1914. James died in 1918, and with the coming of prohibition, the brothers closed the bottling works, and went into the sporting goods trade.

Front: D. W. McCARTHY / "monogram" / STOCKTON, CAL.

Quart and Pint, Bulge Neck, Tooled Blob Top
Amber
Rarity: Scarce in both sizes

HISTORY: No info at this time.

Front: G. W. McINTYRE CO. / RETURN THIS BOTTLE / AND GET 5 CENTS / STOCKTON, CAL.
(in round plate)

½ Gallon, Picnic Beer, Tooled Blob Top
Amber
Rarity: Rare

HISTORY: Probably a wine bottle, since the McIntyre Co. was a wholesale liquor dealer. No other info.

Front: MEAMBER BROS. / BOTTLERS / YREKA, CAL. (in round plate)

Quart, Tooled Crown Top
Amber
Rarity: Rare

HISTORY: Nothing at this time.

Front: H. MEHLMAN / S.L.O. / CAL.

Quart and ½ Pint, Tooled Blob Top
Amber, ½ Pint, $120.00 - 2020 GWA
Rarity: Very Rare in both sizes

HISTORY: nothing at this time

Front: M. MEYER / ASTORIA BREWERY (in round plate)
Re: THIS BOTTLE / NOT TO / BE SOLD

Quart, Tooled blob Top
Aqua
Rarity: Rare

HISTORY: No info at this time; ad is circa 1902.

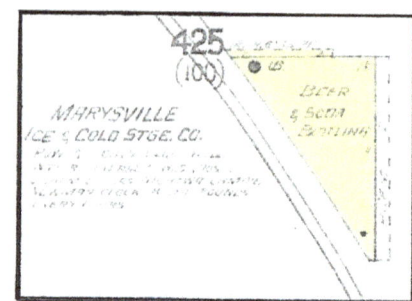

Front: H. METZLER / "eagle on barrel" / SAN FRANCISCO
Quart, Applied Blob Top
Amber
Rarity: Ex. Rare
History: Herman Metzler first comes on the scene in 1876 as a brewer at the Golden Gate Brewery. His brother Charles goes back even further to 1863 when he is listed as a driver for the same Golden Gate Brewery. In 1877 Herman is a brewer and Charles the Proprietor at the Golden Gate Brewery
In 1878, Herman Metzler is listed as Clerk for the San Francisco Stock Brewery. By 1879 he became the brewer at the same S.F. Stock Brewery. This lasted thru 1882.
In 1883, Herman is a saloon owner at Powell and Filbert Sts. and brother Charles is a driver for the S.F. Stock Brewery.
They are both drivers for the S.F. Stock Brewery in 1884. 1885 lists Herman as an agent for the same brewery, then as a driver again in 1886.
1887 is the only year Herman Metzler is listed as a Beer Bottler on his own.
Sometime is 1888 they are both out of the beer business and listed as undertakers.
This bottle would seem to date from 1887, when he is on his own as a bottler.

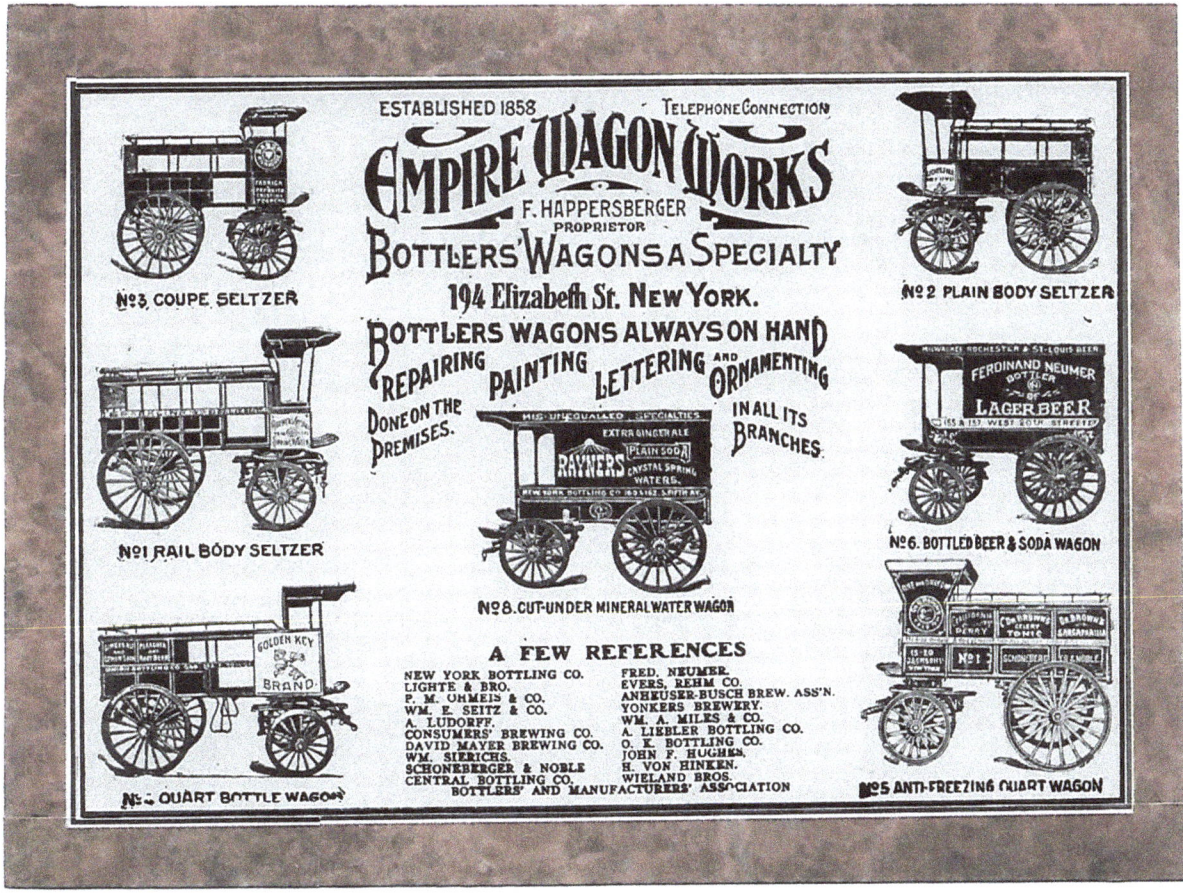

Front: GEO. T. MAGINNIS & CO. / SEATTLE / WASH.

½ Pint, Tooled Crown Top
Amber
Rarity: Scarce

Front: MILWAUKKE BEER / "hops" / GEO. T. MAGINNIS & CO. (in round plate)
Re: BOTTLE / NOT TO / BE SOLD

½ Pint, Tooled Blob Top
Aqua
Rarity: Rare

HISTORY: George Maginnis was the local Seattle area bottler for Olympia Beer in the early 1900's. And judging from the earlier blob top bottle, he was an agent for Milwaukee Beer also.

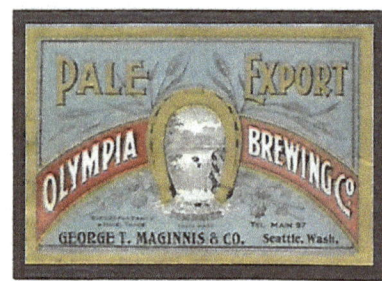

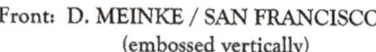

Front: D. MEINKE / SAN FRANCISCO
(embossed vertically)

Quart, Tooled Blob Top
Amber
Rare

HISTORY: The first listing I could find for Dietrich Meinke in the beer business was in 1896. He was a bottler at 2435 Folsom St. Oddly in 1894 and 1897 there is a Richard Meinke also listed as a beer bottler at the same address. This may have been a mistake and that these are the same person.
Meinke moved his bottling business to 2728 Bryant, from 1898 until 1901. In 1902 he is listed but with no address or occupation.
Then in 1903 we find him again listed as a beer bottler, now at 60 Dorland. He lasted at this address until 1906, when he is at 3109 20th.
After the quake in 1907 he and Charles Lunsman are working in partnership at the Bellingham Bay Bottling works, at the same 3109 20th St. address. This lasted until 1910, then in 1911 only his address is given.
In 1912-1913 he is now working for the Tacoma Bottling Co., at 2978 20th n as a forman. In 1914 and 1915 there is a John Meinke at the same address as a bottler. That changes back to D. Meinke in 1916.
Then from 1917 to 1919, John Meinke is listed as both a driver and clerk at 2978 20th St. address.
1920-1921 it is back to Dietrich Meinke as a driver. Again this may be the same person. The bottle with his name should date from 1896 to 1906, when he is listed as a beer bottler.

Front: HENRY C. MEYER / SAN FRANCISCO / CAL.
(embossed vertically)

Quart, Pint and ½ Pint, Tooled Blob Top
Amber
½ Pint, $20.00 - 2020 GWA
Rare in all sizes

HISTORY: There are many listings for a Henry C. Meyer in the directories. These range in years from 1890 - 1903. None have anything to do with beer bottling until 1904. He is then listed as a beer bottler at 1768 Ellis St. In 1905 he moved to 1807 Ellis. There was no listing for 1906 due to the earthquake.
He was still listed as a beer bottler in 1907, now at 1833-1835 Ellis. 1908 finds him as the proprietor of the Northern Bottling Co., and then in 1909 as a representative of the same, at 451-455 7th st.
In 1910 he is just listed as a bottler. No further listings in the beer business. These bottles should date from 1904 into 1906.

Front: DANIEL MINAHAN / VALLEJO / CAL.

Quart, Pint and ½ Pint
Tooled Blob Top
Amber, ½ Pint, $170.00 - 2020 GWA
Rarity: Rare in all sizes

HISTORY: Daniel Minahan and John Plageman took ownership of the old Pioneer Brewery in the late 1880's. They were on the corner of Marin and Carlina Sts. They continued until shutting the doors in 1904.
The ad and map are circa 1901.

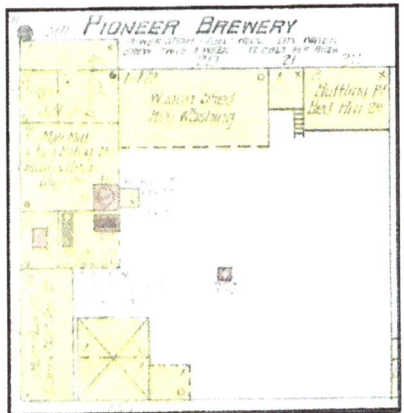

Front: MIRRASOUL / BROS. / S.F. (in round plate)

Quart, Pint and ½ Pint
Tooled Blob Top
Amber
Rarity: Common in the Pint and ½ Pint size
Scarce in the Quart size

HISTORY: Peter Mirrasoul was working for the John Wieland Brewery as early as 1898, in many different jobs. Then in 1904, he joined with his brother John to become bottlers This lasted until 1905, with no address given.. The earthquake in 1906, must have put an end to their business, as there are no further listings in the beer business.

Front: CHAS. MUTZ / WHITE BEER / & / E. RAMMELMEYER

Pint, Tooled Blob Top
Aqua
Rarity: Rare
Locale: Murray, Idaho

HISTORY: Ernest Rammelmeyer operated a brewery in Murray from 1887 until 1888. This bottle should date from the mid 1890's to about 1905, so it would be after his first brewery listing. No other info.

Front: MT. SHASTA BOTTLING WORKS / MUGLER BROS. / SISSON, CAL.

Quart, Tooled Crown Top
Amber
Rarity: Scarce

Front: P. MUGLER / SISSON, CAL.

Quart, Tooled Crown Top
Amber
Rarity: Scarce
Varient: Some have S.F. & P.G.W. on base

Front: PETER MUGLER / BREWER / SISSON / CAL.

Quart, Pint and ½ Pint
Tooled Blob and Crown Top
Amber and Aqua
½ Pint, Amber Blob Top, $70.00 - 2020 GWA
Varient: None Bulge Neck, Slope Shoulders, Ex. Rare
Rarity: Quarts with Blob Top are Rare
 All Crown Tops are Very Rare
 Rare in aqua in all sizes
 Pint and ½ Pints with Blob Top are Scarce

HISTORY: Peter Mugler came to Sisson in 1888, from Kansas. He soon purchased a building that was once a soda works and brewery. He soon became a bottling agent for Rainier Beer and John Wieland products. The brewery was on the corner of Chestnut and Lake Sts. His brother was in the soda business in the same building as well.
Peter Mugler retired in 1901, and his brother Nicholas and his son Albert, Took over the business.
Peter Mugler died in 1912. The map on left and center show the Mt. Shasta Brewery in 1889 and 1897. The map on right show Nicholas Mugler"s Bottling Works in 1905.

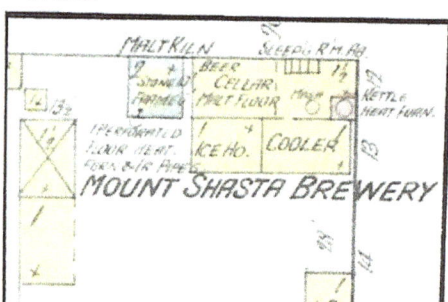

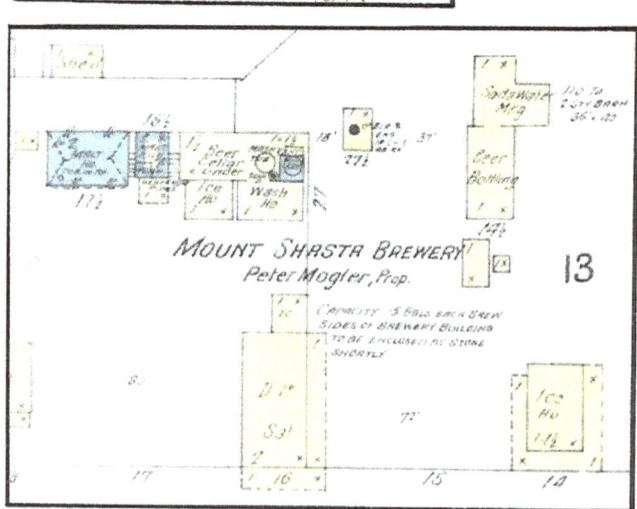

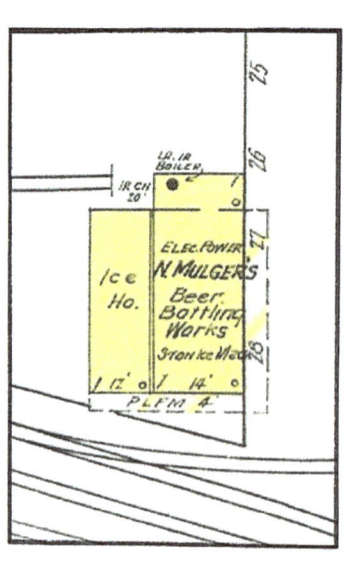

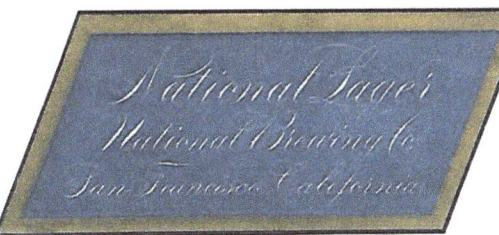

National Lager label trade marked in 1894 by the National Brewing Co. S.F.

Front: NATIONAL BREWING CO. /
SAN FRANCISCO
(embossed vertically)

Quart and Pint, Tooled Blob Top
Amber, Quart, $40.00 - 2005
Rarity: Scarce in both sizes

Front: NATIONAL LAGER / COMPLIMENTS OF
JOS. BICKEL / MARTINEZ, CAL.

3 ½ < 16 Sided, Beer Glass
Rarity: Ex. Rare

Munchener Beer Special Brew label trade marked in 1894 by the National Brewing Co. S.F.

HISTORY: The first listing for the National Brewing Co. was in 1869. They were at O'Farrel & William Sts., with Hansen & Gluck the proprietors. This may have been the same in 1870, as there is no directory for that year.
From 1871 thru 1882 they are at Fulton and Webster.
Charles Hansen only is listed as the prop. in 1883.
Then from 1884 thru 1905, the listing reads, National Brewing Co., Charles Hansen Pres., Armour Laughlin Vice Pres., and Georage Volz, Secretary and Treasurer at the same Fulton and Webster address.
1906 lists the office only at 762 Fulton, this would be just after the earthquake.
Then from 1907 till at least 1918, the listing reverted back to the pre quake form, No further research was done after 1918.

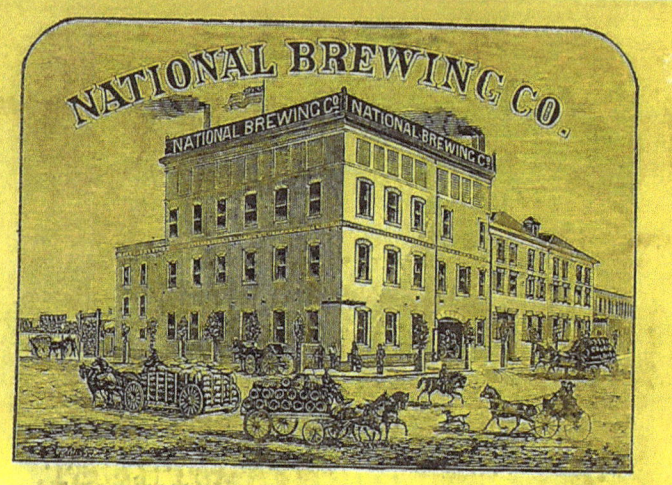

NATIONAL BREWING CO.

CORNER FULTON AND WEBSTER STREETS,
San Francisco.

DEALERS IN

BEER and MALT

Yielding to the manifest wishes of the San Francisco public for a

Genuine Lager Beer,

We have thoroughly renovated our establishment, rebuilt our machinery, added extensive and ample facilities for ICE MANUFACTURE, and effected corresponding increase in our storage vaults.

We are, therefore, now in the field, prepared to face all competitors both as to QUALITY and QUANTITY.

N. B.—Especial attention paid to Country patronage.

Received First Prize for Best Lager Beer at Mechanics' Institute Fair, 1885

Circa 1886 Ad

Front: NATIONAL BOTTLING CO. / TRADE "eagle" MARK / SAN FRANCISCO, CAL. / ADOLPH B. LANG

Quart and Pint, Tooled Blob Top
Amber, Pint, $140.00 - 2009 ABA
Rarity: both sizes are Scarce

Front: NATIONAL BOTTLING CO. / TRADE "eagle" MARK / SAN FRANCISCO, CAL. / AD. B. LANG

Quart, Pint and ½ Pint
Tooled Blob Top
Amber, Clear and Aqua
Rarity: ½ Pints in Clear and Aqua are Rare
Quarts and Pints are Scarce

Front: NATIONAL BOTTLING CO. / TRADE "eagle" MARK / SAN FRANCISCO, CAL.

Pint, Tooled Blob and Crown Top
Amber
Rarity: Crown Tops are Rare
Blob Tops are Scarce

Front: NATIONAL BOTTLING CO. / "eagle" / TRADE MARK / SAN FRANCISCO, CAL. (in round plate)

Quart, Applied Blob Top
Amber
Rarity: Very Rare

HISTORY: *The National Bottling Co. was first listed in 1895, with Fred Sachs, as the proprietor. Located at 337 - 339 Waller. This stayed the same thru 1898. Adolph Lang took over in 1899, and the address changed to 359 - 361 Waller. The listing remained the same until Lang closed thr doors in 1910. Notice the trade mark drawing below. They never used this pattern, only the National Brewing Co. did.*

National Bottling Co. S.F. embossing pattern. Trade marked in 1897 by the National Bottling Co. S.F.

National Standard label. Trade marked in 1894 by the National Bottling Co. S.F.

National Export label, trade marked 1896 by the National Bottling Co. S.F

Front: 524 FULTON STREET / NATIONAL BOTTLING / WORKS / TRADE "eagle" MARK / SAN FRANCISCO, CAL. / NOT TO BE SOLD

    Quart, Tooled Blob and Crown Top
    Amber
    Rarity: Scarce with Blob Top
          Rare with Crown Top

Front: 525 GROVE STREET / NATIONAL BOTTLING / WORKS / TRADE "eagle" MARK / SAN FRANCISCO, CAL. / NOT TO BE SOLD

    Quart, Tooled Blob Top
    Amber, $275.00 - 2007 ABA
    Rarity: Rare

Front: 524 FULTON STREET / NATIONAL BOTTLING WORKS / SAN FRANCISCO, CAL.

    ½ Pint, Tooled Blob Top
    Amber, $80.00 - 2020 GWA
    Rarity: Scarce

Front: 524 FULTON STREET / NATIONAL BOTTLING WORKS / "star" / SAN FRANCISCO, CAL.

    ½ Pint, Tooled Blob top
    Amber
    Rarity: Rare

HISTORY: P. Svetinich & Co. were listed as the proprietors in 1898. This is the first year in the directories, and they were located at 525 Grove.
By 1905 he has added a Mr. Raddich as a partner and moved to 564 Fulton.
They continued until 1916 - 1917, when the props. changed to Svetinich & Sons at the 564 Fulton address. No further listings.

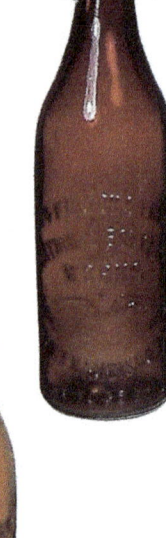

Embossing pattern above trade marked in 1900 by the National Bottling Works, S.F.

Embossing pattern above trade marked in 1900 by the National Bottling Works, S.F.

Front: NATIONAL LAGER BEER / "monogram" / H. ROHRBACHER AGT. / STOCKTON, CAL.

Quart, Pint and ½ Pint
Tooled Blob Top
Bulge Neck
Amber, ½ Pint, $40.00 - 2020 GWA
Rarity: Common in all sizes

HISTORY: I could not find much on this bottler. Henry Rohrbacher did apply for a trade mark for his bottles in 1899. I am assuming this is lager beer from the National Brewing Co. in S.F. His business was very successful, as these bottles are common.

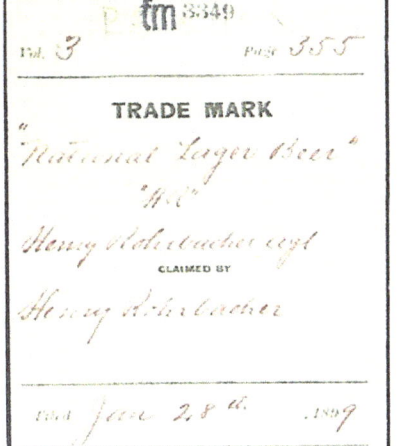

Front: NEFF BROS, BRG. CO'S / WIENER MAERZEN /
BOTTLED BY / H. A. SCHWINHORST /
PUEBLO, COLO. (in round plate)

Pint, Tooled Blob Top
Aqua
Rarity:

HISTORY: The Neff Bros. owner and operated the Western Brewery in Denver, from 1896 until 1915. Map below is circa 1903. I could not find anything on the Schwinhorst Bottling Co. in Pueblo.

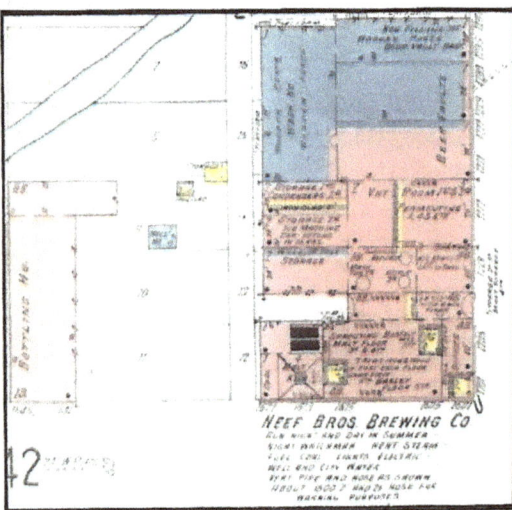

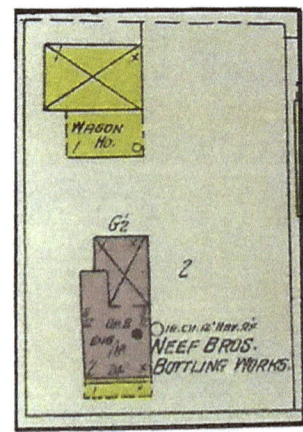

Front: NEW YORK / BREWERY / "monogram" / SPOKANE, WASH.
 (in round plate)

Quart, Tooled Crown Top
Amber
Rarity: Scarce

History: The New York Brewery was in operation from 1886-1903, with Rudolf Gokow, the proprietor. Located at Front and Washington. Map is circa 1902, brewery picture 1891.

Front: NORTH PACIFIC BREWERY / ASTORIA, OR.

Quart and ½ Pint, Tooled Blob and Crown Top
Amber
Varient: spelled "ORE."
Rarity: Blob Tops are Rare
 Crown Tops are Scarce

Front: NORTH PACIFIC BREWERY / ASTORIA, ORE.

Quart and ½ Pint, Tooled Crown Top
Amber, ½ Pint, $30.00 - 2020 GWA
Rarity: Scarce

History: John Kopp and started the North Pacific Brewery in 1884. Located on the waterfront, they were in business until 1916. Kopp died in 1935. Map below is circa 1908, ads are circa 1890's.

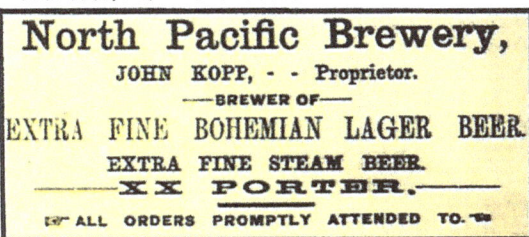

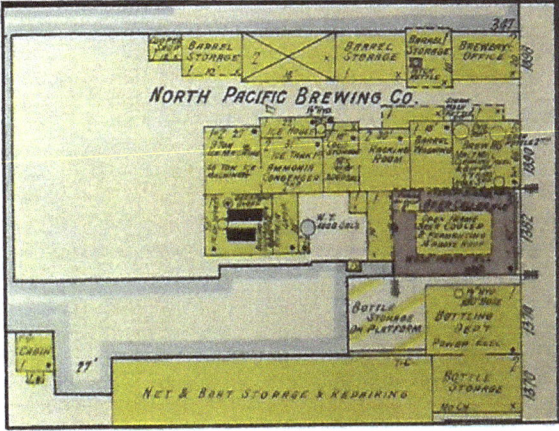

119

Front: NORTH STAR BOTTLING WORKS /
  TRADE "star" MARK / S. F. CAL.
  BOTTLE NOT TO BE SOLD

Quart, Pint and ½ Pint
Tooled Blob Top
Amber and Clear
½ Pint, Clear, $120.00 - 2020 (bruise) GWA
½ Pint, Amber, $60.00 - 2020 GWA
Rarity: Scarce in Amber, all sizes
  Ex. Rare in Clear, ½ Pint
Varient: with "CARL TORNBERG PROP."
  Varients are Ex. Rare

Front: NORTH STAR BOTTLING WORKS /
  TRADE "star" MARK / S. F. CAL.

Quart, Pint and ½ Pint
Tooled Blob Top
Amber
Rarity: Scarce in the ½ Pint size
  Rare in the Quart and Pint size
Varient: with "CARL TORNBERG PROP", Ex. Rare

HISTORY: Carl Tornberg trade marked the name in 1896, even though the first listing does not appear until 1898. The 1898 listing reads, North Star Brewing Co., Carl Tornberg, President, located at Army and Howard.
In 1899 they are listed at 3310 Army with John Pope as president.
The listing stays the same in 1900 and 1901, plus North Star Bottling Works, Carlson and Dahlgren props, at 3317 26th, added.
In 1902 Carlson and Anderson are the proprietors.
This lasted thru 1906. In 1907 - 1914 after the quake, they added Bottlers of Columbia Brewing Co.'s Lager (Tacoma) to the listing, now at 3355 26th.
The listing remained unchanged until 1915 - 1917, when it read only, North Star Bottling Works.
1918 brought the last listing.
Map below in circa 1899, brewery fronting on Army St.

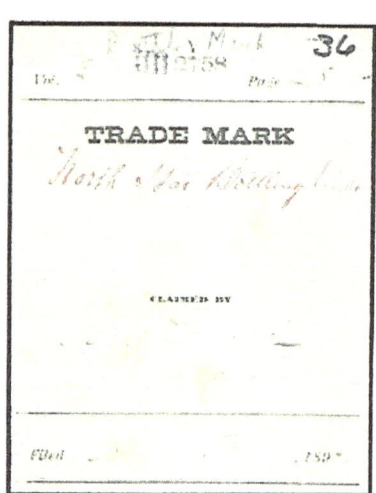

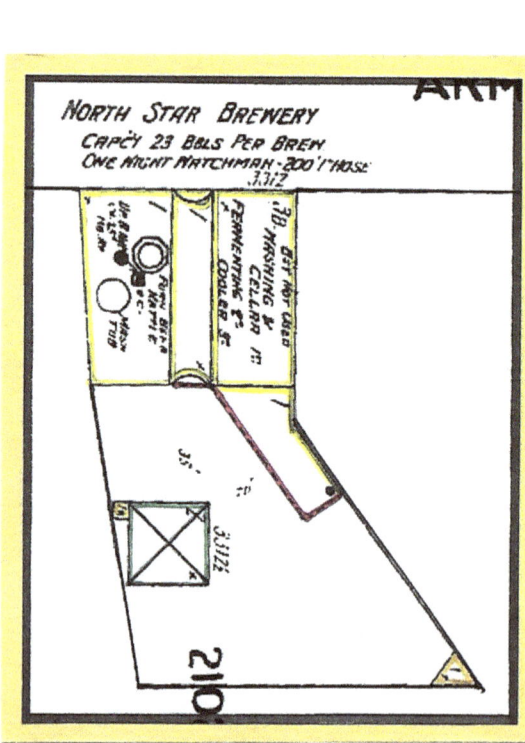

Front: THE NORTH YAKIMA / BREWING & MALTING CO. / NORTH YAKIMA / WASH.

    Pint, Tooled Crown Top
    Amber
    Rarity: Scarce

Front: THE NORTH YAKIMA / BREWING & MALTING CO. / NORTH YAKIMA

    Quart, Tooled Crown Top
    Amber
    Rarity: Scarce

    HISTORY: Information from OldBrewerys.com states that they were open from 1905 to 1915, located at 25 Front St. Map below is circa 1905. I think the brewery was operating before 1905, just from the size of the complex on the map. No other info at this time.

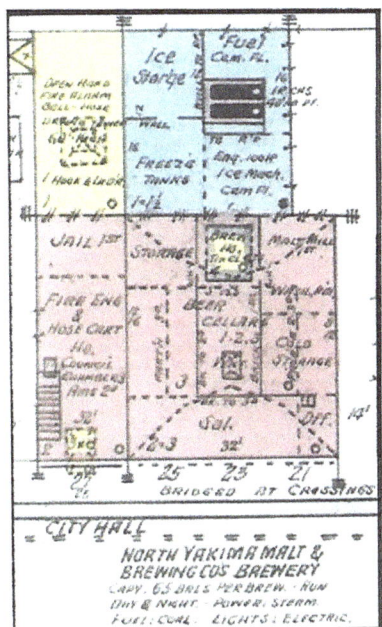

Front: FRANK O'GRADY / "monogram" / VALLEJO, CAL.

    Quart, Tooled Crown Top
    Aqua
    Rarity: Ex. Rare

    HISTORY: Frank O'Grady was the owner on the Empire Soda Works in Vallejo for many years. This bottle probably held soda water. It is post 1900.

Front: OHIO BOTTLING WORKS / 122 N. MAIN ST. / L.A.

    Quart, and Pint
    Tooled Blob Top
    Aqua
    Rarity: Rare

    HISTORY: No info at this time.

Front: OAKLAND BOTTLING CO. / "monogram" /
OAKLAND, CAL. (in round plate) /
BOTTLE NOT TO BE SOLD

Quart, Pint and ½ Pint
Tooled Blob Top
Amber, ½ Pint, $50.00 - 2020 GWA
Rarity: Quart and Pint are Common
½ Pint is Scarce

Front: OAKLAND BOTTLING CO. / "monogram" /
OAKLAND, CAL.

5 ½" Sample Size, Tooled Blob Top
Amber
Rarity: Ex. Rare

Front: OAKLAND BOTTLING CO. / "monogram" /
OAKLAND CAL. (in round plate)
Base: S. F. & P. G. W.

Quart, with Bulge Neck
Tooled Blob Top
Amber
Rarity: Scarce

Front: OAKLAND BOTTLING CO. OAKLAND CAL.
(embossed around shoulder)

Quart and Pint, Tooled Blob Top
Amber
Rarity: all sizes are Common
Varient: Embossed in two lines, Rare

HISTORY: D. Ahrens, Charles Franck, and Frederick and Joeseph Stromberg, established the Oakland Bottling Co. in 1892. They were located at 19th and Broadway. They were initially bottlers of Fredericksburg and Wielands Beer. By 1903, they had added Lohengrin Lager from the Chicago Brewery in San Francisco. Also in 1903, Carl Plaut took over as manager. This lasted until 1907, when John Heaney was listed as the new manager. There is no directory for 1908, and no further listings for them. Carl Plaur went on to become president of the Oakland Brewing & Malting Co. from 1909 until at least 1915.
The embossing pattern, see drawing, was trade marked in 1898, by D.H. Ahrens. Map is circa 1902.

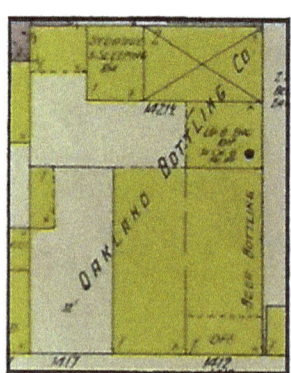

Pint Oakland Bottling Co. bottle with a label for Fredericksburg Lager Beer.

Pint Oakland Bottling Co. bottle with a label for Wieland's Extra Pale.

Front: OLYMPIA BEER / H. C. K. & CO. / OAKLAND, CAL.

Quart and Pint
Tooled Crown Top
Amber
Rarity: Scarce in both sizes

HISTORY: H.C. Kattenhorn took over the Olympia Beer agency in Oakland in 1907. He was located at 815-819 Cypress. Prior to Kattenhorn, Tillman and Welander were the agents in 1906, located at 1154 7TH. No further listings

---

Front: OLYMPIA BEER CO. / S. F. CAL.

Quart, Pint and ½ Pint
Tooled Crown Top
Amber and Aqua
Rarity: ½ Pint in Amber is Rare
All sizes are scarce in aqua

HISTORY: The first listing for the Olympia Beer Co. in San Francisco was in 1905-06. G. & M. Harris were the agents at 1423 Sansome. Daniel Rosenblum took over as the agent from 1907 to 1912 at various addresses. The final listing was in 1913 with the Olympic Beer Co. as the agent at 265 Market.

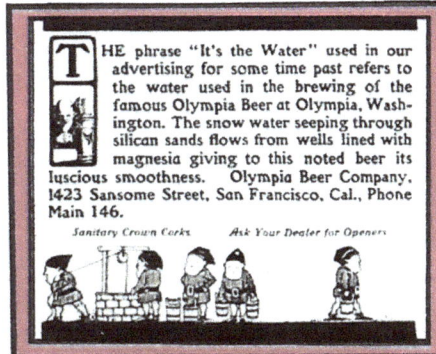

Front: P. B. / MILWAUKEE (in round plate)
Base: S. F. & P.G.W.

Quart, Pint and ½ Pint
Bulge Neck
Tooled Blob Top
Amber, ½ Pint, $60.00 - 2020 GWA
Rarity: Scarce in the Quart and Pint size
Rare in the ½ Pint size

HISTORY: Wm Wolff was the first agent I could find for Pabst Beer in San Francisco.
This would date from 1892 to 1899.
John Rapp is listed as the sole bottler in 1896.
1899 lists the Pabst Beer Bottling Establishment with John Rapp and Son,
located at 6th and King. This was the last year for Wm. Wolff on the listing.
1900-1901, the Royal Eagle Dist. were listed as the agents at 501-505
Market St.
Then in 1902, Thos. Collins & Co. became the agents at various addresses
until 1912.
1912 - 1914 has the Blue Ribbon Beer Co. the agents at 158 5th.
In 1915 thru 1918 the Pabst Brewing Co. were listed as the agents at 172 5th.
No further research was done after 1918.
I believe this bottle should date to when John Rapp was the bottler.

Front: PACIFIC BOTTLING CO. / J monogram / S. F.
(in round plate)

Quart, Pint and ½ Pint
Tooled Blob Top
Amber, ½ Pint, $200.00 - 2020 GWA
Yellow, Quart, $140.00 - 2005 ABA
Varient: "JW" in the monogram
½ Pint, $110.00 - 2020 GWA
Varient: Bulge Neck with S. F. & P.G.W. on base
Rarity: all varients are Very Rare

HISTORY: Theodore Wiese and John Jacobs started the Pacific Bottling
Works in 1900. They wre located at 2639 Folsom.
They are not listed in 1901 or 1902.
The 1903 listing has a Pacific Bottling Works at 2539 Folsom.
1900 seems to be the only year they were in business together.
J. Jacobs is at 2539 Folsom in 1904, listed as a Beer Bottler.
No further listings in the beer business for either of them
The bottle with the "J" monogram would date 1904 only.
The bottle with the "JW" monogram would seem to date from
the 1900 date.

Front: A. PALMTAG & CO. / EUREKA, CAL.

   Quart, Pint and ½ Pint
   Tooled Blob and Crown Top
   Amber, Quart, Blob Top, $40.00 - 2001 ABA
           Pint, Blob Top, $50.00 - 2001 ABA
   Rarity: All Crown Tops are Rare
          ½ Pint Blob Top is Very Rare
          Scarce in the Quart and Pint sizes

HISTORY: Palmtag was involved with the Humboldt Brewery in Eureka as a part owner in the early 1900's. I do not know what relationship these bottles have with the brewery. He may have had a separate bottling business.

Front: JAMES PEREIRA / SANTA CLARA / CALIF.
          (embossed vertically)

   Quart, Tooled Blob and Crown Top
   Amber, Blob Top, $40.00 - 2001 ABA
   Rarity: Common in all varients

HISTORY: Pereira was listed as a bottler at 799 Franklin St. in 1909. This is the only directory I had access to, but I am sure he was in business for a few years before and after this date.

Front: PEARSON BROS. / PLACERVILLE
          (embossed vertically)

   ½ Pint, Tooled Blob Top
   Aqua, $1400.00 - 2020 GWA
   Rarity: Ex. Rare

HISTORY: The Pearson Bros. were wholesale liquor merchants and bottlers of all kinds of sodas, syrups and cider, dating from the 1850's in Placerville. They also had outlets in Bodie and Carosn City, Nevada.
After the death of John Pearson in 1891, John Jr. expanded the beer, wine and cider business. After he passed, his wife ran the business until 1920.
Of the many bottles this firm used, this is the only one that resembles a beer type bottle. It was probably in use in the early 1900's.

PEARSON BROS.
BOTTLERS
Manufacturers of Soda Water and other
Ærated Beveridges
Placerville

Front: H. A. PETERSON / WATSONVILLE / CAL.

   Quart, Pint, ½ Pint
   Tooled Blob Top
   Amber, Quart, $40.00 - 2020 GWA
          ½ Pint, $70.00 - 2020 GWA
   Rarity: Quart and Pint are Rare
          ½ Pint is Ex. Rare

Front: WATSONVILLE / BOTTLING WORKS / H. A. PETERSON / PROP.

   Quart and Pint
   Tooled Blob Top
   Amber, Quart, $170.00 - 2020 GWA
          Pint, $50.00 - 2020 GWA
   Varient: some have P.C.G.W. on base
   Rarity: Scarce in all varients

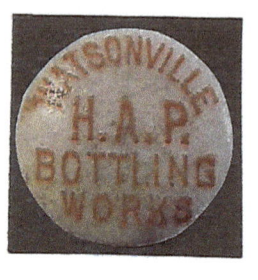

HISTORY: No info at this time. I could not even find them on the Sanborn maps. The maps below are circa 1886, 1892, and then on the bottom, 1892 also. It appears that the Watsonville Brewery of 1886, changed the name to the Pajaro Brewery by 1892, and then built a newer plant, in use by 1892. I could find no connection between these breweries and the bottles pictured.

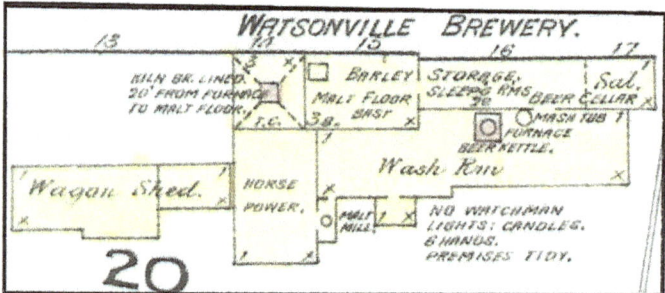
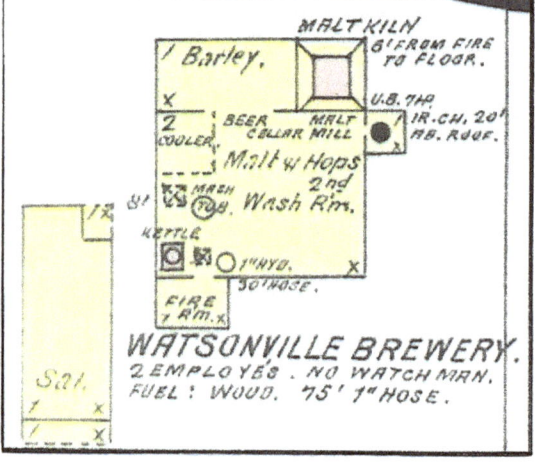
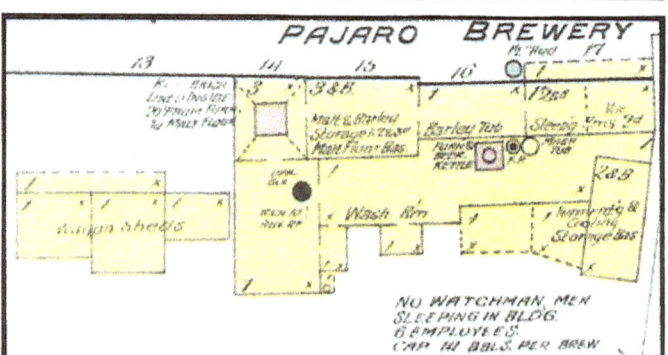

Front: TONY PHILIPPS / S. F. CAL.

   Quart, Pint and ½ Pint
   Tooled Blob Top
   Amber
   Rarity: Rare in the Quart and Pint size
          Very Rare in the ½ Pint size

Front: PHILIPPS BOTTLING CO. / "monogram" / SAN FRANCISCO, CAL.

   ½ Pint, Tooled Blob Top
   Amber, $220.00 - 2020 ABA
   Rarity: Very Rare

   HISTORY: *Antone Philipps was in the beer business for a very short time. In 1900 and 1901 he was listed as a Beer Bottler, with no address given. No other info.*

Front: T. F. PHILLIPS / COLUSA, CAL.

   Quart, Tooled Crown Top
   Amber
   Rarity: Rare

   HISTORY: *The map below is circa 1889. This bottle is not the same era, but I could find nothing else in Colusa unless one of the soda works used it. I did find a T.F. Phillips as the owner of the Colusa Soda Works from 1900 to around 1920. This bottle may have contained soda. The map of the soda works is 1918. It was on the corner of 3rd and Market.*

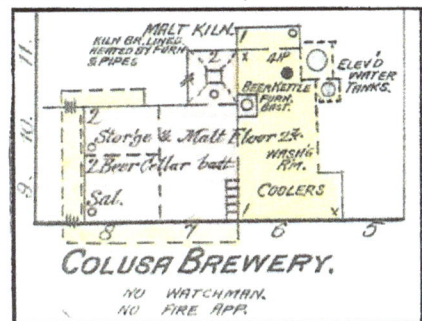 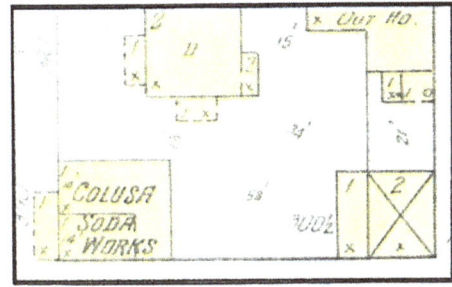

Front: A. & R. POSTEL / "walking bear" / S.F. CAL.
  Quart, Applied Blob Top
  Amber
  Rarity: Ex. Rare

Front: C. D. POSTEL / T. "sheaf of hops" M. / S.F. CAL.
  Quart, Applied Blob and Ring Top
  Amber, Blob Top, $3000.00 - 2005 ABA
  Yellow Amber, Ring Top, $4400.00 - 2017 (repaired) ABA
  Rarity: Very Rare with Blob Top
  Ex. Rare with Ring Top

  HISTORY: Christian D. Postel started in the grocery business in the late 1870's. His store was located at the corner of Pacific and Taylor Sts. His store was a success and he employed his two sons, Arnold and Rudolph to learn the business.
  In 1881 he financed Arnold in a second store, and brother Rudolph joined him in 1883. In 1884 the brothers sold their store and became beer bottlers. Christian saw the sons success and sold his store also and went in the beer bottling business.
  In 1884 he was listed at 539 California as a Beer Bottler. Then in 1885 he moved to 1424 Taylor.
  Rudolph was listed at 122 San Jose Ave. as a bottler in 1885 also.
  In 1886 the two brothers are listed together as bottlers of Fredericksburg Beer at 919 Dolores, cor Bush and Sansome.
  Christian only lasted about two years in the beer business and retired.
  The Postel Bros. and Albert Lau, were listed as proprietors of the Cosmopolitan Saloon and agents for Fredericksburg Beer by 1888. This Was located at Bush & Kearney Sts.
  Fredericksburg bought the bottling works in 1888, ending the Postel Bros. venture in the beer business in San Francisco.

Front: PREBLE & JONES
  Quart, Applied Ring Top
  Amber
  Rarity: Ex. Rare

  HISTORY: Charles B. Preble and Charles A. Jones were listed as proprietors of the California and Oregon Cider Works, from 1881 thru 1883. They were located at 218 Davis. 1884-85, finds only Preble with the company, no mention of Jones. This is the last time the Company was listed.
  The short time they were in business together would account for the extreme rarity of this bottle, with maybe 3 known. The author dug one of these is Pittsburgh Ca. in the mid 1970's.
  Preble and Jones trade marked the label at right, for Golden Champagne Cider, in 1881.

Front: CHAS. R. PUCKHABER / "monogram" / FRESNO, CAL.
    (in round plate)

Quart, Tooled Crown Top
Amber, $80.00 - 2010 ABA
Rarity: Rare

Front: PROPERTY OF / CHAS. R. PUCKHABER /
    BEERS / FRESNO, CAL.

Quart, Pint and ½ Pint
Tooled Blob and Crown Top
Amber, ½ Pint, Blob Top, $375.00 - 2020 GWA
    ½ Pint, Crown Top, $140.00 - 2010 ABA
    Quart, Blob Top, $650.00 - 2009 ABA
Varient: Some have a Bulge Neck
Rarity: Ex. Rare in the Quart size
    All other varients are Very Rare

Front: CHAS. R. PUCKHABER / "monogram" /
    856-858 I STR. / FRESNO, CAL.

Quart, Tooled Crown Top
Amber, $80.00 - 2010 ABA
Rarity: Rare

HISTORY: No info at this time.

Front: PUEBLO BREWERY / PUEBLO, COLO.
    (in round plate)

Pint, Tooled Blob Top
Aqua
Rarity: Scarce

HISTORY: No info at this time.

Front: J. PROLL BOTTLING WORKS / BOTTLING /
    U. S. LAGER / S.F. CAL.

Quart, Pint and ½ Pint
Tooled Blob Top
Amber, ½ Pint, $425.00 - 2006 ABA
Rarity: Quart and Pint sizes are Rare
    ½ Pint is Very Rare

HISTORY: The first listing I could find of Justus Proll in the beer industry was in
    1888. Listed as a Beer Bottler, at 528 Hayes. This changed in 1890,
    when he is listed with Antone Proll at the same address.
    1891 - 1898, he is again on his own at the Hayes St. address.
    1899 - 1904, he is listed at 535 Ivy, then in 1905, at 477 Ivy.
    After the 1906 earthquake he has moved to 1358 8th, where he
    remained until 1914, when he went out of the beer bottling business.

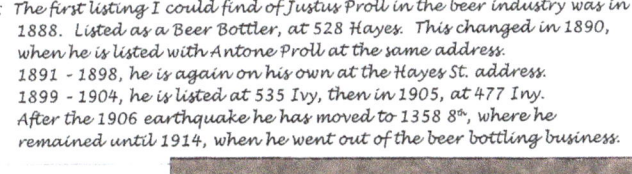

Front: PUGET SOUND BREWING CO. / TACOMA
             (embossed vertically)
Re: THIS BOTTLE IS NOT SOLD
Base: S. F. & P.G.W.

   Pint, Tooled Blob Top, Bulge Neck
   Amber
   Rarity: Rare

Front: BOTTLE TO BE / RETURNED / PUGET SOUND / BREWING CO. / LAGER BEER / TACOMA / WASH.

   Quart, Tooled Blob Top, Bulge Neck
   Amber
   Rarity: Rare

Front: PACIFIC & PUGET SOUND / BOTTLING / CO. / SEATTLE / WASH. (in round plate)

   ½ Pint, Tooled Blob Top
   Amber, $60.00 - 2020 (chip), GWA
   Rarity: Very Rare

Front: PACIFIC & PUGET SOUND / BOTTLING CO. / SEATTLE / WASH.

   Pint and ½ Pint, Tooled Crown Top
   Amber
   Rarity: Rare

HISTORY: Anton Huth and John Scholl founded the Puget Sound Brewery in 1888. Located at 25th and Jefferson, with P.A. Kalenborn as the manager.
The company was incorporated in 1891. Shortly after, Huth bought out his partner, in 1894. By 1897, Huth had brought in a new partner, S.S. Loeb
At that point they had merged with another Tacoma brewery and became the Pacific Brewing and Malting Co.

Front: RAINIER / BEER BOTTLING WORKS / RENO, NEV.
(embossed vertically)

Quart and Pint, Tooled Crown Top
Amber
Quart, $160.00 - 2009 ABA
Rare in both sizes

HISTORY: Rainier Beer was created by Andrew Hemrich who started the Seattle Brewing and Malting Co. The Rainier Bottling Works and brewery got its start in Reno about 1905. They were owned by the Seattle Brewing and Malting Co. and E. Herrick was the manager in Reno at 328 Spokane St. Rainier beer was very popular and the company expanded into many western cities with brewerys and bottling plants. The Reno branch closed with the onset of prohibition in 1918. Ad below from the Tonopah Bonanza, March 11, 1905.
Map below showing the Rainier Plant in Reno in 1918,
The other map is 1906, and shows the Buffalo Beer Depot and Reno Bottling Works, across the tracks the Wieland Bottling Works and Beer Depot is shown. All accessible by train.

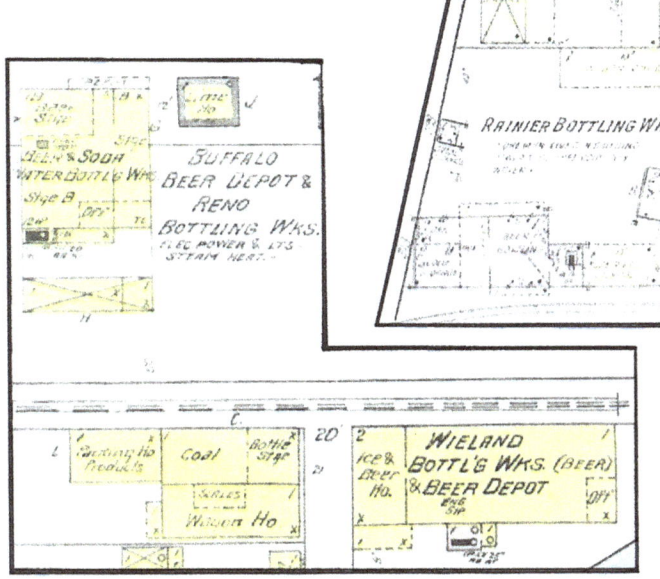
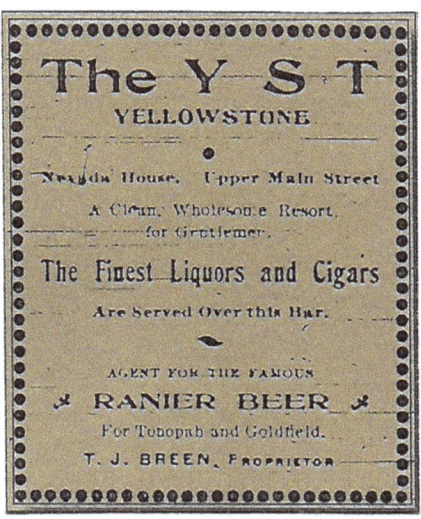

Front: RAINIER BEER / FRESNO / BOTTLING

Quart, Tooled Crown Top
Amber
Rarity: Scarce

Front: RAINIER BEER / "star" / FRESNO BOTTLING

Quart, Pint and ½ Pint
Tooled Crown Top
Amber
Rarity: Rare in the Quart and Pint size
Very Rare in the ½ Pint size

HISTORY: Jacob Richter was the agent in Fresno for Rainier Beer, during the time frame these bottles should have been in use. I do not know the relationship, if any, of Richter and the Fresno Bottling Co. They may be one and the same.

Front: RAINIER / BEER / SAETTLE / U.S.A.
 5 ¼" Sample, Tooled Blob Top
 Amber, $110.00 - 2020 GWA
 Rarity: Scarce

Front: RAINIER / SEATTLE / BREWING &
  MALTING / COMPANY / BEER

 Quart, Pint and /2 Pint
 Tooled Blob and Crown Top
 Amber, Clear and Green
 Clear, Pint, Blob Top, $60.00 - 2000 ABA
 Amber, ½ Pint, Blob Top, $80.00 - 2020 GWA
 Green, Pint, Blob Top, $120.00 - 2000 ABA
 Rarity: Blob Tops in Amber are Scarce
    Blob Tops in Green are Very Rare
    Crown Tops in Green are Rare
    Crown Tops in Amber are Scarce
    Clear varients are all rare

HISTORY: Hemrich & Kopp started their Seattle brewery in 1883. They eventually became the Bay View Brewig Co. In late 1892, they merged with two other local breweries to form the Seattle Brewing & Malting Co. The name for their flagship brand was "RAiNIER". The company lasted until prohibition in various forms and locations.

Front: JOHN RAPP & SON / S. F. CAL.

Quart, Pint and ½ Pint
Tooled Blob and Crown Top
Amber and Clear
Deep Amber, Pint, $190.00 - 2019
½ Pint, Clear with Blob Top, $80.00 - 2007 ABA
Pint, Yellow with Blob Top, $200.00 - 2017 ABA
Rarity: All are common in Amber
Clear, ½ Pint with Blob Top is Rare
Clear with Crown Top is Very Rare

Front: JOHN RAPP & SON / S. F. CAL.
Base: S. F. & P.G.W.

Quart, Pint and ½ Pint
Tooled Blob Top, Bulge Neck
Amber
Rarity: Scarce in all sizes

HISTORY: The first listing for John Rapp in the beer business was in 1886, as a Beer Bottler, at 519 Chestnut.
In 1887-1888 he is in business with George Goeppert & Co.
1889 - 1894, he is in partners with Debary as proprietors of the U.S. Bottling Co., at McAllister & Mason. In 1895, they moved to 6th and King Sts.
In 1896 John Rapp's son joined him and Debarry is no longer listed. They are the proprietors of the U.S. Beer Bottling Co., at the 6th and King address.
This remained the same in 1897.
In 1898, they are also Bottlers for Pabst and U.S. Beer.
1899-1900, They were bottlers for Pabst and Rainier Beer.
The listing changed from 1901 - 1909, it read, John Rapp & Son, rainier Beer Agency, 8th & Townsend.
In 1910 the address again changed to 1500 Bryant. This was unchanged until 1918, when research was stopped.
Map below is circa 1899, bottling plant photo is 1915.

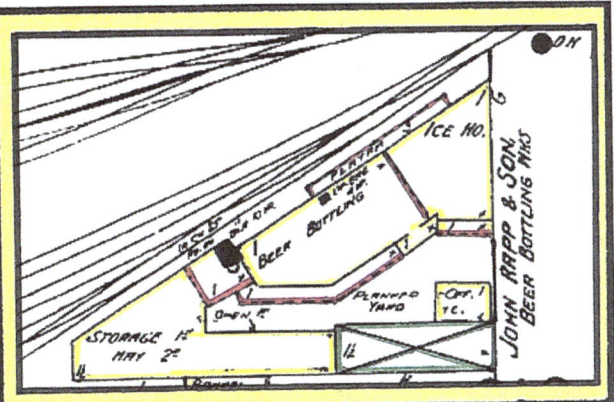

133

Front: RASPILLER / "eagle" / BREWING CO. / WEST BERKELEY

Quart, Pint and ½ Pint
Toole Blob and Crown Top
Amber, ½ Pint, Blob Top, $140.00 - 2020 GWA
        Quart, Blob Top, $110.00 - 2019 ABA
        Pint, Crown Top, $60.00 - 2019 ABA
Yellow, ½ Pint, Blob Top, $750.00 - 2019 ABA
Varient: Eagle is smaller
    Amber, ½ Pint, Blob Top, $425.00 - 2019 ABA
        Quart, Blob Top, $325.00 - 2019 ABA
Rarity: Crown Tops are Rare in all sizes
       Blob Tops are Scarce in all sizes
       Varients are Very Rare

HISTORY: Joseph Raspiller and John Wohlfrom started the American Brewery in 1893. It was located on San Pablo Ave and Francisco. Wohlfrom left the company in 1898 and Raspiller became the sole proprietor.
The name was finally changed in 1904, becoming the Raspiller Brewing Co. The business prospered until 1910 when Raspiller shut the doors and went to work for the Golden West Brewery.
Photo of the brewery is circa 1910, and the map is circa 1903.
The Victorian style house is a depot. Caption said Las Vegas in 1900. There is no way that this is Las Vegas. It was nothing but a watering hole for the horses and a stage stop in 1900. It is probably Oakland, Hayward or maybe Pinole to the north.

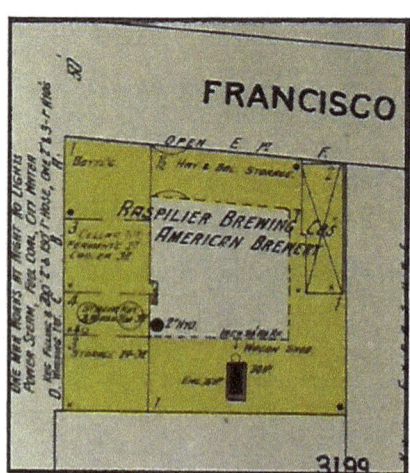

Front: RED LION / BREWERY / SAN FRANCISCO

Pint, Tooled Blob Top
Amber
Very Rare

Front: RED LION LAGER BEER

Label only
5 ½" sample, Tooled Blob Top
Amber
Ex. Rare

Front: RED LION BEER / "lion" / S.F.

½ Pint, Tooled Crown Top
Clear, $100.00 - 2010 ABA
Very Rare

History: In 1888, Jacob Stuber and Albert Weikert established a small Weiss beer brewery at the corner of Baker and Geary Sts. In 1893 they expanded and called the plant the San Francisco Weiss Beer Brewery.

In 1898, Weikert left the business and long time employee Joseph Rohrer bought into the company, becoming J. Stuber & Co. Rohrer left after only a few years and Charles Lentz became a partner in 1903. He talked Stuber into dropping the Weiss beer in favor of the more popular stout, porter and ale. The company then reorganized as the Red Lion Brewery.

The brewery survived the earthquake in 1906, but Lentz left the company. Even though the brewery survived the quake, the bottling plant did not. August Lang became the new bottler. The pint blob top bottle predates the quake and is circa 1904.

Stuber continued on as the sole proprietor, and at the age of 91, was hoping to retire. In Dec. of 1907 he sold controlling interest to Alfred Goscinsky and Paul Hartman. The new investers were not interested in brewing beer, just bottling for other brewers. There is no listing for the Red Lion Brewery in the city directory in 1907. Only Gasinsky and Hartman Beer Bottlers. The Red Lion beers were bottler by Lang the following year with no mention of the bottling works.

The new company lasted only a year and Stuber took it back in 1908. He found new investors in Morris Rotheschild and Bernard Davidow. In January 1909 They renamed the brewery the Red Lion Ale and Porter Brewing Co. and resumed brewing their products.

Apparently the new owners were no better at keeping Stubers plant in the black. August Lang & Co. had been bottling Red Lion products since 1906, and was still a major creditor. With the brewery facing bankruptcy, Lang exchanged dept for an interest in the brewery, just to keep it operating and prevent a major loss to his company. By Nov. 1910, Lang had control and Guss Lang Jr. was plant manager. It was reorganized as the August Lang Brewing Association in 1911.

With the popularity of lager, the Lang's decided to drop the ale, porter and stout brews and brew only lager. The first batch was shipped on May 6th of 1912. At that point they discontinued the Tivoli Lager. About the same time, the Lang's sold their interest in the bottling plant to Fredericksburg's parent company and could comcentrate all their efforts on the Red Lion product.

The directory for 1913 listed the Aug. Lang Brewing Assn at Harrison & Mariposa Sts, along with the Red Lion depot. This would indicate that the brewery had clsed in late 1912, but the bottling works was still in operation. In 1914 it Became the Red Lion Beer Agency, but now at 612 Alabama St, which was the address for Oakland Brewing and Malting agent. The moves did not meet expectations and after 30 years in the bottling business, August Lang went into the real estate and insurance business.

Ads circa 1912. History courtesy of Gary Flynn, brewerygems.com.

Front: RENO / BREWING CO. / RENO, NEV.

Quart, Pint and ½ Pint, Tooled Blob Top
Amber
Clear, ½ Pint, $350.00 - 2020 (chip) ABA
Common in the Quart
Scarce in the Pint size
½ Pint in Clear and Amber is Ex. Rare

HISTORY: In the early days of Reno, the Reno Brewery name was used by a few different owners. None of these produced an embossed bottle. That did not happen until 1903, when a group of men from Montana purchased property and built a two story brick brewery at 990 E. 4th St. John Maurer, Peter Dohr and Jacob Hook held all the stock. Later in 1904 they announced plans to build a new six story building to handle increased business. It was completed within a year and two new products were introduced, "MALT ROSE" and "ROYAL LAGER". The products were so popular cold storage facilities were built in Lovelock, Fallon, Yerington and Truckee, Cal. A new bottling plant was built after 1910, and by 1916 production was at 40,000 barrels a year. Prohibition ended beer production in 1918, but the soda water and other non alcoholic products, were produced until 1933. The Sanborn map below is circa 1906. It shows the brewery facing E. 4th and Spokane Sts.

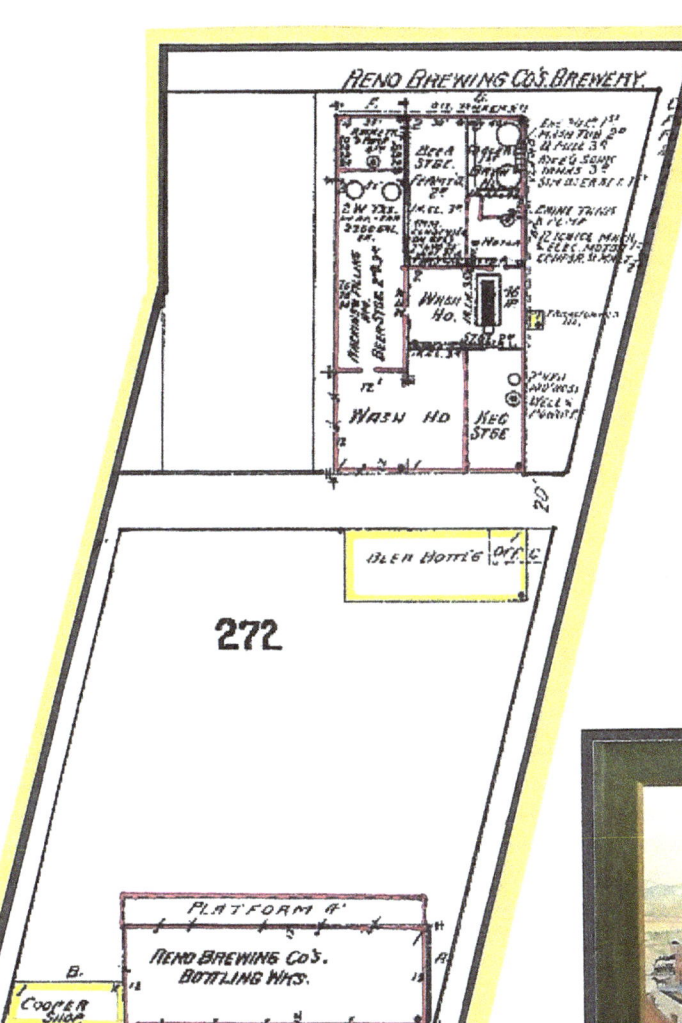
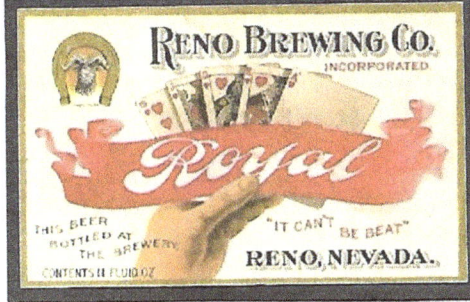

Front: RICHMOND / BOTTLING / WORKS

Quart, Pint and ½ Pint, Tooled Blob Top
Clear and Amber
½ Pint, Clear, $30.00 - 2020 GWA
½ Pint, Amber, $20.00 - 2020 GWA
Scarce in all sizes in Amber
Very Rare, ½ Pint in Clear
Locale: San Francisco, Cal.

HISTORY: The first listing I could find for the Richmond Bottling Works was in 1904. Carl Zimmerman was listed as the proprietor at 417 32nd Ave. In 1907 the address changed to 33rd Ave near Pt. Lobos.
Then in 1908, Zimmerman & Ruhland where listed as the proprietors at 32nd and Clement. At this time they were also agents for Valley Brew Lager from Stockton., see label below.
The listing remained the same in 1909. Then no further listings could be found.

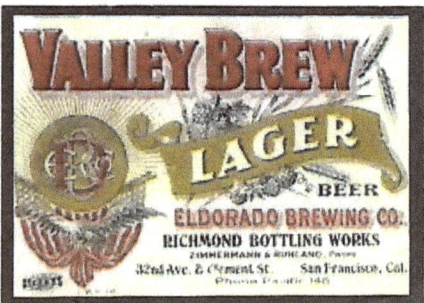

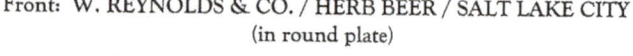

Front: W. REYNOLDS & CO. / HERB BEER / SALT LAKE CITY
(in round plate)

Pint, Applied Blob and Double Collar Top
Green and Amber
Rarity: Green is Ex. Rare
        Amber is Rare

HISTORY: Walter Reynolds was in business in the 1880's
         No other info at this time.

Front: JACOB RICHTER / FRESNO, CAL.

½ Pint, Tooled Crown Top
Amber
Rarity: Rare

HISTORY: In 1895, Jacob Richter opened a soda works in Fresno. By 1896 he had aquired an agency for Buffalo Beer. Needing a larger building he moved to the corner of I and Mono Sts. Rainier Beer was then added and Richter was very busy up to prohibition. the soda works continued on with his sons running the operation. On a side note, he has a bad explosion in the soda plant in 1911, killing a plant worker and shutting down operation temporarily. The photo below is after the move to the Mono St. address and the ad is circa 1897.

ARRIVED!   ARRIVED!

2 Carloads of Pabst Keg Beer

I have taken the agency of this famous Keg Beer, and the people of Fresno and surrounding country will this coming season have the opportunity of drinking a fine palatable Beer for 5¢ per glass, and the same will be for sale in all first-class saloons. The Pabst Beer needs no recommendation, as it has a world-wide reputation. Same will be sold at

$12.00 PER BARREL,

Which is within the reach of every dealer to handle. The cooperage in Eastern packages is larger than the California cooperage, thereby making the price as low as inferior qualities. For particulars inquire of

Jac Richter,

Agent for Pabst and Buffalo Beer.

All kinds of Sodas, Seltzers, Phosphates, Ginger Ale, Etc., on hand.

TELEPHONE MAIN 30.   P. O. 599.   DEPOT—707 I STREET, FRESNO.

Front ROSEBURG BREWING CO. / "monogram" / ROSEBURG, OR.

Quart, Tooled Crown Top
Amber
Rarity: Scarce

HISTORY: I could not find much on this brewery. The map below shows the brewery in 1903, but states it is not in operation at that time, with the buildings being vacant. The photo is pre 1906, and the beer tray is circa 1910. No other info.

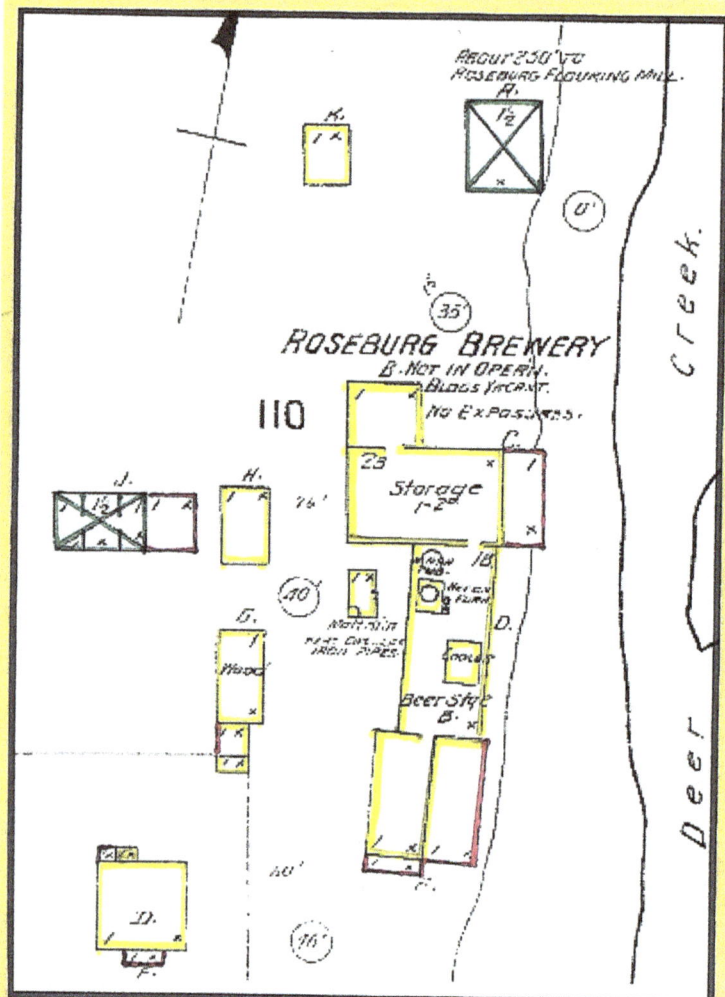

Front: RUHSTALLER'S / GILT EDGE / LAGER / SACRAMENTO, CAL.
(in round plate)

Quart and Pint
Tooled Crown Top
Bulge Neck
Amber
Rarity: common in both sizes

HISTORY: Frank Ruhstaller came to Sacramento in 1865. He went to work for the City Brewery, and became forman after a few weeks on the job. After about a year he went to works for the Pacific Brewery.
In 1881 he purchased the City Brewery. He made many improvements, and greatly increased production.
In 1895, the City Brewery was also known as the Sacramento Brewing Company. Ruhstaller's family became a major share holder in the Buffalo Brewing Comapany, but continued to use the Ruhstaller brand separately. He had a depot in San Francisco to help distribute his beer.
Even though the Buffalo and Sacramento Brewing Company had merged, the two companies kept their business identities separate. They each had their board of directors and managers. In 1913, Frank Ruhstaller became president of the company.
Map circa 1895 and 1913. Some of the history notes courtesy of John Wendler.

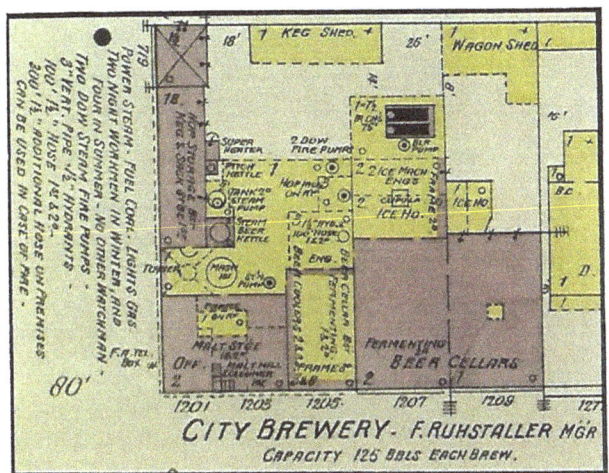
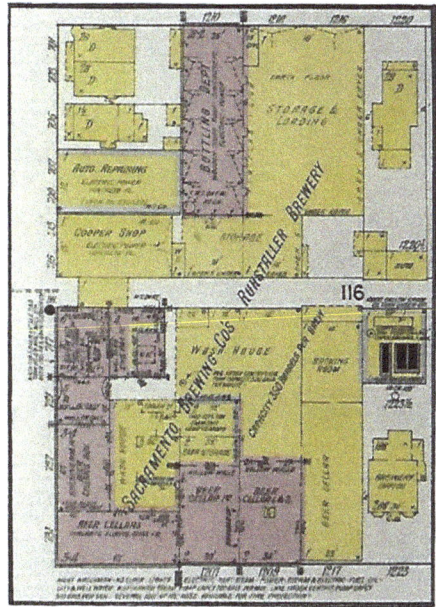

Front: S (fancy letter in round plate)

Quart, applied Blob Top
Green, $120.00 - 2019 ABA
Rarity: Rare
Note: I do not believe this bottle and the one below are connected in any way.

Front: S L / TRADE MARK (in round plate)

Quart and Pint, Applied Blob Top
Aqua
Rarity: Common in the Quart size
         Scarce in the Pint size
Varient: "S" only, Common

History: There has been much speculation about these bottles over the years. Eric McGuire has uncovered some new info that appears to have solved the mystery. Schmidt & Lowell of Stockton, patented the label below in 1887. As you can plainly see, the monogram is the same as the bottle embossing. Also, the billhead from Schmidt & Lowell states the products that they were dealers in at that time. This bottle could have held any of them, including the Champagne Cider. The map below shows the Schmidt Sarsaparilla and Iron Water Works on East Weber in 1895. They must have moved sometime after 1887.

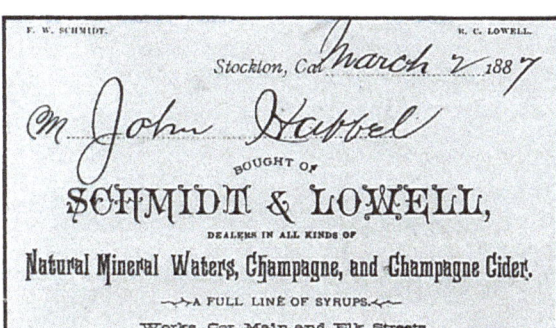

143

Front: SALINAS / BREWING CO. / SALINAS / CAL.

Quart, Pint and ½ Pint, Tooled Blob Top
Amber, Quart, $40.00 - 2020 GWA
Pint, $40.00 - 2020 GWA
Rare in the ½ Pint size
Scarce in Pint and Quart sizes

Front: SALINAS VALLEY / BOTTLING CO. / SALINAS, CAL.

Pint and ½ Pint, Tooled Blob Top
Amber, ½ Pint, $40.00 - 2020 GWA
Pint, $40.00 - 2020 GWA
Scarce in both sizes

HISTORY: The Salinas Brewery first commenced operations in 1874. Lurz & Hagner were the proprietors. The brewery was located on Castroville St. at this time, with an output of 240 barrels per year. In 1877 Mr. Hagner sold his share to John Menke. The business grew and by 1891 production had increased to 2000 barrels a year.

The death of Henry Lurz in 1889 ended the partnership. By 1891 John Menke was sole proprietor and built a new steam brewery on San Juan St. in Salinas. It was completed in 1892. The company has increased its output to about 8000 barrel a year, at this time.

Menke operated the plant for thirteen more years, and in 1904, he formed a stock company to raise capital for improvements to the brewery. Menke was the president, principal stock holder and chairman of the corporation. William F. Voss was secretary and manager of the brewery. There were seven members on the board of directors. At this time Menke removed himself from the day to day brewery operations to oversee the First National Bank of Salinas, which he had established in 1892.

In 1905 steam beer was still being produced and a lager beer called "SCHLOSS BRAU" was added to the product line. They ahd outgrown the old frame building, and in 1907 the corporation increased the capital stock to build a new brick brewery. It included a 30 ton ice machine and a bottling shop that could handle the new crown cap bottles. The new five story structure was located at 347 N. Main St. and resumed production in the spring of 1908. See litho below. They were now bottling their "SALINAS LAGER" and "SALINAS STEAM BEER" in crown top bottles. At this time the brew master was John Bauer, who was succeeded by Joseph Eckhart of Vallejo, who bought out Bauer's interest. This continued until prohibition. History notes courtesy of Gary Flynn, breweygems.com.

Photo below circa 1895. Sanborn insurance map in circa 1900 and shows the brewery fronting N. San Juan St. in Salinas. Labels are mostly 1905 to 1918.

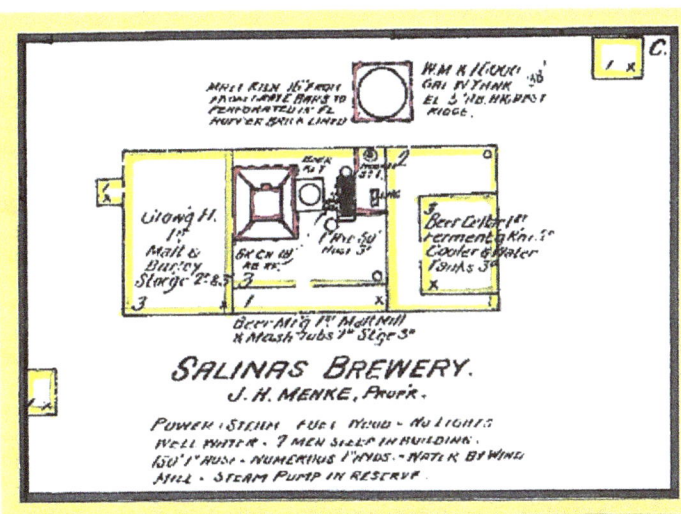

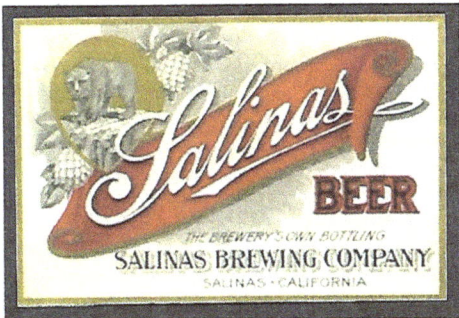

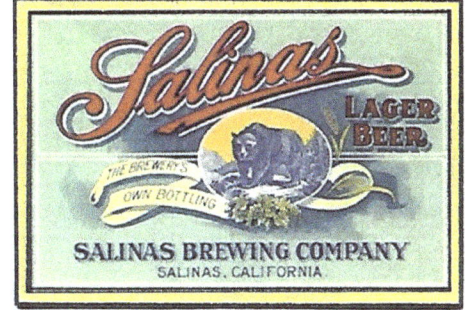

Front: SANTA CLARA / COUNTY / BOTTLING
CO. / SAN JOSE

Quart, Pint and ½ Pint
Tooled Blob and Crown Top
Rarity: Common in Quart and Pint size with
 Blob Top
 All Crown Tops are Scarce
 ½ Pint Blob Top in Scarce

HISTORY: No info at this time. Map is circa 1915.

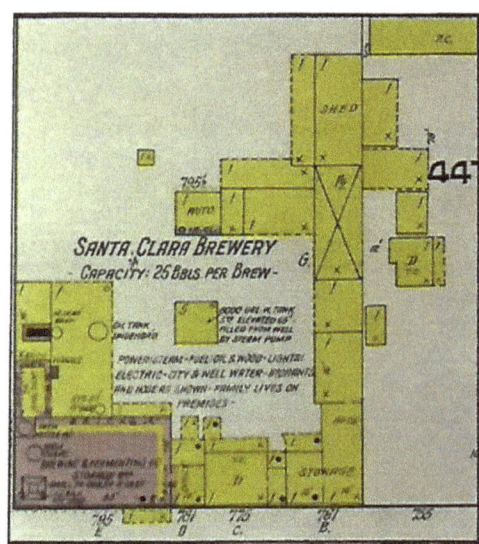

Front: SALT LAKE CITY / BREWING CO.
 (in round plate)

½ Pint, Tooled Blob Top
Amber
Rarity: Rare

HISTORY: No info at this time.

Front: SANTA CRUZ / BREWING CO. / SANTA CRUZ, CAL.
(embossed vertically)

Quart, Tooled Crown Top
Amber
Rarity: Rare

HISTORY: Labels below are circa 1907. No other info at this time.

Front: SAN DIEGO / BREWING CO. / SAN DIEGO, CAL.
(in round plate)

Pint and ½ Pint
Tooled Blob and Crown Top
Amber
Rarity: ½ Pint with Blob Top is Rare
All others are Scarce

Front: SAN DIEGO BREWING CO. / SAN DIEGO, CAL.
(embossed vertically)

Quart, Tooled Blob and Crown Top
Amber
Rarity: Scarce

Front: SAN DIEGO / BREWING CO. / SAN DIEGO, CAL.
Base: S. F. & P.G.W.

Quart, Pint and ½ Pint
Tooled Crown Top
Amber
Varient: Base in plain
Rarity: all varients are scarce

HISTORY: I could find no directories before 1903, so these dates could vary.
1904 has Jacob Gruendike as the proprietor, located at 32 and Bay Front.
In 1905 the Brewery has moved to 1509-1515 G. St, with Ernest Causton as sec.
1906 - 1907, has George Stadler the manager on Front, corner of California.
No further listings.
Map is circa 1906.

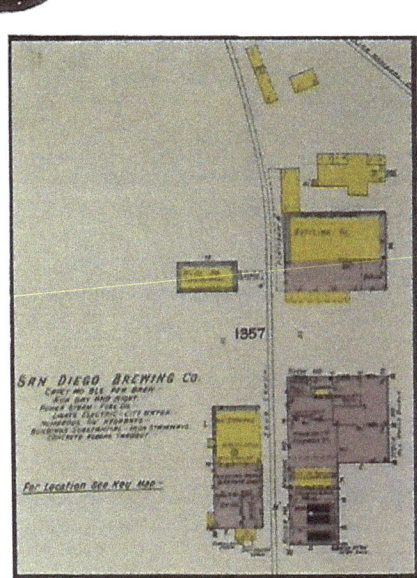

147

Front: SAN JOSE BOTTLING CO. / C. MAURER
(embossed vertically)

Quart, Tooled Blob Top
Amber
Rarity: Scarce

Front: SAN JOSE BOTTLING CO. / SAN JOSE, CAL.
(embossed vertically)

Quart, Pint and ½ Pint
Applied and Tooled Blob Top
Bulge Neck
Amber
Red Amber, ½ Pint, Applied Top, $150.00 - 2006 ABA
Pint, Applied Top, $180.00 - 2006 ABA
Rarity: Rare with Applied Top in all sizes
Common with Tooled Top in all sizes

Front: SAN JOSE BOTTLING CO. /
C. MAURER, PROP.

Quart, and Pint, Tooled Blob Top
Amber
Rarity: Scarce in all sizes

Front: SAN JOSE / BOTTLING CO. / C. MAURER
(embossed vertically)

Quart, Pint and ½ Pint
Tooled Blob and Crown Top
Amber
Rarity: Quarts and Pints with Blob Top are Common
All other varients are Scarce

Front: PROPERTY OF / C. MAURER /
SAN JOSE, CAL. (in round plate)
Base: S. F. & P.G.W.

Quart, and ½ Pint, Tooled Blob Top
Amber, ½ Pint, $275.00 - 2020 GWA
Rarity: Rare in both sizes

HISTORY: Christian Maurer was first listed in 1891. He was an agent for Fredericksburg Brewery. This lasted until 1896, when he stared the San Jose Bottling Co., and was still an agent for Fredericksburg. His business address was at 370 S. Fernando St. He continued until 1900 when he took on a partner, a Mr. Blumcke.
Blumcke lasted until 1905 when Maurer's son, William joined the company.
Christian must have retired before 1911, because then the company was listed as the Maurer Bros. (Carl & William). This lasted at the same Fernando St. address until 1916, when they closed the doors. They remained agents for Fredericksburg Beer the entire time.

Front: SANTA ROSA BOTTLING CO. / HUDSON & PALMER / SANTA ROSA, CAL.

Quart, Pint and ½ Pint
Tooled Blob and Crown Top
Amber and Aqua
Rarity: All sizes are Rare with Blob Top
         All Crown Tops are Rare
         Quart Crown Top in Amber is Ex. Rare

HISTORY: In 1889 William Hudson and his father-in-law James Palmer, purchase an interest in the Santa Rosa Bottling Works. The partnership included W.W. Skaggs, and became known as Hudson & Skaggs.
Later in 1889, Skaggs sells his share to Hudson and Palmer.
Palmer died in 1901, and in 1909, Hudson leased the bottling company to John Gist and Fred Jones.
This lasted until 1924, when Hudson sold the business to Robert Callori.
The plant was first located on 2nd St., but was soon moved to 3rd and Roberts.
Map below circa 1904, and the two pics are circa early 1900's. An interior view of the bottling plant, and the plant on 3rd St.

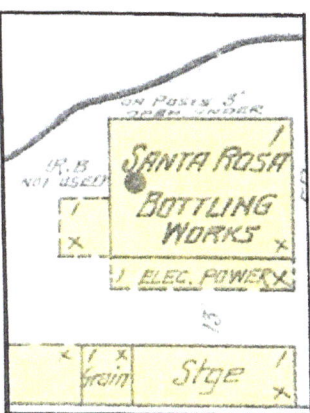

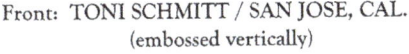

Front: TONI SCHMITT / SAN JOSE, CAL.
(embossed vertically)

Quart and Pint, Tooled Blob Top
Amber
Rarity: Rare in both sizes
HISTORY: no info at this time

Front: L. L. SCHULER / PALACE BREWERY / ALAMEDA / CAL.

Quart, Tooled Top
Amber
Rarity: Ex. Rare
HISTORY: L. Schuler operated the Palace Brewery from 1891 - 1907. Map is circa 1897.

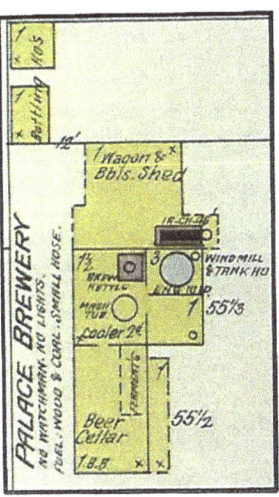

Front: SANTA FE BOTTLING CO. / C. V. & CO. / S. F.

Quart, Pint and ½ Pint
Tooled Blob Top
Amber, ½ Pint, $50.00 - 2020 GWA
Rarity: Scarce in the Quart and Pint sizes
Rare in the ½ Pint size

History: 1905 was the only year I could find a listing for this company. Cuneo and Vannucci were the proprietors at 420 Broadway. states they were lager and steam beer bottlers

Front: RUDOLPH SCHERF SAN JOSE CAL.
(embossed around shoulder)

Quart, and Pint
Tooled Blob and Crown Top
Amber
Rarity: Common with Blob Top in both sizes
Rare with a Crown Top in both sizes

HISTORY: No info at this time.

Front: SCHLITZ / MILWAUKEE BEER / WM. LAGEMANN / S. F.

½ Pint, Tooled Blob Top
Bulge Neck
Amber
Rarity: Ex. Rare

History: 1895 is the only years that Lagemann shows up in the directories. It has him as the proprietor of the Schlitz Bottling Works, at 712 14th. No other info. This would account for the extreme rarity of this bottle.

Front: SCHLITZ MILWAUKEE BEER / NADEAU & WALLER AGTS. / PORTLAND

½ Pint, Tooled Blob Top
Bulge Neck
Amber
Rarity: Very Rare

HISTORY: No info at this time.

Front: WM. SCHIMMEL / SAN JOSE, CAL.
(embossed vertically)

Quart, Pint and ½ Pint
Tooled Blob Top
Amber, ½ Pint, $170.00 - 2020 GWA
Rarity: Rare in all sizes

HISTORY: No info available.

Front: JOS. SCHWARZ / BREWING CO. / S. F. CAL.

Quart, and Pint. Tooled Blob Top
Amber
Rarity: Rare in all sizes

HISTORY: Joseph Schwarz was in the brewing business a very long time. First listing was in 1871, with no directory in 1870. By 1875 he was listed with Joseph Matt as proprietors of the North Beach Brewery at 420 Chestnut. This is the only time that Matt is listed as a partner.
From 1876 until 1914, the listing reads Joseph Schwarz Brewing Co., North Beach Brewery, at the Chestnut St. address. 1914 is the last year he appears in the beer business. Ads are circa 1895 and 1896.

Front: C. SCHNEER & CO. / SACRAMENTO, CAL.

    Pint and ½ Pint,
Tooled Blob Top
Amber, ½ Pint, $80.00 - 2001 ABA
Rarity: Scarce in both sizes

Front: SCHNERR & CO. / SACRAMENTO / CAL. / TRADE MARK REGISTERED / BOTTLES NEVER SOLD

    Pint, Tooled Crown Top
Aqua
Rarity: Scarce

    HISTORY: *The Schnerr Brothers were the proprietors of the Capitol Soda Works from 1892 until 1908. In 1895, they were also agents for Fredericksburg Beer. First located at 111-1113 Front St. and then in 1898 Constant Schnerr died and his son moved to 310 K St. They closed the doors in 1908.*

Front: PH. SCHNEIDER BREWING CO. / TRINIDAD / COLO.
        (in round plate)

    ½ Pint, Tooled Blob and Crown Top
Aqua and Clear
Varient: no slug plate
Rarity: Scarce in all varients

Front: PH. SCHNEIDER / BREWING CO. / TRINIDAD / COLO. (in round plate)
Re: THIS BOTTLE / NOT TO / BE SOLD

    ½ Pint, Tooled Crown Top
Aqua
Rarity: Scarce

Front: PH/ SCHNEIDER / BREWING CO. / TRINIDAD / COLO.
Re: CENTURY

    Pint, Tooled Crown Top
Aqua
Rarity: Scarce

    HISTORY: *The Ph. Schneider Brewing Co. was in business from 1892 - 1915. Located at Covert and Plum Sts. Photo is circa 1900, map circa 1895.*

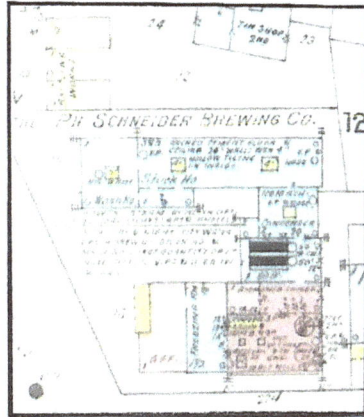

Front: S. F. STOCK BREWERY / S. F. S. B. / SAN
        FRANCISCO, CAL.

    Quart, Pint, and ½ Pint
    Tooled Blob Top
    Amber, Pint, $30.00 - 2017 ABA
    Rarity: All sizes are Rare

Front: S. F. S. B. (near base)

    Quart, Pint and ½ Pint
    Tooled Blob Top
    Amber
    Rarity: All sizes are Rare

    History: The first listing was in 1867. There was no directory in 1866, so this date could overlap into the previous year. Listed as the S.F. Stock Brewery at Powell and Francisco. This address stayed the same thru out the years. In 1871 a Mr. Schearze was listed as the proprietor. From 1876, F. Bruns was listed as the prop., the from 1877 to 1880 Wm. Schmidt was the prop. Henry Bruns took over in 1881, until they closed the doors in 1898.
    Label at right was trade marked in 1881.

Front: S. F. WEISS BREWERY / STUBER & CO.

    ½ Pint, Tooled Blob Top
    Amber, $475.00 - 2020 GWA
    Rarity: Ex. Rare

    HISTORY: 1894 was the first listing for S.F. Weiss Brewery. Stuber & Co. were the proprietors. In 1894, he was still in charge, but from 1895 until 1898, Stuber & Weikert wre the proprietors. In 1899 J. Stuber & Co. are again the Props. From 1900 until the last year, 1904, no props. were listed. The address the entire time was the corner of Geary and Baker.

Front: S. F. BEER / J. STRAUSS AGT. / AST. O.

    Quart, Applied Blob Top
    Amber
    Rarity: Ex. Rare

    HISTORY: No info at this Time.

Front: SEBASTOPOL / BOTTLING WORKS / CAL.
        (embossed vertically)

    Quart and Pint, Tooled Blob Top
    Amber
    Rarity: Common in both sizes

    History: Sebastopol Bottling Works dates from 1905 to 1909, with the Zimmerman family as owner. The name was changed to the Enterprise Bottling Works at the end of 1909, when Fred Matthews took over majority ownership. This lasted until 1917. They were an agent for the Enterprise Brewery of San Francisco.

Front: SEAL ROCK / BOTTLING CO. / JOHN
       KROGER / SAN FRANCISCO, CAL.

Quart, Pint and ½ Pint
Applied and Tooled Blob Top
Green, Quart only
Amber, ½ Pint, Tooled Top, $100.00 - 2020 (chip) GWA
       Quart, Tooled Top, $210.00 - 2009 GWA
Rarity: Rare in Quart and Pint size
       Ex. Rare in the ½ Pint size
       Green Quart is Ex. Rare

HISTORY: Seal Rock Bottling was first listed in 1900 at
       909 York St. This lasted until 1902, with no
       more mention of Seal Rock Bottling. John
       Kroger was still listed as a beer bottler at the
       same address as late as 1917. The name was
       trade marked in 1899, see drawing.

Front: JOHN R. SEIFERT / BOTTLER / SAN DIEGO
       (embossed vertically)

Quart and Pint, Tooled Crown Top
Amber
Varient: "BOTTLERS"
Rarity: Very Rare in all varients

Front: JOHN R. SEIFERT / BOTTLER / SAN DIEGO, CAL.

½ Pint, Tooled Blob Top
Clear
Rarity: Very Rare

Front: JOHN R. SEIFERT / SAN DIEGO / CAL.
       (in round plate)

½ Pint, Tooled Blob Top
Clear
Rarity: Very Rare

HISTORY: John Seifert was a wholesale wine and liquor dealer,
       located at 842 5th. He was an agent in the San Diego
       area for Rainier Beer, Pabst, and for the San
       Francisco Breweries Ltd., in 1905. No further info.

Front: S. F. BOTTLING CO. / FREITAS & RODGERS /
       S. F. CAL. (embossed vertically)

½ Pint, Bulge Neck
Tooled Blob Top
Rarity: Very Rare

HISTORY: I could not find much on this company. In 1901 it
       was listed as the S.F. Bottle Works at 925 Fulton,
       with M. Rodgers & co. as the proprietor. No mention
       of Mr. Freitas. I am not sure this is even the same
       company.

Front: SEATTLE BREWING & MALTING CO. / "star" /
       SEATTLE, WASH.

  5 ¼", Tooled Blob Top
  Amber, $120.00 - 2020 GWA
  Rarity: Very Rare

Front: SEATTLE BREWING & MALTING CO. /
       SEATTLE, WASH.

  ½ Pint, Tooled Blob Top
  Green
  Rarity: Very Rare

  HISTORY: The Seattle Brewing and Malting Co. was a consolidation of three breweries. In 1892, they were the Bay View, Claussen-Sweeney and the Albert Braun Brewing Co. Andrew Hemrich was the president. In less than 10 years, this company would grow to become the largest brewery on the west coast.
  There were distribution agents all over the west including, John Rapp and Son in San Francisco, Kirchner & Manti in Oakland, Cal, the Fresno Bottling Works, and the Ranier Beer Bottling Works in Reno, Nevada.
  In 1902, the Pacific Bottling Works became the bottler and Agent in Vancouver, B.C. These were the green crown top bottles shown here. Maps circa 1904. History and brewiana courtesy of Gary Flynn, brewerygems.com

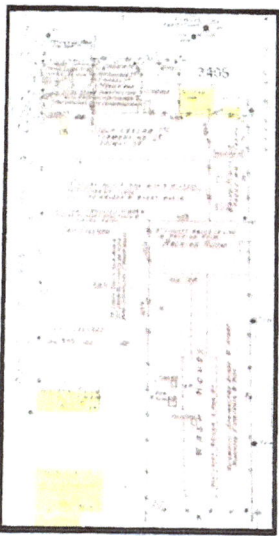   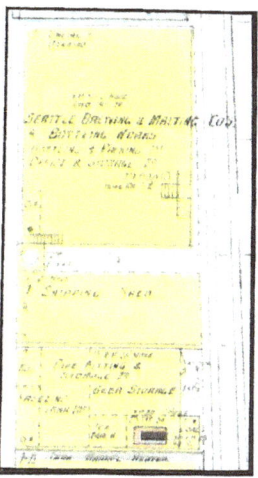

Front: SIERRA BOTTLING CO. / "monogram" / WIELAND'S BEST /
        JAMESTOWN, CAL.

   Quart, Pint and ½ Pint, Tooled Blob Top
   Amber, ½ Pint, $70.00 - 2020 (chip) GWA
           Quart, $650.00 - 2012 ABA
   Rarity: Very Rare in the Quart and Pint sizes
           Ex. Rare in the ½ Pint size

Front: SIERRA BOTTLING CO. / WIELAND'S BEST /
        JAMESTOWN, CAL.

   Quart, Tooled Blob Top
   Amber, $400.00 - 2001 ABA
   Rarity: Very Rare

   HISTORY: Nothing available at this time.

Front: SILVER BOW / "bow and arrow" /
        BREWING CO.   (in round plate)

   Quart, Tooled Crown Top
   Amber
   Rarity: Rare

   HISTORY: The Silver Bow, Montana Brewery was
        founded by Christian Nissler in 1871. He op-
        erated it until he died in 1901. It then
        changed hands, and was known as the Capitol
        Brewery and Chrystal Springs Brewery, until it
        closed for good in 1912. Ad at right circa 1876.

Front: SWAN BREWERY CO. / "swan" / XXX ALE
              (in round plate)
Re: THIS BOTTLE / NEVER SOLD / BY THE CO.

   ½ Pint, Applied Blob Top
   Amber, $2300.00 - 2020 GWA
   Yellow Green, $1500.00 - 2020 GWA
   Grass Green, $1100.00 - 2020 GWA
   Rarity: Rare in Amber
           Common in Green

   HISTORY: There was no directory in 1870, so the 1871 first
        listing could also be 1870. Shepard and Wilmot were the
        proprietors at 527 Valencia. From 1872 - 1875, Frederick
        Elliott joined Charles Wilmot.
        In John Bigbee was added as a partner. Then in 1876,
        Frederick Clay is listed as the President, and the other
        three proprietors have moved on.
        Then from 1877 thru the closing in 1881, George Hudson
        was the Prop. at 15th and Dolores. Hudson trade marked
        the label below in 1879.

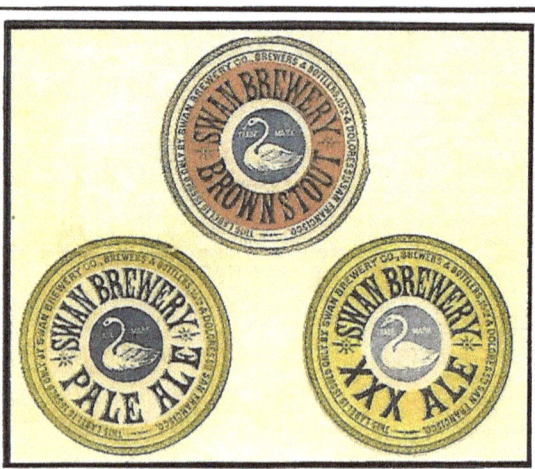

Front: SONOMA BREWING CO. / "monogram" / SONOMA, CAL.
(in round plate)

Quart, Pint and ½ Pint
Tooled Double Collar Export Top
Amber, ½ Pint, $70.00 - 2020 GWA
Rarity: Scarce in all sizes

HISTORY: The Sonoma Brewery Co. was up and running from 1905 - 1916. Wendler states that John Steiner incorporated the business in 1910. The export style bottles are earlier then that date, so they were operating at least 5 years before incorporation.
The Brewery and bottling works were located on East 2nd, next to the railroad tracks.
The company started to have financial issues in 1911, and Steiner resigned as president. The legal problems continued until they closed the doors sometime in 1916.
Some of the history notes and ads are courtesy of John Wendler.
Map is circa 1911, ads are 1910 and 1912.

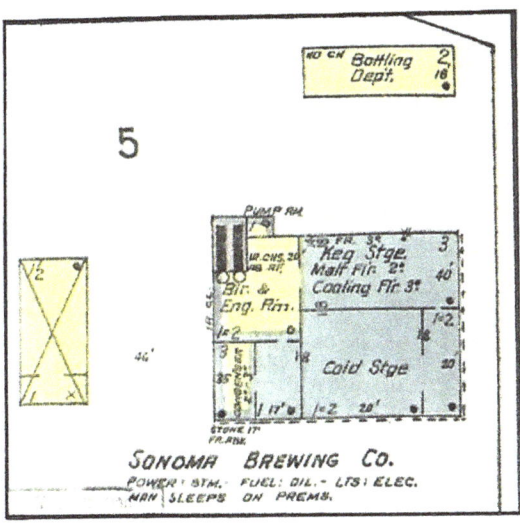

Front: SOUTHERN CALIFORNIA / BEER / BOTTLING ASS'N / LOS ANGELES, CAL.

Quart and ½ Pint, Bulge Neck
Tooled Blob Top
Amner, ½ Pint, $210.00 - 2020 (chip) GWA
Rarity: Very Rare in both sizes

HISTORY: No info at this time.

Front: SOUTHWESTERN LAGER / "monogram" / BEER BOTTLING (in round plate)

½ Pint, Tooled Blob Top
Amber
Rarity: Very Rare
Locale: Albuquerque, N.M.

HISTORY: The history of this brewery is somewhat confusing, depending on where you find it. Joe Demars and John Koenig founded the brewery in 1884- 1885. It was then taken over Jacob and Henry Loebs in 1885- 1887. Harry Rankin joined with the Loebs after 1887, it appears business was very good and at the start of the 1900's, it was one of Albuquerque's largest employers. In 1915, they changed the name to Western Brewing and Ice Co. Map below is circa 1908, newspaper ads circa 1905, trays circa 1910 and photo and label circa 1910 also. The bottle pictured here should date from the 1890's.

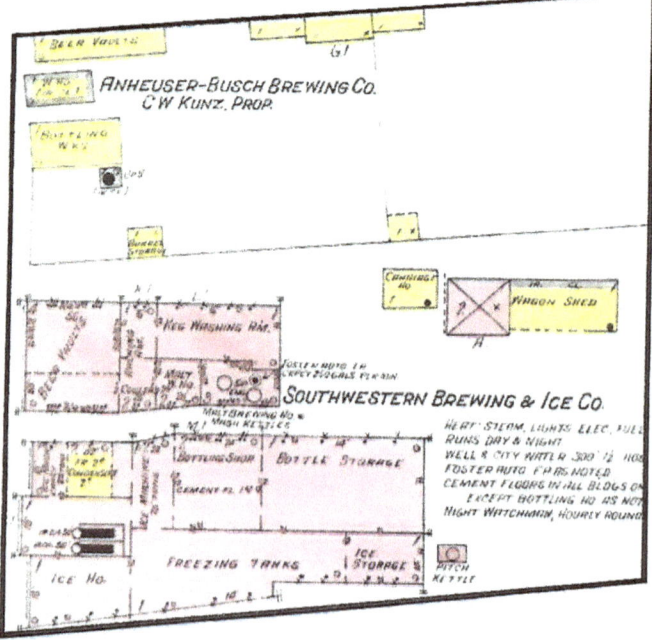

Front: STANDARD / S. F. / BOTTLING CO.

    Quart, Pint and ½ Pint
    Tooled Blob and Crown Top
    Amber, ½ Pint, $20.00- 2020 GWA
    Rarity: Scarce in all varients

    HISTORY: There was only one listing for this company. 1905 had them at Beach between Dupont and Stockton, with B. Hessel as the Proprietor. They were agents for the Los Angeles Brewing Co.

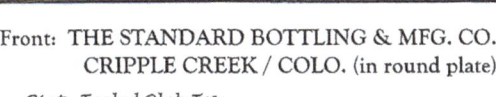

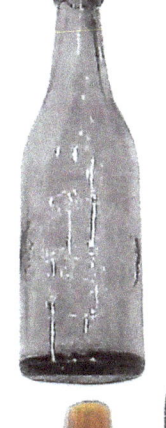

Front: THE STANDARD BOTTLING & MFG. CO. / CRIPPLE CREEK / COLO. (in round plate)

    Pint, Tooled Blob Top
    Aqua
    Rarity: Scarce

    HISTORY: No info at this time.

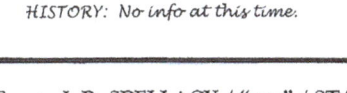

Front: J. R. SPELLACY / "star" / STAR BOTTLING CO. / S. F.

    ½ Pint, Tooled Blob Top
    Amber, $100.00- 2020 GWA
    Rarity: Rare

    HISTORY: John R. Spellacy was listed as a Beer Bottler in 1899, no address given. 1900-1901, he is a driver for the Hibernia Brewery. No further listings.

Front: J. GEO. STEIGER / "cross in shield" / 5 CEDAR AVE. S. F. (all in round plate)

    Quart, Tooled Blob top
    Amber, $900.00- 2017 (chip) ABA
    Rarity: Very Rare

    HISTORY: George Steiger is first listed in the beer business in 1890. He was with the Boca Bottling Co. at 615 Laguna. Then he was not listed in 1891 or 1892. Then from 1893 to 1897 he is listed as a Beer Bottler at 5 Cedar St. 1898 has him as John G. Steiger, Beer Bottler at 810 Alvarado. 1898 - 1900 he listed as J. George Steiger at the same Alvarado St. address. No listing for him in 1901, then George J. Steiger is listed as a driver for the Enterprise Brewing Co. from 1902- 1905. No further listings in the beer business.

Front: STAR BREWERY / VANCOUVER, WASH.
 (in round plate)

Quart and Pint, Bulge Neck
Tooled Blob Top
Amber
Rarity: Rare

History: The Star Brewery was a successor to one of the first breweries in the Washington Territory. It was originally established in 1856, by John Muench, near Fort Vancouver. In 1859, Henry Weinhard bought the brewery from Muench. In 1862 Weinhard sold the brewery to Anton Young, and he operated the brewery until 1894.
In 1894 Young retired and then sold the brewery to Louis Gerlinger, who changed the name to the Star Brewery Co. in 1897.
In 1904, the company was purchased by the Northern Brewery Co. These bottles should date from the 1890's period. Picture of the brewery is circa 1900, and the ad is circa 1890.
History and ad courtesy of Gary Flynn, brewergems.com.

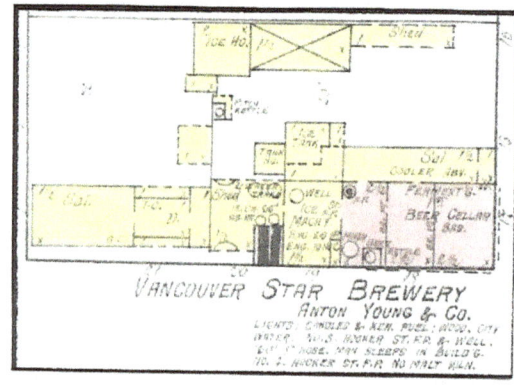
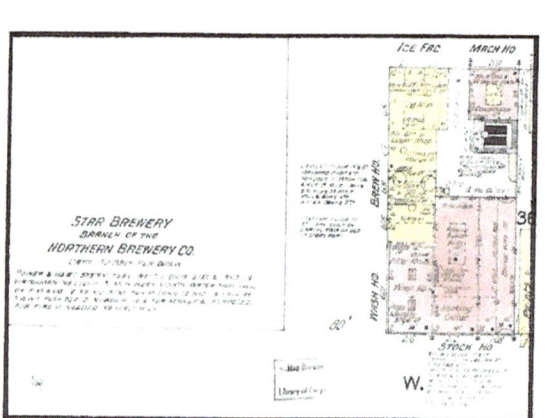

Front: ST. HELENA BOTTLING / AND / COLD STORAGE CO. / ST. HELENA / CAL.

Quart, Pint and ½ Pint
Tooled Blob and Crown Top
Amber
Rarity: Common in all sizes with Blob Top
Scarce in all sizes with Crown Top

HISTORY: In 1901, Priest and Meyer were the first proprietors of the St. Helena Rainier Beer Agency. Mr. Priest was also involved with the Priest Soda Works. In 1904, Romanso Cook took over the business. The St. Helena Bottling and Cold Storage Co. purchased the Rainier agency in 1905, and kept Romanso Cook on as manager. I am not sure what the "R" on the bottle stopper stands for, but it is probably for Rainier. The map below shows the business on Madrona in 1910. The brewery on Hunt predates the bottling works and is probably not related. Ads and history notes courtesy of John Wendler. Ads are circa 1905 and 1914.

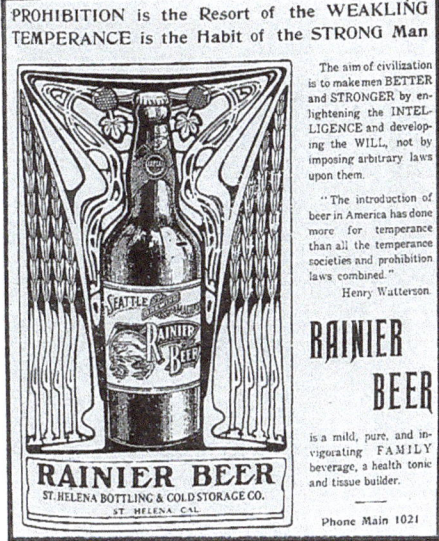
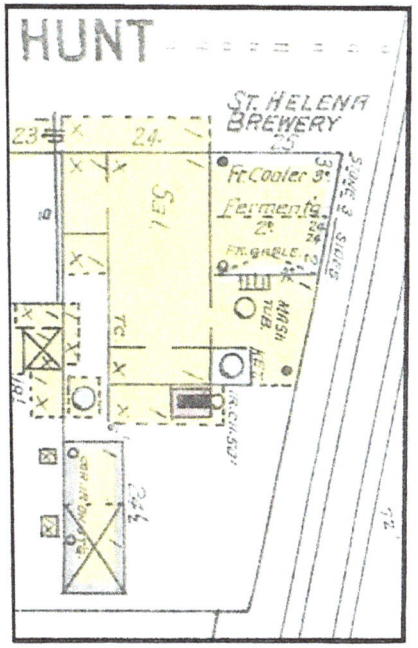
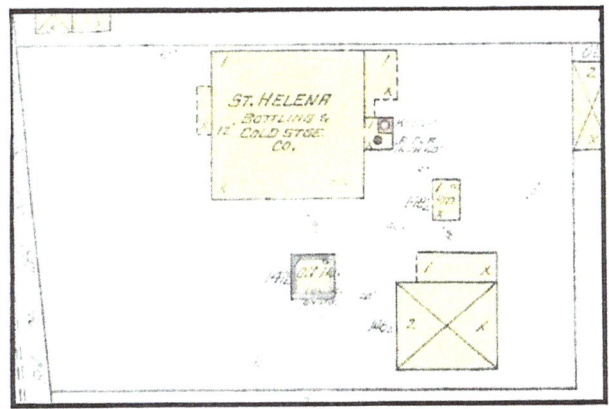

Front: ST. LOUIS BOTTLING CO. / McC. & B. / VALLEJO, CAL.

Quart, Pint and ½ Pint
Tooled Blob and Crown Top
Amber and Aqua
Varient: some have S.F. & P.G.W. on base, with Bulge Neck
½ Pint, Amber, $30.00 - 2020 GWA
Rarity: ½ Pints in Aqua are Common
 ½ Pints in Amber are Rare
 Quarts and Pints in Amber with Blob Top are Common
 Aqua Quart is Rare
 Quarts and Pints with Crown Top are Scarce
 Base embossed are Scarce

HISTORY: James McCauley and John Brennan formed a partnership in 1890. By 1901 they had built a new bottling works on Maine, see map. They were an agent for Rainier Beer and the Buffalo Brewing Co. The partnership lasted until 1914. They were very successful as most of these bottles are not rare. They trade marked the embossing pattern in 1899. Map is circa 1901. History courtesy of John Wendler.

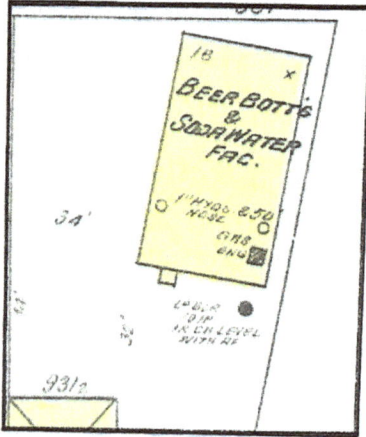

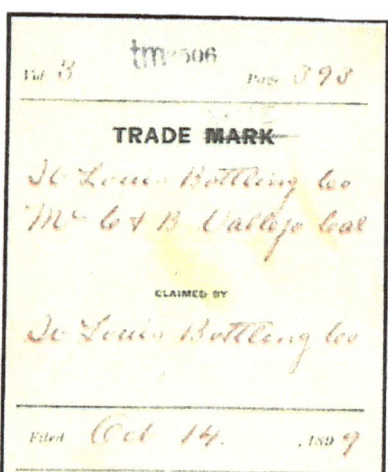

Front: STOCKTON WHOLESALE LIQUOR CO. / "monogram" / STOCKTON, CAL. (in round plate)

½ Gallon Picnic Beer
Tooled Blob Top
Amber
Rarity: Very Rare

HISTORY: No info available. This bottle probably held wine.

Front: H. W. STOLL & CO. / TRADE 'star" MARK / LOS ANGELES, CAL.

Quart and Pint
Applied and Tooled Blob Top
Bulge Neck
Amber
Rarity: Rare in the Quart size
 Scarce in the Pint size
 All Tooled Tops are Scarce

HISTORY: Henry Stoll moved to Los Angeles in 1867. By 1868 he had established the Los Angeles Soda Water Works. It was located on Sansavain St. Eventually Henry's brother, Phillip joined the firm, and then in 1880 he bought a partnership. They bottled soda, sarsaparilla, beer and syrups.

Front: JOHN STROHM / "monogram" / JACKSON, CAL.

Quart, Pint and ½ Pint, Tooled Crown Top
Amber
Quart, $160.00 - 2001 ABA
Pint and ½ Pint sizes are Rare
Quart is Scarce

History: John Strohm came to America in the late 1870's. He worked as a brewer in St. Louis, Cleveland and in Mexico before coming to Amador Co. in 1886. The original Jackson Brewery was established in 1860. Upon arriving in Jackosn, Strohm decided to rent the small plant. He used only the best hops and barley and soon was very successful. At this point he bought the business for $5000.00 from A. Chicazola, F. Hoffman and J. Holtz.

The brewery was on Sutter Rd. and Mattley St. In the 1890's he had added a saloon facing Sutter Rd. By 1898, a newer Brewery complex was built across Sutter Rd. It consisted of an ice factory, malt mill, beer cellar, beer kettle and copperage, with sleeping rooms on the second floofr of the new brick building. The old brewery was converted to the bottling plant with the facing the street. His dwelling was next door. Sometime around 1896 he added a soda works next to the new brewery complex.

Strohm delivered his beer in kegs to Mokelumne Hill, Pine Grove, Butte City, Pioneer, Cook's Station, Ione, Drytown, Plymouth, and other locations in horse drawn wagons. The beer was in kegs with bottles coming later. The brewery was in operation until prohibition, and then was converted to a creamery. John died in 1937.
Map below in circa 1898.

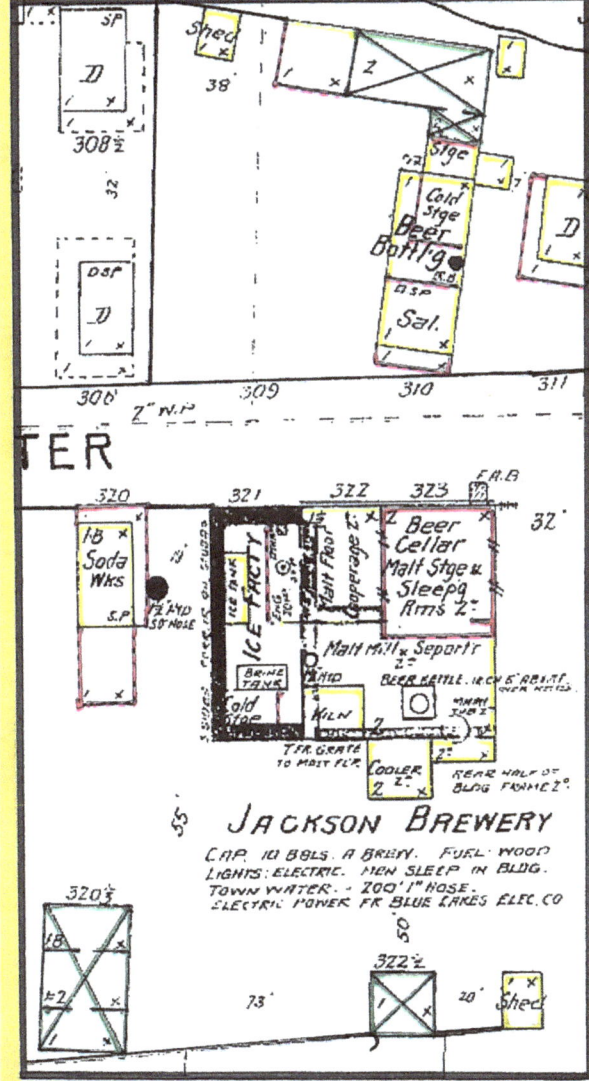

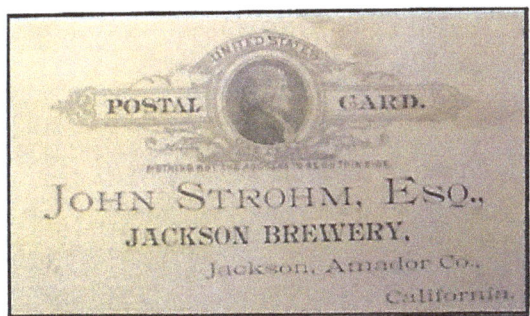

Picture below appears to be 1890's. John Strohm is probably the gentleman on the left. Circa 1918 calendar and a label for a malt product, no doubt put out during the prohibition era. Note is says less than 1% acholhol.

Front: SUNRISE BOTTLING CO. / E. STIRNKORB /
SAN FRANCISCO (embossed vertically)

Quart, Pint and ½ Pint, Tooled Blob Top
Amber, ½ Pint, $140.00 - 2020 GWA
Rarity: Quart and Pint size are Rare
½ Pint is Very Rare

Front: SUNRISE / BOTTLING CO. / STIRNKORB
BROS. / S. F. CAL. (embossed vertically)

Quart, Pint and ½ Pint, Tooled Blob Top
Amber, ½ Pint, $130.00 - 2020 GWA
Rarity: Quart and Pint size are Rare
½ Pint is Very Rare

HISTORY: I could only find one listing for the Sunrise Bottling Co. In 1905 the proprietors were the Stirnkorb Bros., at 3936 Sacramento.

Front: SUNSET BOTTLING CO. / SAN FRANCISCO

Quart, Tooled Blob Top
Amber
Rarity: Rare

Front: SUNSET BOTTLING CO. / "monogram" /
SAN FRANCISCO, CAL. (in round plate)

Quart, Tooled Blob top
Amber
Rarity: Scarce

Front: SUNSET BOTTLING CO. / "monogram" /
SAN FRANCISCO, CAL.

Quart, Pint and ½ Pint
Tooled Blob Top
Amber, ½ Pint, $70.00 - 2020 GWA
Rarity: Scarce in all sizes

HISTORY: The Sunset Bottling Co. was first listed in 1903, as Sunset Bottling Co., Bottlers of the Famous United States Lager, Props. Sorich & Sosich. Located at 1529 Howard. Listing was the same in 1904, and in 1905 also, except no props were listed. No further mention of this bottler.

Front: SUESSDORF & LAYMAN / "monogram" /
MOKELUMNE HILL

Quart, Tooled Blob Top
Amber, $375.00 - 2011 ABA
Rarity: Very Rare

HISTORY: Mokelumne Hill is a very early Gold Rush town. Its first brwery dates to 1852. It was called the Mokelumne Hill Brewery and operated by Suessdorf and Himminghofen. A second brewery was operated by Taft and Disbrow in 1858. The Suessdorf and Layman partnership was from 1899 to 1901. Before that Augusta Suessdorf operated the brewey alone from 1898 into 1899. Sometime is 1901, Suessdorf left the partnership to Andrew Layman, and he ran it from 1901 - 1904. The brewery was located on Church St. and was torn down in 1912. Map circa 1890.

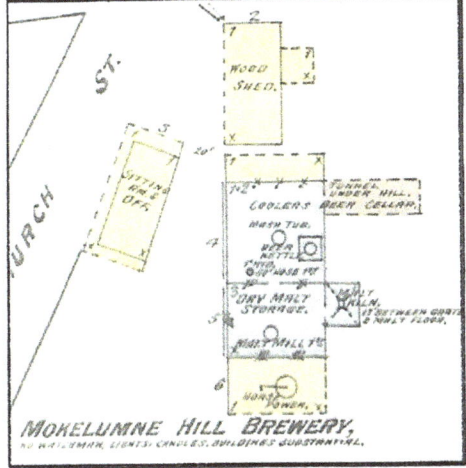

Front: TACOMA / BEER CO. / OAKLAND / CAL.

    Quart, Tooled Crown Top
    Bulge Neck
    Amber
    Rarity: Very Rare

    HISTORY: The Tacoma Beer Co. was listed in Oakland for the first time in 1906. They were doing business at 1068 5th. By 1907, they had moved to 104 4th, with Carl Lind as the manager. There was no directory in 1908, and the listing was the same in 1909.
    1910 brought some changes. Now we have Edward Conner as the proprietor, across the Webster Street bridge in Alameda. This remained unchanged in 1911. The last listing was in 1912, and stated that the Tacoma Bottling Works were the proprietors, at the same Alameda address. No further listings.

Front: TACOMA / BOTTLING CO. / S. F. CAL.

    Quart, Pint and ½ Pint
    Tooled Blob and Crown Top
    Amber and Aqua
    Amber, ½ Pint, Blob Top, $50.00- 2020 GWA
    Rarity: Very Rare in Aqua
          Common in Amber, all varients

    HISTORY: The first listing was in 1906. Bottlers of Tacoma Beer, at 2360 Harrison. This remained the same until 1910, when George Alpers was added to the listing as Manager. The next change was in 1917, with a new address of 675 Treat, no manager listed. The listing was unchanged in 1918, when research was stopped.

Front: PROPERTY / OF / OTTO TULLMAN / BOTTLING WORKS / SAN LUIS OBISPO / BOTTLE IS NOT TO BE SOLD

    Quart, Tooled Crown Top
    Aqua
    Rarity: Very Rare

    History: There was a brewery in San Luis Obispo from 1884 - 1888, under the Otto Tullman name. This bottle is much more recent than that brewery, Most likely 1905 - 1915 era. He also had an ice and cold storage plant on Pismo and Walker Sts. from at least 1905 to 1909. He could have had his bottling works associated with that.

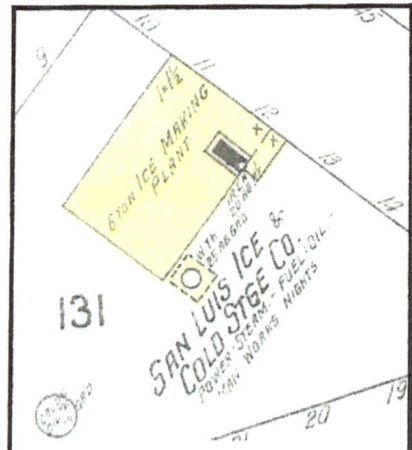

Front: GEO. A. TICOULET / SAC.
  Quart, Tooled Crown Top
  Amber
  Rarity: Common

Front: GEO. A. TICOULET / SAC.
  Quart, Pint and ½ Pint
  Tooled Blob Top
  Amber
  Rarity: Common in the Quart and Pint size
          Rare in the ½ Pint size

Front: TICOULET & BESHORMAN / SAC. CAL.
  Quart, Pint and ½ Pint, Tooled Blob Top
  Amber, ½ Pint, $20.00- 2020 GWA
  Rarity: Scarce in all Sizes

  HISTORY: George Ticoulet and Henry Beshorman started their bottling works in 1905. Beshorman left the firm in 1906, and Ticoulet ran it until he closed the doors in 1909. They were agents for Rainier Beer, and located at 1420 J Street.

Front: TOBENER BROS. / BOTTLERS / VALLECITO, CAL.
  Quart and ½ Pint, Tooled Blob Top
  Bulge Neck
  Amber
  Rarity: Very Rare in both sizes

  HISTORY: No info avavilable.

Front: JOHN TONS / "monogram" / STOCKTON / CAL.
       (in round plate)
  Re: THIS BOTTLE IS NEVER SOLD
  Quart, Tooled Blob Top
  Bulge Neck
  Amber
  Rarity: Scarce

Front: JOHN TONS / "monogram" / STOCKTON / CAL.
  Quart, Pint and ½ Pint, Tooled Blob and Crown Top
  Amber, ½ Pint, Blob Top, $20.00- 2020 GWA
  Varient: monogram is different
  Rarity: Common in all Varients

Front: JOHN TONS / "monogram" / STOCKTON / CAL.
  Base: S.F. & P.G.W.
  Quart, Pint and ½ Pint, Tooled Blob Top
  Bulge Neck
  Amber
  Rarity: Common in all Sizes

Front: JOHN TONS / "monogram" / STOCKTON, CAL.
  Quart, Pint and ½ Pint, Tooled Blob Top
  Amber
  Rarity: Common in all Sizes

  HISTORY: John F. Tons was an agent for John Wieland's Brewery in Stockton, From 1890 until 1903. Located at 12 East Weber. He was very successful, as these bottles are common.

Front: C. THOMAS / TRUCKEE

½ Pint, Tooled Top
Bulge Neck
Amber, $800.00 - 1998 ABA
Ex. Rare

History: Charles Thomas started a soda works in Truckee in 1885. This venture lasted until 1921. He took over the old St. Louis Brewery of Grazer & Stoll in 1897. They had operated this brewery from 1881 to at least 1886. After it closed and the Boca Brewery down river burnt down they was no beer supply locally, so Thomas had a ready market for his beer. He ran both the soda works and brewery at the same time in different locations in town.
It was called the Eureka Brewery in the business directories.
He brewed "THOMAS STEAM BEER", "EUREKA STEAM BEER, and "FELSON LAGER". Thomas had trouble finding a dependable brewer. and the quality of his beer suffered because of this. He finally sold the business sometime in 1911.

Both the Hutchinson style soda bottles and the ½ pint beers are ex. rare. There are only 2 or 3 beers known to exist at this time. Map is circa 1907.

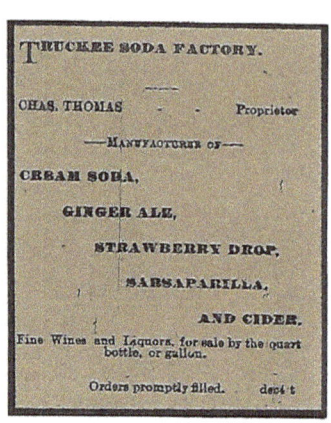

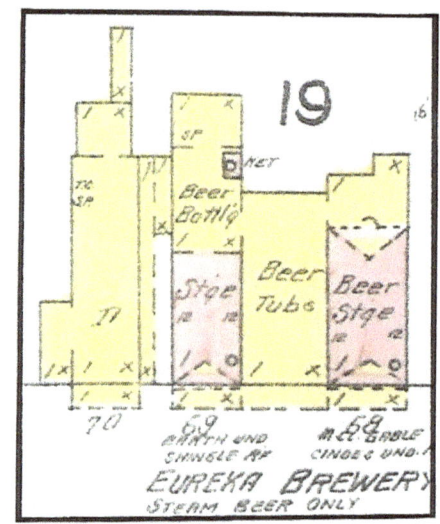

168

Front: D. TWEEDIE / RED "hand" HAND / TRADE MARK / SAN FRANCISCO / THIS BOTTLE NEVER SOLD

Quart, Pint and ½ Pint
Applied and Tooled Blob Top
Amber and Clear
½ Pint, Amber, Tooled Top, $130.00 - 2020 GWA
$400.00 - 2017 ABA
Rarity: Clear ½ Pint is Very Rare
Applied Tops, all sizes are Ex. Rare
Tooled Tops, all sizes are Rare

Front: D. TWEEDIE / RED "hand" HAND / TRADE MARK / SAN FRANCISCO / THIS BOTTLE NEVER SOLD

½ Pint, Tooled Blob Top
Bulge Neck
Amber
Rarity: Ex. Rare

Front: T (on shoulder) / D. TWEEDIE / RED "hand" HAND / TRADE MARK / SAN FRANCISCO / THIS BOTTLE NEVER SOLD

Quart, Pint and ½ Pint
Applied Blob Top
Green, Quart, $650.00 - 1997 ABA
Green, ½ Pint, $750.00 - 2017 ABA
Rarity: Very Rare in all sizes

HISTORY: *The first listing for Daniel Tweedie was as a clerk in 1887. In 1888 he is a Beer Bottler and then a salesman in 1889.*
1890, has him as a driver for the Phoenix Brewery.
1891 - 1892 he is again a Beer Bottler
1893 listing, Daniel Tweedie, Proprietor Sunrise Bottling Co., at 504 24th. In 1894 he is a bottler at the same address.
He finally establishes his own bottling works in 1895.
Daniel Tweedie Prop, Tweedies Bottling Works, 229 - 231 24th.
This remained the same in 1896, with the listing changing in 1897 to, Tweedie & Goldberg, Porter Beer Bottlers, 2973 - 2975 24th St.
The listing changed again in 1898 to, Daniel Tweedie, bottler of Porter, Ale, Lager Beer, with the new address of 409 - 419 8th.
1899 brought another address change to 2015 Folsom. This remained the same until 1901 when he went out of business. Tweedie trade marked the RED HAND brand in 1894. See drawing above.

Front: UKIAH BOTTLING WORKS / UKIAH / CAL.

    Quart and Pint,
    Tooled Blob and Crown Top
    Amber
    Rarity: Scarce with Blob Top
          Ex. Rare with Crown Top

Front: UKIAH BREWING & ICE CO. / "barrel" / UKIAH, CAL.

    ½ Pint, Tooled Crown Top
    Aqua
    Rarity: Rare

    HISTORY: The Ukiah Bottling Works was located at the end of Clay St, at the railroad tracks. I found that the Ukiah Brewery was taken over by Max Weiss of the Roseburg Oregon Brewing & Ice Co. in 1912. It has not been in operation since 1908. They updated the apparatus and operations. I do not know if this occurred in this building. Closed for good in 1917. The Ukiah Brewing and Ice Co. was located at Clara and Mason Sts. in 1911. They were an agent for Grace Bros. Beer, of Santa Rosa. Bottling Works map circa 1898, Ice Co. circa 1911.

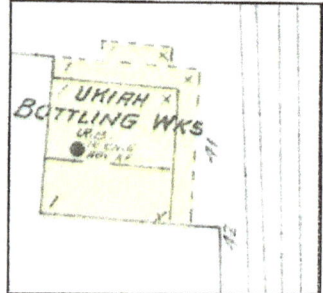
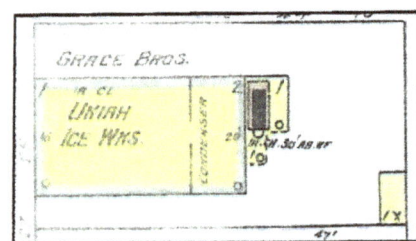

Front: UNION BREWING CO. / "monogram" / ANAHEIM, CAL.

    Quart, Tooled Crown Top
    Amber
    Rarity: Scarce

    HISTORY: The Brewery seems to have been operating from at least 1907 - 1915. Map is circa 1911. No other info.

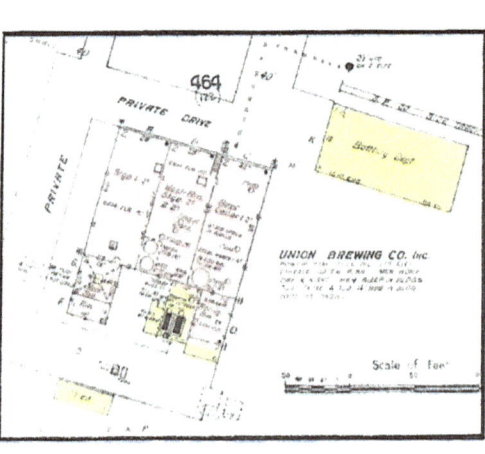

Front: UNION BREWING / AND / MALTING CO. / S. F. CAL.

Quart, Pint and ½ Pint
Tooled Blob and Crown Top
Amber and Clear
½ Pint, Amber, with Blob Top, $50.00 - 2020 GWA
Pint, Amber, Blob Top, $30.00 - 2006 ABA
Rarity: All Crown Tops are Scarce
All Amber Blob Tops are Common
Clear, ½ Pint with Blob Top is Ex. Rare

Front: TRADE MARK / XX / UNION BREWING CO. / PORTER / S. F. (in large shield)

½ Pint, Tooled Blob Top
Amber
Rarity: Very Rare

HISTORY: In 1893 and 1894, they were listed as the Union Brewing Co., located at 325 Clementina.
Then in 1895 and 1996 they had moved to the corner of Solano and Florida.
By 1897 the name had changed to the Union Brewing Co, Inc. with Henning Thode as President, now located at 18ᵀᴴ and Florida. This stayed the same thru 1904.
In 1905 the same Union Brewing is listed with the Bottling Works added at 423-427 Valencia St. The 1906 listing dropped the bottling works from the description.
Cascade Bottling Works was added in 1907 thru 1910 with everything else being the same.
From 1910 until closing in 1917 the listing reads Union Brewing and Malting Co. with H. Thode as Preodent, still at the 18ᵗʰ and Florida address. They shut the doors in 1918, due to prohibition.
Map below is circa 1899 at 18ᵀᴴ and Florida

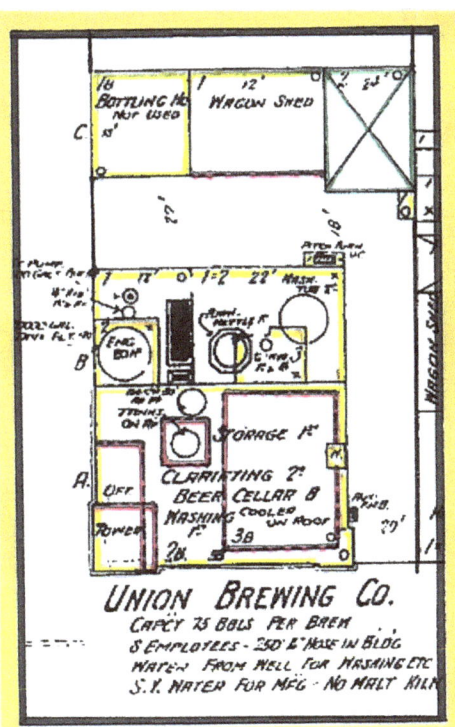

171

Front: U. S. BOTTLING CO. / JOHN FAUSER & CO. / S.F. CAL.
(embossed vertically)

Pint and ½ Pint, Applied Blob Top
Red Amber
Pint, $110.00 - 2017 ABA
½ Pint, $80.00 - 2017 ABA
Rarity: Rare in both sizes
Note: ½ Pint has a bulge neck

Front: U.S. BOTTLING CO. / JOHN FAUSER & CO. / SAN FRANCISCO (embossed vertically)

Quart and Pint
Applied and Tooled Blob Top
Red Amber
Quart, Applied Top, $130.00 - 2010 ABA
Rarity: Scarce with Applied Top in both sizes
Common with Tooled Top in both sizes

Front: LITTLE FAUSER / U. S. / LAGER

½ Pint, Tooled Blob Top
Amber and Clear
Rarity: Rare

HISTORY: In 1890, John Fauser & Co. was listed as a bottler of United States Lager Beer, located at 126 Guerrero. This continued until 1893, when his widow was listed as the "& CO."
1896 brought William and George Fauser in the business also. There was no listing in 1906 or 1907 for any Fauser in the beer bottling trade.
In 1908 the listing read, John Fauser & Co., G J & W. Fauser props for the Phoenix Bottling Works at 162 Guerrero. This lasted to at least 1918, when research was stopped. The bottles here should date in the 1890 to about 1900 era.

Front: U. S. BOTTLING CO./ TRADE U. S. MARK /
RAPP & DEBARRY / S. F. CAL. / THIS
BOTTLE NOT TO BE SOLD

½ Pint, Applied and Tooled Blob Top
Bulge Neck
Amber, Tooled Top, $180.00 - 2010 ABA
Rarity: Very Rare

Front: U. S. BOTTLING CO. / TRADE U. S. MARK /
RAPP & DEBARRY / SAN FRANCISCO /
CAL. / THIS BOTTLE NOT TO BE SOLD

Quart, Applied Blob Top
Red Amber
Rarity: Very Rare

Front: U. S. BOTTLING CO. / US / RAPP &
DEBARRY / S. F. CAL.

Quart, Tooled Blob Top
Amber
Rarity: Rare

Front: U. S. BOTTLING CO. / TRADE U. S. MARK /
J. RAPP & SON / S. F. CAL. / THIS
BOTTLE NOT TO BE SOLD

Quart and Pint, Tooled Blob Top
Amber
Rarity: Rare in both sizes

Front: UNITED STATES / "shield" / BOTTLING WORKS /
J. B. CUNEO / BOTTLE NOT TO BE SOLD

Quart and Pint, Tooled Blob Top
Amber, Quart, $800.00 - 2010 ABA
Varient: Some have Bulge Neck
Rarity: Rare in all varients
Note: The embossing patterns were trade marked
in 1899, by J. B. Cuneo. See drawing.

Front: U. S. LAGER BEER / "crossed flags" / J. B. CUNEO /
S. F. / BOTTLE NOT TO BE SOLD

Quart, Pint and ½ Pint
Tooled Blob Top, Bulge Neck
Amber, ½ Pint, $1700.00 - 2020 GWA
Rarity: Very Rare in all sizes.

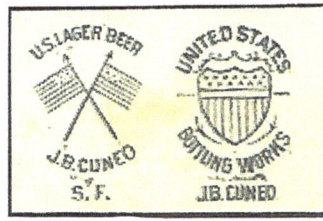

United States Lager Beer label trade marked in 1890 by Rapp & DeBarry S.F.

United States Lager Beer label trade marked in 1893 by Rapp & DeBarry S.F.

HISTORY: 1889 is the first listing for the United States Bottling Co. They were located at Franklin and McAlister Sts. Rapp and Debarry were the proprietors. They remained at this location until 1899 when John Rapp and Son became the proprietors. They were at 6th and King, and were bottlers of Pabst and U.S. Lager.
There was no listing in 1900.
In 1901 the United States Bottling works was at 3017 20th, with J. B. Cuneo as the prop.
The next move was in 1903, Cuneo moved to 2194 Folsom.
The next year found them on the move again, this time to 3109 20th. They remained there in 1905.
The earthquake brought no listing for 1906, but Cuneo is listed again as a bottler in 1907 and 1908.
The bottles listed here should all date before 1901.
There was a United States Brewery listed from 1872 to 1909 at various locations around San Francisco. They had many managers over the years, and I am not sure about a connection to any of these bottles. I doubt that there is one.

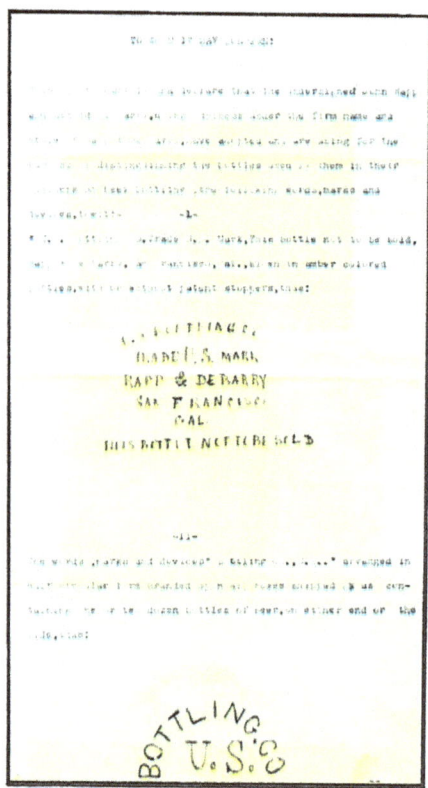

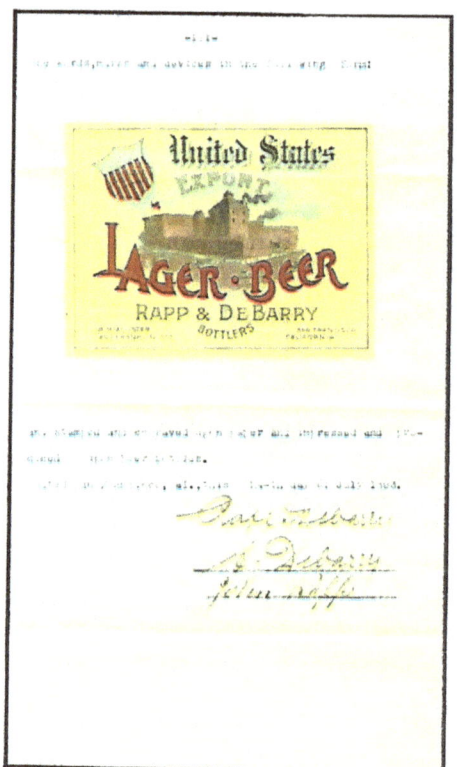

Front: VALLEJO / BOTTLING WORKS / H & K / VALLEJO, CAL.
(embossed vertically)

Quart, Tooled Blob Top
Amber
Rarity: Rare
Note: No pic at this time. Looks like the Doty bottle below.

Front: VALLEJO / BOTTLING WORKS / C. E. DOTY / VALLEJO, CAL.
(embossed vertically)

Quart, Pint and ½ Pint
Tooled Blob and Crown Top
Amber
Rarity: Rare in Quart and Pint size with either top
Very Rare in the ½ Pint size with either top

HISTORY: Charles Doty was a wholesale liquor distributor and an agent Enterprise Beer from about 1904 to sometime in 1910. Ad circa 1905. He was doing business at the corner of Colusa and Pennsylvania in Vallejo. I do not know if the H & K bottle preceeds this one or comes after.

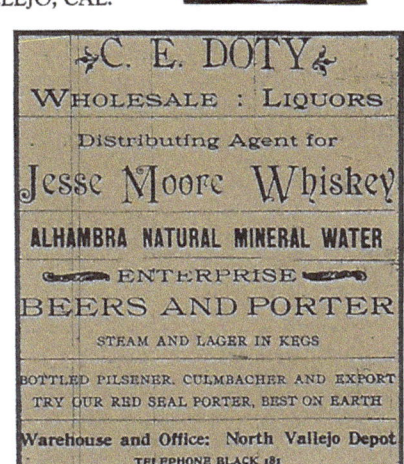

Front: C. J. VATH & CO. / SAN JOSE

Quart, Pint and ½ Pint
Tooled Blob and Crown Top
Amber and Clear
½ Pint, Amber, Blob Top $30.00 - 2020 GWA
½ Pint, Clear, Blob Top, $120.00 - 2020 GWA
Rarity: Common in all Amber varients
Clear, ½ Pint is Very Rare

HISTORY: In 1901, Charles Vath moved to San Jose from San Francisco, where he was a butcher for 10 years. He then established a bottling business for beer and soda. His big break came in 1902, when he acquired the bottling and distribution agency for Rainier Beer products in the San Jose area. He was located on 4th and Virginia. He continued operations until 1919, when he was shut down by prohibition. History notes courtesy of John Wendler. Map is circa: 1915.

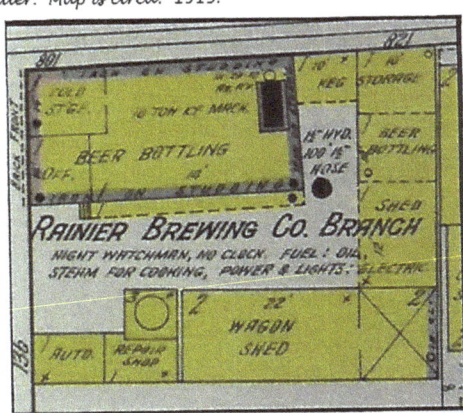

Front: VIKING BREWING CO. / "ship" / SAN FRANCISCO, CAL.

Quart and Pint
Tooled Blob Top
Amber
Rarity: Ex. Rare in both sizes

HISTORY: The Viking Brewing Co., Inc. was listed rom 1895 - 1897 with L. Knudsem as president. The address in 1895 was 108 Alabama and then in 1896 and 1897 it was 28th and Hampshire Sts. No further listings.

Front: A. L. VAN VALEY / BOTTLING WORKS /
        EVERETT, WASH. (in round plae)

½ Pint, Tooled Blob Top
Amber
Rarity: Rare

HISTORY: The Van Valey Bottling Works was located on Broadway, next to the Standard Steam Laundry in 1914. The photo looks to be about the same era.

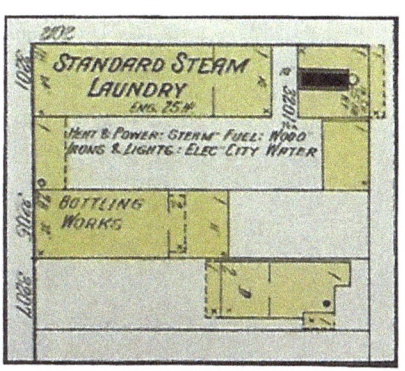 

Front: THE WALTER / BREWING CO. / PUEBLO
        COLO (in round plate)

Quart and Pint, with Bulge Neck
Tooled Blob and Crown Top
Amber and Aqua
Rarity: Rare in Amber
        Scarce in Aqua

Front: THE / WALTER BREWING CO. / PUEBLO /
        COLO. (in round plate)
Re: BOTTLE / NOT TO / BE SOLD

Quart, Pint and ½ Pint
Tooled Blob and Crown Top
Amber and Aqua
½ Pint, Amber, Blob Top, $70.00 - 2020 GWA
Rarity: Rare in amber
        Scarce in Aqua
Varient: Some have bulge neck.

HISTORY: No info at this time. Map below in circa 1904.

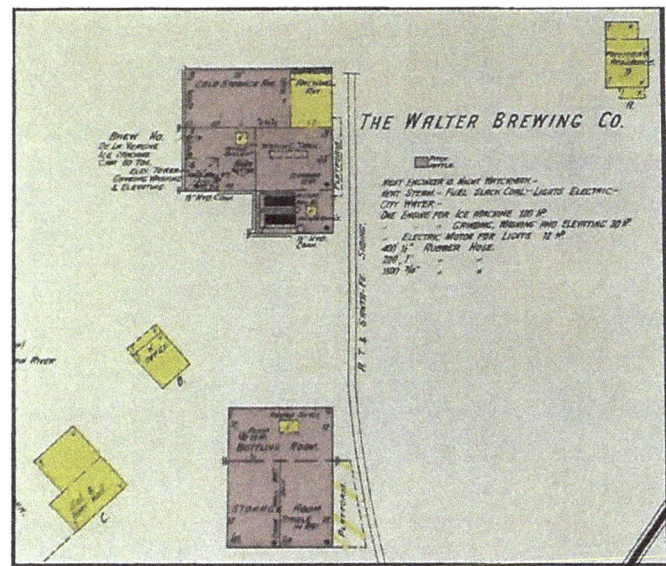

177

Front: HENRY WAGENER / BREWING CO.

Quart, Tooled Crown Top
Bulge Neck
Amber
Rarity: Rare

HISTORY: Henry Wagener first established his brewery in 1864 as the California Brewery. Located at 17 2nd St. South in Salt Lake City. In 1894, the name was changed to the Wagener Brewing Co. This remained the same until prohibition forced them to close the doors in 1815. This was Utah's first brewery. Maps are circa 1889.

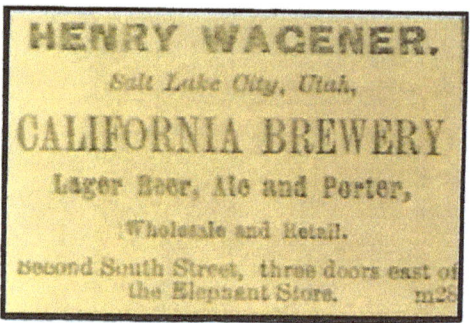

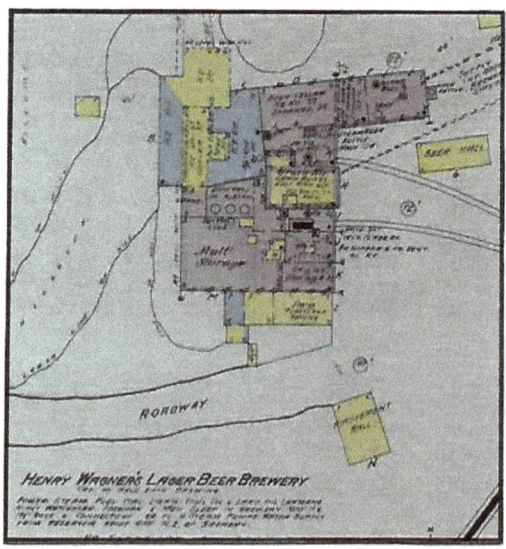

Front: HENRY WEINHARD / EXPORT BEER /
PORTLAND, OR. (embossed vertically)

Quart, Tooled Blob Top
Bulge Neck
Amber, $150.00- 2013 ABA
Rarity: Scarce

Front: H. WEINHARD / PORTLAND OR.
(in round plate)
Re: BOTTLE NOT / TO BE SOLD

½ Pint, Tooled Blob and Crown Top
Amber, Blob Top, $30.00- 2020 GWA
Clear, Blob Top, $65.00- 2017 ABA
Rarity: Scarce in all varients

Front: HENRY WEINHARD / CITY
BREWERY / PORTLAND OR.
(in round plate)

Quart, Tooled Blob and Crown Top
Bulge Neck
Amber
Rarity: Rare with Blob Top
Scarce with Crown Top

Front: HENRY WEINHARD / PORTLAND / ORE.
(in round plate)

Pint, Tooled Blob Top
Bulge Neck
Amber
Rarity: Rare

Front: H. WEINHARD / BREWERY /
PORTLAND, ORE.
Re: BOTTLE / NOT TO / BE SOLD

½ Pint, Tooled and ABM Crown Top
Amber
Varient: reverse is blank
Rarity: Scarce with Crown Top
Rare with ABM Top
Varient is Rare

HISTORY: Henry Weinhard came from Germany and made his way to Washington state. He found a job with John Meney, a local brewer. He eventually bought the brewery from Meney and operated it for about 4 years.
By 1862, he had bought out the Saxer Brewery in Portland. His patner in this venture was George Bottler. In 1866 he then bought out Bottlers share. His next acquisition was the old City Brewery, which became the Weinhard Brewery. He soon had agencys up and down the west coast. Brewery barrel room picture is circa 1910, building pic 1892. Map 1889.

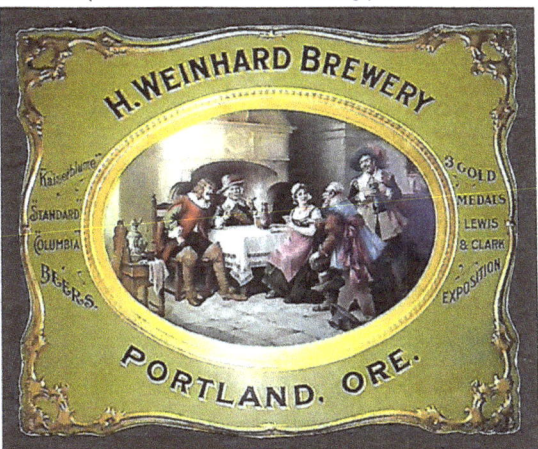

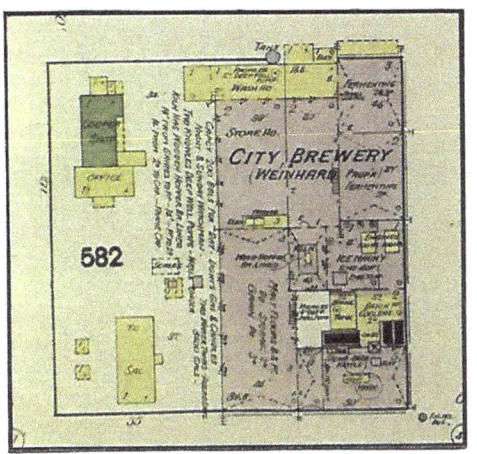

181

Front: W. B. CO. S. F. / "sun" / TRADE MARK
(in round plate)

½ Pint, Applied Blob Top
Aqua, $4400.00 - 2019 ABA
         $2750.00 - 2020 GWA
Rarity: Ex. Rare

HISTORY: The first listing for Charles Wilmot was in 1869. He was listed as a brewer. There is no directory for 1870.
From 1871 to 1876, he was a superintendent with the Swan Brewery.
The Wilmot Brewing Co. was first listed in 1877. Charles Wilmot was the president, doing business at 324 - 328 Guerrrero.
The 1878 - 1879 listing states, Wilmot Brewing Co., Manufacturers of XXX Ales & Porters, 324 - 328 Guerrero. There is also a Samuel Wilmot listed at the same address, I am assuming this is his brother.
In 1880 the Wilmot Brewing Co. appears to be gone, as Harry Wilmot is a brewer and Charles Wilmot is a forman at the San Francisco Stock Brewery at 1413 Valencia.
This is the last mention of the Wilmots in the brewery business.
The bottle should date from 1877 to 1879.

Front: G. W / ANGELS

½ Pint, Tooled Blob Top
Bulge Neck
Amber, $100.00 - 2020 GWA
Rarity: Rare
Note: This is the split size for George Werly, Angels Camp.

Front GEO. WERLY / ANGELS

Quart, Tooled Crown Top
Amber
Rarity: Very Rare
Locale: Angles Camp, Cal.

HISTORY: No info at this time.

Front WESTERN / BREWERY / NEFF / BROS. / DENVER, COLO. (in round plate)

Pint, Tooled Blob Top
Aqua
Rarity: Scarce

HISTORY: In 1891, the Neff Bros bought the Western Brewery from John Dostal. It was located on 12th and Raritan in Denver. They ran it very successfully until prohibition came in 1918, and they were forced to close the doors. Map circa 1903, ads circa 1905 to 1912.

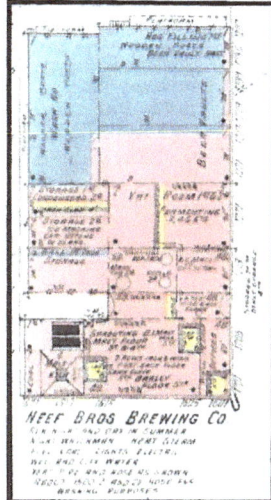

THE NEEF BROS. BREWING COMPANY,
CELEBRATED
Wiener Maerzen
THE BEER THAT WILL MAKE COLORADO FAMOUS.

A STRICTLY COLORADO PRODUCT.
NEEF BROS. BREWING CO.
Weiner Maerzen and Gold Belt Beers
Comparison Solicited with any and all Eastern High-Priced Beers.
Purity and Quality Guaranteed.
FAMILYS SUPPLIED.   PHONE MAIN 1105

183

Front: WESTERN BOTTLING CO. / D & K (in shield" /
        SAN FRANCISCO, CAL.

Quart, Tooled Blob Top
Amber
Rarity: Rare

HISTORY: Dohrman & Kerth were the proprietors of the Western Bottling Co. 1899.
        They were located at Montgomery and Chestnut Sts.
        The directory page for 1900 was missing, so this bottle may have been
        used in that year also. None the less it is very rare. No further listings.

Front: WESTERN BOTTLING COMPANY / S. F. CAL.
        (in horseshoe) / 'bear" (in the middle)

Pint and ½ Pint
Tooled Crown Top
Amber and Aqua
Rarity: Very Rare in all varients

HISTORY: This is a different Western Bottling Co. then the one listed above. It was
        first listed in 1906, at 895 Alabama.
        This stayed the same thru 1911, with D. Griffin and C. and J. Herlihy
        added as proprietors in 1908.
        1912 brought an address change to 3136 Army.
        In 1914, Ginger Ale and Soda Water Mfg. was added to the listing.
        They must have went out of business after 1916, as there are no further
        listings. This may have been a soda instead of a beer, even though it
        resembles many beers of that period. Used for a very short time, as it
        is very rare.

Front: WIENER BOTTLING CO. / 914 ELLIS ST. / SAN FRANCISCO

Quart, Applied Blob and Ring Top
Amber, $4200.00 - 2017 (chip) ABA
Rarity: Ex. Rare

HISTORY: 1886 was the only year Alois Wiener was listed
        in the beer business. He was a bottler with no
        address given. He probably used this bottle
        for less than a year.

Front: PROPERTY OF / GEO. WISSEMANN / SACRAMENTO,
        CAL. / THIS BOTTLE NOT TO BE SOLD

Quart and Pint, Tooled Blob Top
Bulge Neck
Amber
Rarity: Very Rare in both sizes.

HISTORY: George Wissemann operated a saloon on 4th St.
        starting in 1885. In 1891, while he was still op-
        erating his saloon, he became an agent for Lemp's
        St. Louis Lager. By 1893, he aws also an agent for
        Pabst. These two beers were probably bottled in his
        bottles by a local bottler.
        These bottles should date from the late 1890's, to
        The early 1900's, when he entered the wholesale
        Liquor business with Michael Cronin.

BEER IS BREAD

Bread in a liquid form, and therefore more easy Digestable, more Palatable, and for this reason

More Nutritious than Oven Bread.

Beer is a most Wholesome Beverage

provided it is brewed properly and has the necessary

AGE, STRENGTH AND PURITY.

These qualities can be found in the Beer brewed by the

John Wieland,
Fredericksburg and
Chicago Breweries.

The undersigned keeps on hand always a complete stock of both keg and bottled Beer, comprising the following brands:

BLUE SEAL,
EXTRA PALE,
STANDARD,
CULMBACHER,
BOCH, and Special Brew
DOUBLE EXTRA BROWN STOUT.

Give our Beer a Trial and you will Use no other.

It is highly recommended by the leading Physicians on account of its Superior Qualities.

Unsurpassed as a TONIC and APPETIZER.

PLEASE ADDRESS

JACOB ADLOFF, Agent.

Depot and Bottling Works Junction of North Main, Mission and Chavez Streets.

P. O. Box 1231, Station C. Telephone 468.

All orders will receive careful and prompt attention.

☞ FAMILY TRADE SOLICITED.

Front: JOHN WIELAND'S / EXPORT BEER / S. F.
        (embossed vertically)

½ Pint, Applied Double Collar Top
Bulge Neck
Olive Amber
Rarity: Very Rare

Front: JOHN WIELAND'S / EXPORT BEER / S. F.
        (embossed vertically)

5 ½ Sample, Tooled Blob Top
Amber, $140.00 - 2020 GWA
Rarity: Very Rare

Front: WIELAND'S / "crown" / W / LITTLE POP
Re: CAL / BOTTLING / CO.
        (all letters etched)

½ Pint, Tooled Blob and Crown Top
Clear, Aqua and Amber
Rarity: Scarce in Clear and Aqua
        Rare in Amber

Front: JOHN WIELAND / EXPORT BEER /
       JOHN TONS, AGENT
        (embossed vertically)

Quart, Applied Blob Top
Bulge Neck
Amber
Rarity: Rare

Front: JOHN WIELAND'S / EXPORT BEER / S.F.
        (embossed vertically)

Pint and ½ Pint, Applied Blob Top
Bulge Neck
Red Amber, $180.00 - 2017 ABA
Rarity: Scarce in both sizes

HISTORY: Hoelscher & Wieland were the proprietors of the Philadelphis Brewery as early as 1861. They were located on 2nd St. Wieland was at this address the entire time he was in business. In 1868, the listing changed to just John Wieland as the sole proprietor.
This remained the same until 1885, when the estate of John Wieland was listed, followed by the widow in 1886.
1887-1888 has Herman Wieland the president. . I am not sure if this is a brother or son.
1889-1890 has John H. Wieland as the president. I am assuming that this is a son of John Wieland.
Then in 1891 thru 1902, the listing just says John Wieland Brewery, 228-240 2ND.
Sometime in 1903, they were bought out by the San Francisco Brewies Ltd., an English company. The listings continued the same until prohibition in 1918, when research was stopped. Map circa 1887.

Philadelphia Brewery PB beer label. Trade marked in 1881 by John Wieland.

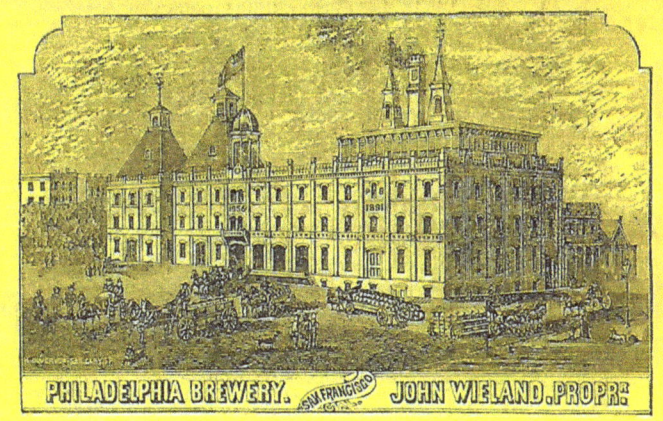

PHILADELPHIA BREWERY

PHILADELPHIA BREWERY.   **JOHN WIELAND, PROPR.**

COR. SECOND AND FOLSOM STS.

SAN FRANCISCO.

The Amount of Beer Sold during the Year 1885 was about 68,000 Barrels.

We take the present opportunity of thanking our friends and customers for the liberal support heretofore extended to the

PHILADELPHIA BREWERY

And notify them that we have added to our establishment

New and Extensive Buildings.

We are now ready to supply the market with the Favorite

JOHN WIELAND'S LAGER!

THE SAME IS OF EXCELLENT QUALITY AND

SUPERIOR TO ALL IMPORTED BEERS.

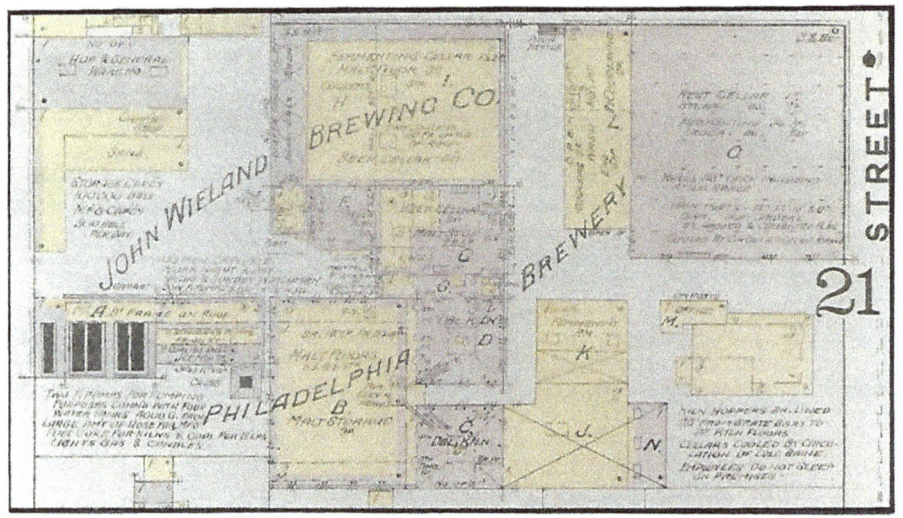

Front: IRA WILBER / LEWISTOWN / MONT.

½ Pint, ABM Crown Top
Amber
Rarity: Scarce

HISTORY: Ira Wilber was the local Agent for Pabst Beer in 1915. I don't know if he used the Bottling Works shown on the 1908 map, but it was the only one in town at the time. No other info.

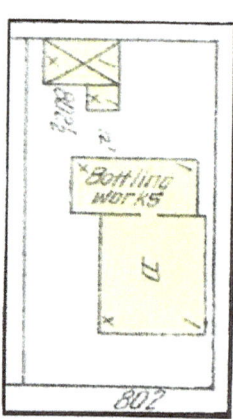

Front: W. E. WILLIAMS & CO. / STOCKTON
Base: S. F. & P.G.W.

Quart and Pint
Tooled Crown Top
Amber
Rarity: Rare in the Quart size
Scarce in the Pint size

HISTORY: no info at this time

Front CLAUS WREDEN / "monogram" / BREWEING CO. / S.F

Quart, Pint and ½ Pint
Tooled Blob Top
Amber
Rarity: Common in the Quart and Pint sizes
Scarce in the ½ Pint size

HISTORY: *Claus Wreden was listed as Proprietor of the Washington Brewery located on the corner of Washington and Taylor Sts, as early as 1873.*
This lasted until 1899, when the same address now has the Claus Wreden Brewing Co. on it.
He was in business until 1917, when the coming of prohibition forced him to shut the doors on one of San Francisco's oldest brewerys.
The bottle shown here should date after 1900 to 1917.

Front: WREDEN'S / LAGER / OAKLAND / CAL.

Quart, Pint, and ½ Pint
Tooled Blob Top
Amber
½ Pint, $20.00 - 2020 (chip) GWA
Quart, $40.00 - 2001 ABA
Rarity: Scarce in the Quart and Pint size
Rare in the ½ Pint size

HISTORY: *The first listing I could find was in 1905.*
Wreden's Lager Beer, F. Rebstock Agent. They were located at 6th and Webster.
The listing remained the same thru 107. There was no directory in 1908, so they may have still been in business during that year. No further listings.

Front: T. W. WRIGHT & CO. / PUEBLO / AGENTS FOR /
       LEMPS ST. LOUIS BEER
              (in round plate)

  Pint, Tooled Blob Top
  Aqua
  Varient: "A.A. GROME AGT."
  Rarity: All varients are Rare

  HISTORY: no info at this time

Front: WUNDER BOTTLING WORKS / P. GREENWALD /
       STOCKTON, CAL.

  Quart, Pint and ½ Pint
  Tooled Blob and Crown Top
  Amber, ½ Pint, Blob Top, $20.00 - 2020 GWA
         Quart,, Blob Top, $40.00 - 2017 ABA
  Rarity; All sizes are Scarce with a Crown Top
          Quarts and Pints are Scarce with a blob Top
          ½ Pint with a Blob Top is Rare

  HISTORY: P. Greenwald was one of the many agents for the
           Wunder Brwery in California.

Front: WUNDER BOTTLING / CO. / W. NOETHIG /
       SACRAMENTO, CAL.

  Quart and Pint
  Tooled Blob Top
  Amber
  Rarity: Scarce in both sizes

  History: Not listed in the 1900 or 1905 Sacramento directories. I could not
           find any other sources to search. Probably another ahent of the
           Wunder Brewery in San Francisco.

Front: WUNDER BOTTLING WORKS / J. ESCHELSON / OAKLAND, CAL.

   Pint, and ½ Pint, Tooled Blob Top
   Amber
   ½ Pint, $50.00 - 2020 GWA
   Rarity: Rare in both sizes

Front: WUNDER / BOTTLING WORKS / OAKLAND, CAL.
            (embossed vertically)

   Quart, Pint and ½ Pint
   Tooled Blob Top
   Amber
   Rarity: Common in all sizes

Front: WUNDER BOTTLING / WORKS / OAKLAND, CAL.

   ½ Pint, Tooled Blob Top
   Amber
   Rarity: Common

Front: WUNDER BOTTLING / WORKS / HENRY TILL / OAKLAND, CAL.

   Quart, Pint and ½ Pint
   Tooled Blob Top
   Amber
   ½ Pint, $130.00 - 2020 GWA
   Rarity: Rare in the Quart and Pint size
              Very Rare in the ½ Pint size.

HISTORY: There were no business directories available for the years 1891 thru 1902, and the year 1908. Henry Till shows up as the proprietor of the Wunder Bottling Works in 1903. They were located at 223 8TH, and were the agents for Wunder Beer in Alameda Co.
By 1904, they had moved to 931 Webster and 6TH, with Julius Stirn the manager in 1907.
1909 - 1910 has Jos. Oskea as the manager, with the plant now located on Broadway. No further listings.
I could find no mention of J. Eschelson, he was probably with the company sometime before 1903, when there were no directories.
This company had to be an offshoot of the S.F. Wunder Beer Co, but I could not find any info on it.

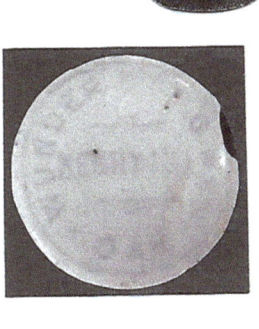

Front: WUNDER BOTTLING CO. / "monogram" / SAN FRANCISCO, CAL.

Quart, Pint and ½ Pint
Tooled Blob Top
Amber
½ Pint, $50.00 - 2020 GWA
Pint, $40.00 - 2005 ABA
Rarity: Common in all sizes

HISTORY: The Wunder Brewing Co. Inc. was first listed in 1899. John C. Wunder was the president and they were located at the corner of Greenwich & Scott. This lasted until 1909.
The Wunder Bottling Co. was listed from 1902 to 1908, with an address of 6th and Howard. William Cohen was the manager of the bottling plant.
I am assuming John Wunder owned both of these businesses, as the name is spelled the same, not being 'Wonder'.
In 1895 John Wunder had founded the San Diego Brewing Co., before moving north and purchasing the Bavarian Brewery of San Francisco, which became the Wunder Brewering Co.

Front: NICK ZUCK / "eagle" / SAN FRANCISCO

Quart, Applied Blob and Ring Top
Amber
Rarity: Ex. Rare

HISTORY: Nicholas Zuck was first listed in the saloon business in 1881. It was located at 4th and King Sts. 1882 finds him as a teamster.
He was listed as a beer bottler in 1883. The directory page for 1884 was missing, so it is possible that he also used this bottle in that year also,.
It is one of the rarest western beers, used for only about a year.

ADDENDUM
STYLES OF CALIFORNIA BEER STOPPERS

HUTTER STOPPER

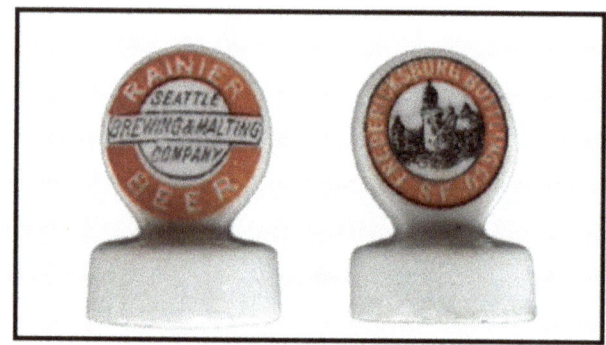

STAND UP CORK BOTTOM STOPPER

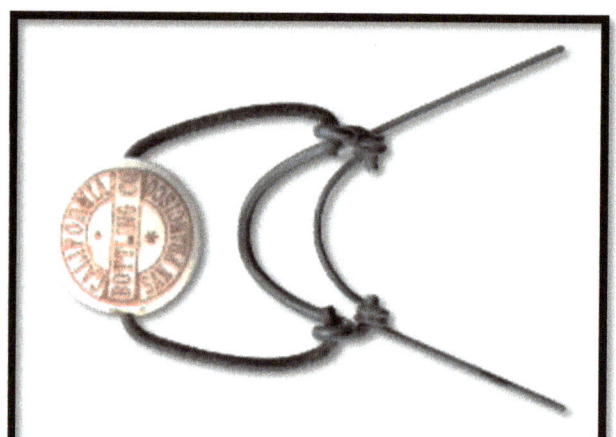

VERY RARE UNUSED HUTTER STOPPER

FLAT CROWN COVER STOPPER WITH CORK

Initials to the left of each porcelain stopper signifies the contributor. I believe this is the first-time porcelain stoppers have been shown as a group there will be additions with time.

The addition of porcelain stoppers is the idea of Michael Burgess and is greatly appreciated as they are "go-with's" to any beer book that has crown top bottles.

JB	John Burton		RS	Richard Siri
RH	Ralph Hollibaugh		BW	Bob Welch
JC	John Cartwright		DB	Dan Brown
RM	Richard McClellan		D&HJ	DeAnna & Helmut Jordt
BH	Brent Henningsen		AM	Alan Miller
			MB	Michael Burgess

RH — E. F. HUBLER, PROP. (ANGELS)

RH — G. WERLY (ANGELS CAMP)

RS — MARTIN BROS. (ANGELS CAMP, CAL.)

BW — KENISON & JOPHNSON CO. (ANGELS CAMP, CAL.)

	EUREKA		EUREKA
BW	DELANEY & YOUNG	JC	DELANEY & YOUNG
	EUREKA, CAL.		EUREKA, CAL.
RS	HUMBOLDT BREWING CO.	RS	"HUMBOLDT BEER"
	FERNDALE, CAL.		FORT BRAGG, CAL.
MB	MONROE CIDER & VINEGAR CO.	BW	STANDARD BOTTLING CO.

	FRESNO, CAL.		HEALDSBURG
RH	J. RICHTER BOTTLING WORKS	JB	F. O. BRANDT
	HEALDSBURG		LOS ANGELES, CAL.
JB	F. O. BRANDT	BW	R.W. STOLL & CO.
	LOS ANGELES, CAL.		LOS ANGELES, CAL.
BW	MAIER & ZOBELEN BREWERY	BW	MAIER & ZOBELEN BREWERY

	LOS ANGELES, CAL.		MADERA, CAL.
BW	MAIER & ZOBELEN BREWERY	BW	BORELLO & PORTER

	MARTINEZ, CAL.		Mc CLOUD, CAL
RH	C.C. BOTTLING CO.	BW	M. LEONARDINI

	MOKELUMME HILL		OAKLAND
MB	SUESSDORF & LAYMAN	RH	AHRENS BOTTLING CO.

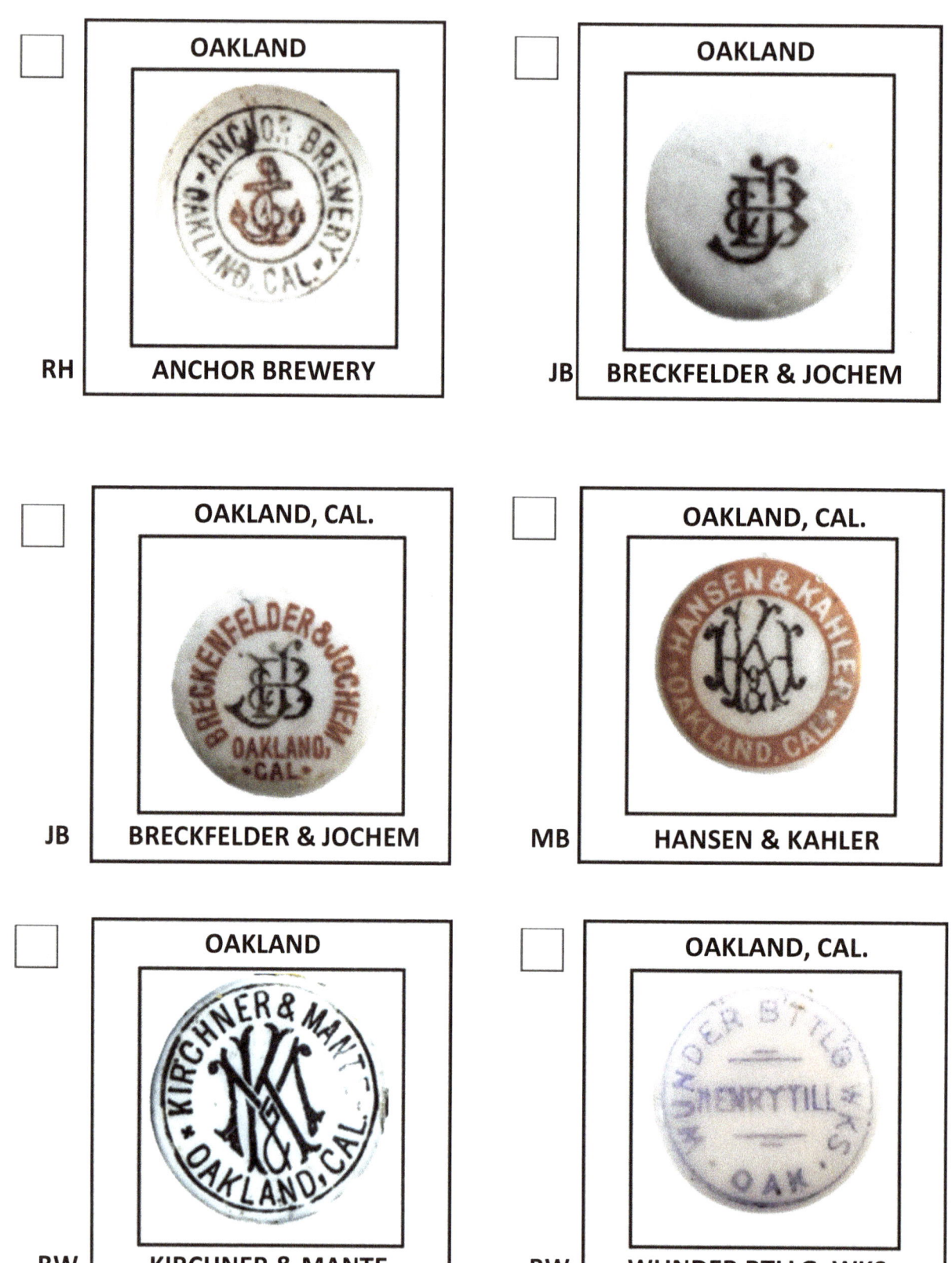

	OAKLAND		OAKLAND
RH	ANCHOR BREWERY	JB	BRECKFELDER & JOCHEM
	OAKLAND, CAL.		OAKLAND, CAL.
JB	BRECKFELDER & JOCHEM	MB	HANSEN & KAHLER
	OAKLAND		OAKLAND, CAL.
BW	KIRCHNER & MANTE	BW	WUNDER BTLLG. WKS.

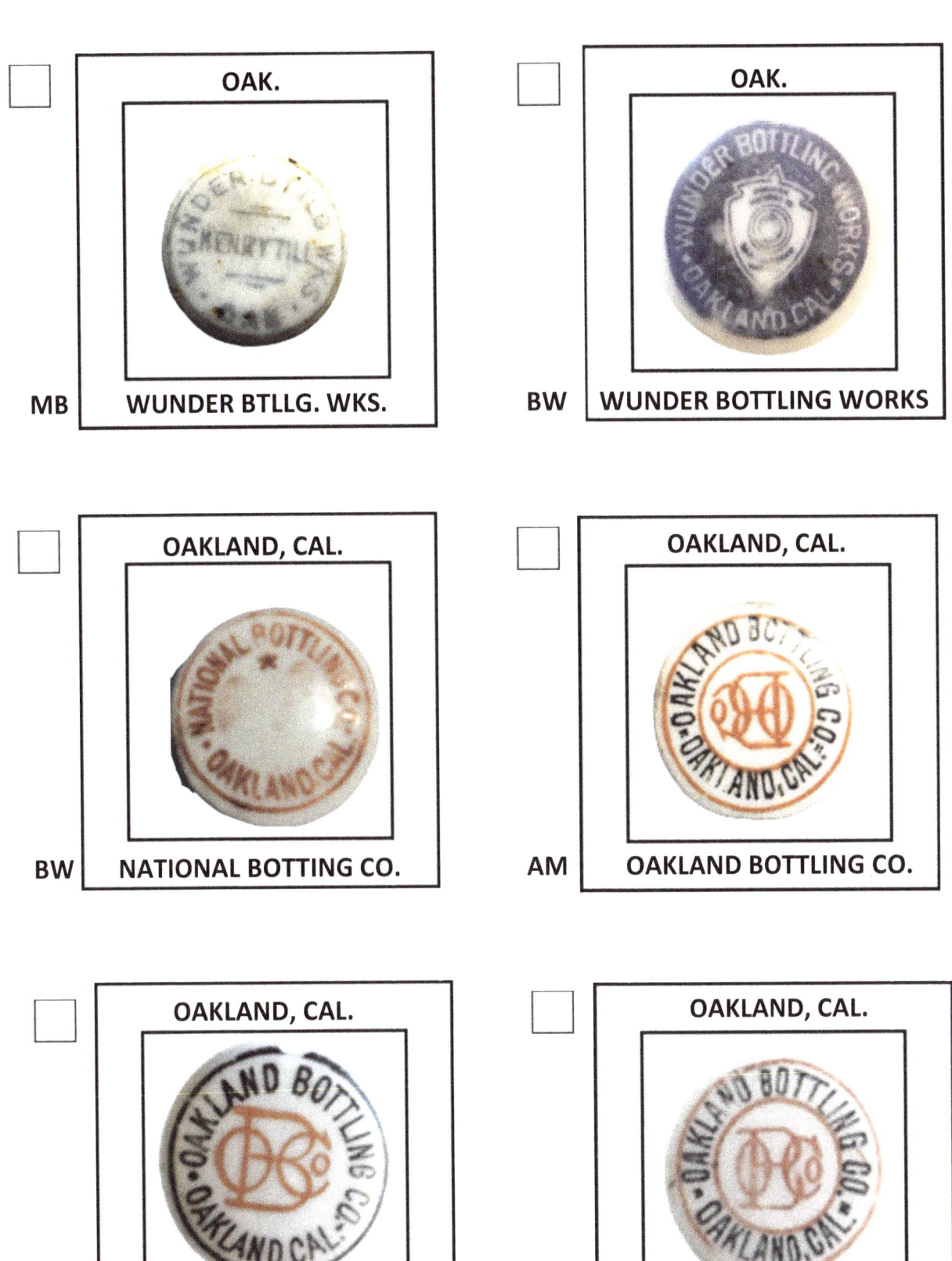

SACRAMENTO

RH — COMPLIMENTS BUFFALO BREWING CO.

SACRAMENTO

MB — BUFFALO BREWING CO.

SACRAMENTO

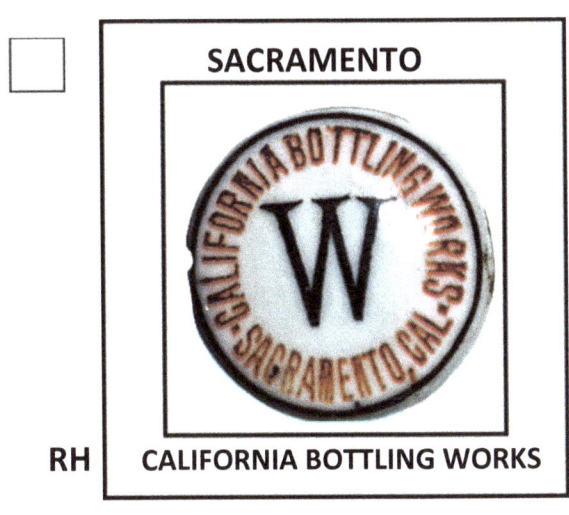

RH — CALIFORNIA BOTTLING WORKS

SACRAMENTO

BW — G. E. V. WISSMAN

SACRAMENTO

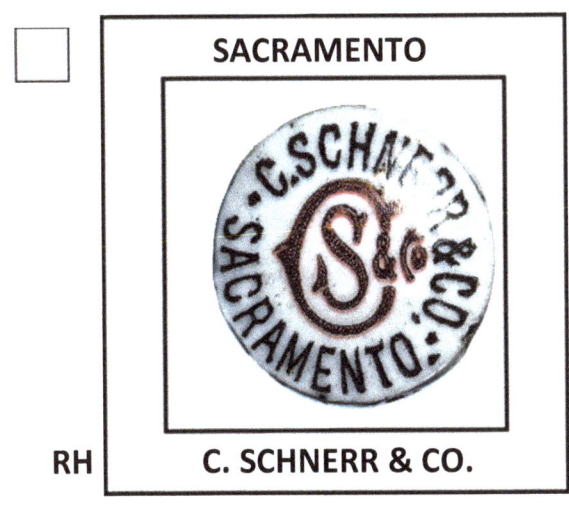

RH — C. SCHNERR & CO.

SACRAMENTO

RH — THEO. BLAUTH SONS CO. INC.

	SACRAMENTO		SACRAMENTO
MB	GEO. A. TICOULET	MB	TICOULET & BESHORMAN

	SALINAS		SAN FRANCISCO
BW	SALINAS VALLEY BOTTLING CO.	BW	ALBANY BREWERY

	SAN FRANCISCO		SAN FRANCISCO
RH	ANDERSON BOTTLING CO.	RH	BUFFALO BREWING CO. S. F. AGENCY

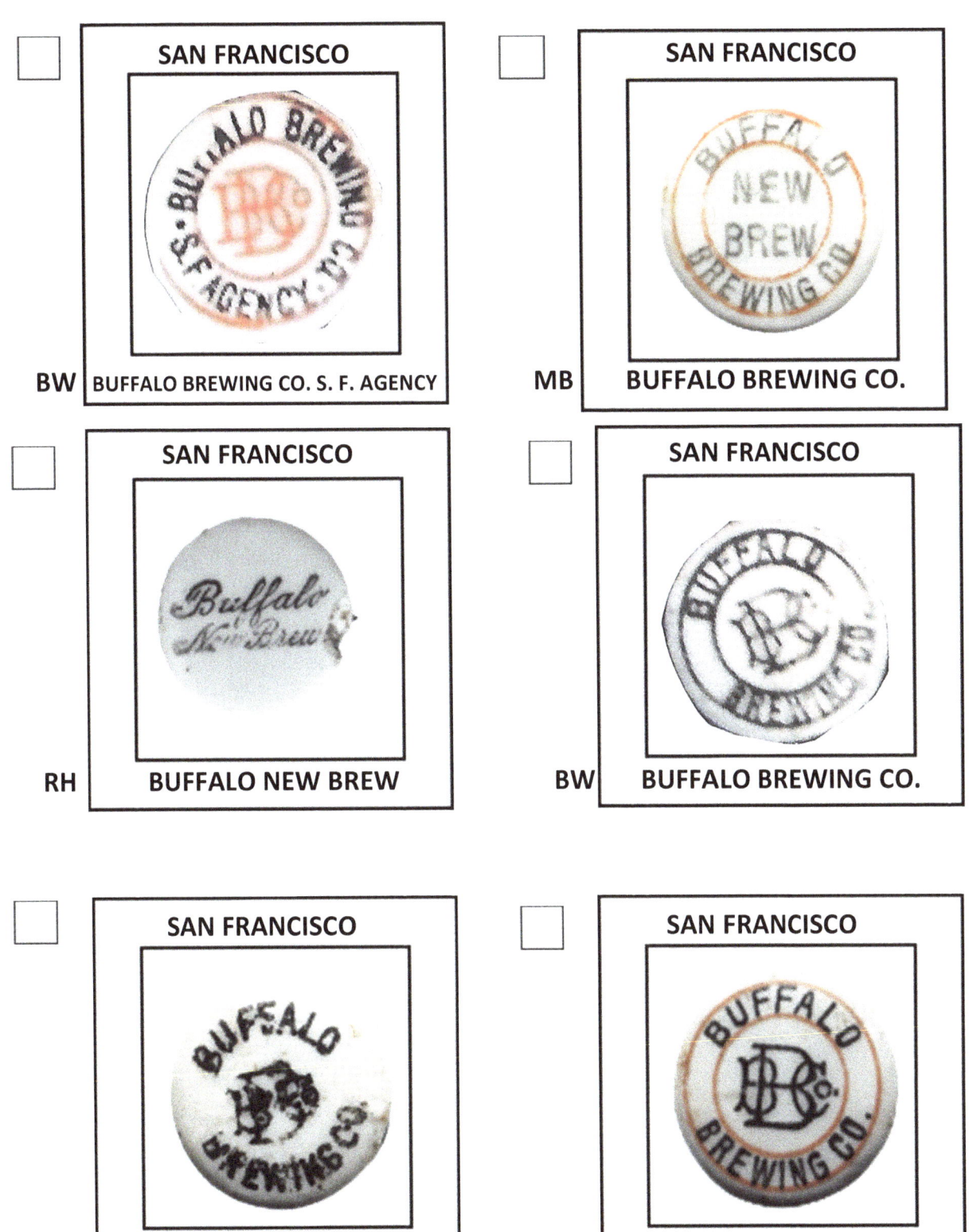

	SAN FRANCISCO		SAN FRANCISCO
MB	CALFORNIA BOTTLING CO.	JB	CALIFORNIA BOTTLING CO.
BW	CALIFORNIA BOTTLING CO.	DB	CALIFORNIA BOTTLING Co.
JB	MILWAUKEE BREWERY	RH	J. B. CUNEO

	SAN FRANCISCO		SAN FRANCISCO
BW	EAGLE BREWING Co.	BW	EAGLE BREWING Co. S.F. CAL.

	SAN FRANCISCO		SAN FRANCISCO
BW	EAGLE BREWING Co. S. F. CAL.	RH	ENTERPRISE BREW'G CO

	SAN FRANCISCO		SAN FRANCISCO
MB	ENTERPRISE BREW'G CO.	RH	ENTERPRISE BREW'G CO.

	SAN FRANCISCO			SAN FRANCISCO

BW	FRANKS BROS		RH	JOHN FAUSER & CO.

	SAN FRANCISCO			SAN FRANCISCO
	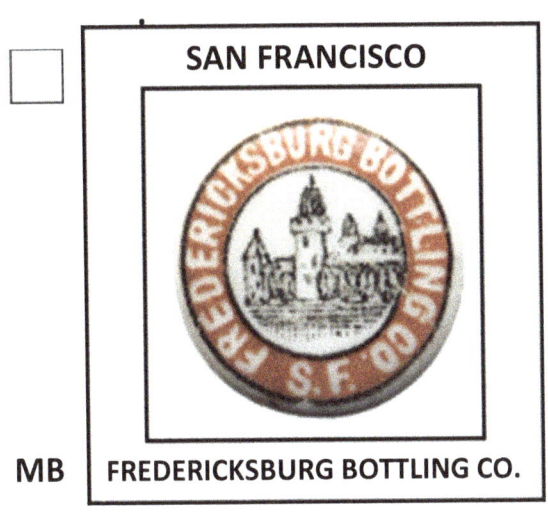			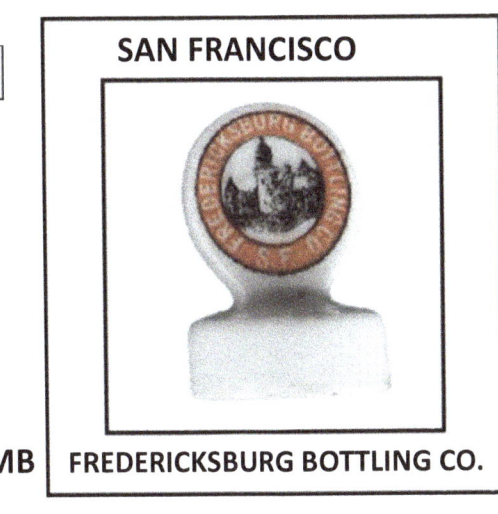
MB	FREDERICKSBURG BOTTLING CO.		MB	FREDERICKSBURG BOTTLING CO.

	SAN FRANCISCO			SAN FRANCISCO
				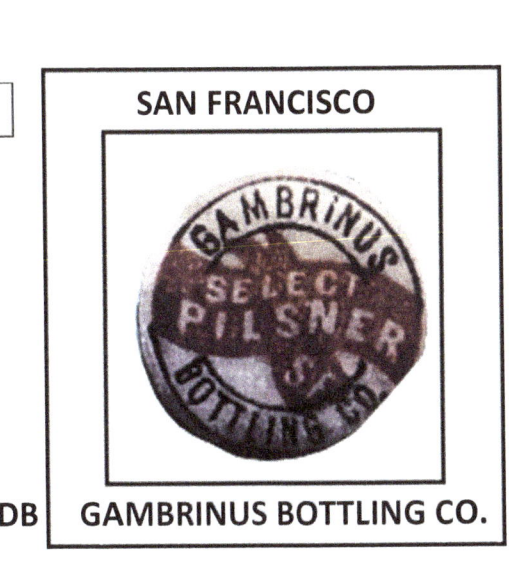
RH	GAMBRINUS BOTTLING CO.		DB	GAMBRINUS BOTTLING CO.

☐	**SAN FRANCISCO**	☐	**SAN FRANCISCO**
MB	N. CERVELLI gray color	MB	NATIONAL BOTTLING WORKS
☐	**SAN FRANCISCO**	☐	**SAN FRANCISCO**
JB	NATIONAL BOTTLING CO.	MB	NATIONAL BOTTLING CO.
☐	**SAN FRANCISCO**	☐	**SAN FRANCISCO**
RH	NORTH STAR BOTTLING WORKS	BW	PACIFIC BOTTLING CO.

	SAN FRANCISCO		SAN FRANCISCO
MB	RICHMOND BOTTLING WORKS	MB	JOHN RAPP & SON
RH	RHINE GOLD BOTTLING CO.	JB	SANTA FE BOTTLING CO.
DB	SEAL ROCK BOTTLING CO.	DB	SUNRISE BOTTLING CO.

	SAN FRANCISCO		SAN FRANCISCO
MB 	SUNSET BOTTLING CO.	BW 	STANDARD BOTTLING CO.
	SAN FRANCISCO		SAN FRANCISCO
BW 	STANDARD BOTTLING Co.	MB	UNION BREWING & MALTING CO.
	SAN FRANCISCO		SAN FRANCISCO
MB 	UNITED STATES BOTTLING WORKS	DB 	UNITED STATES BOTTLING WORKS

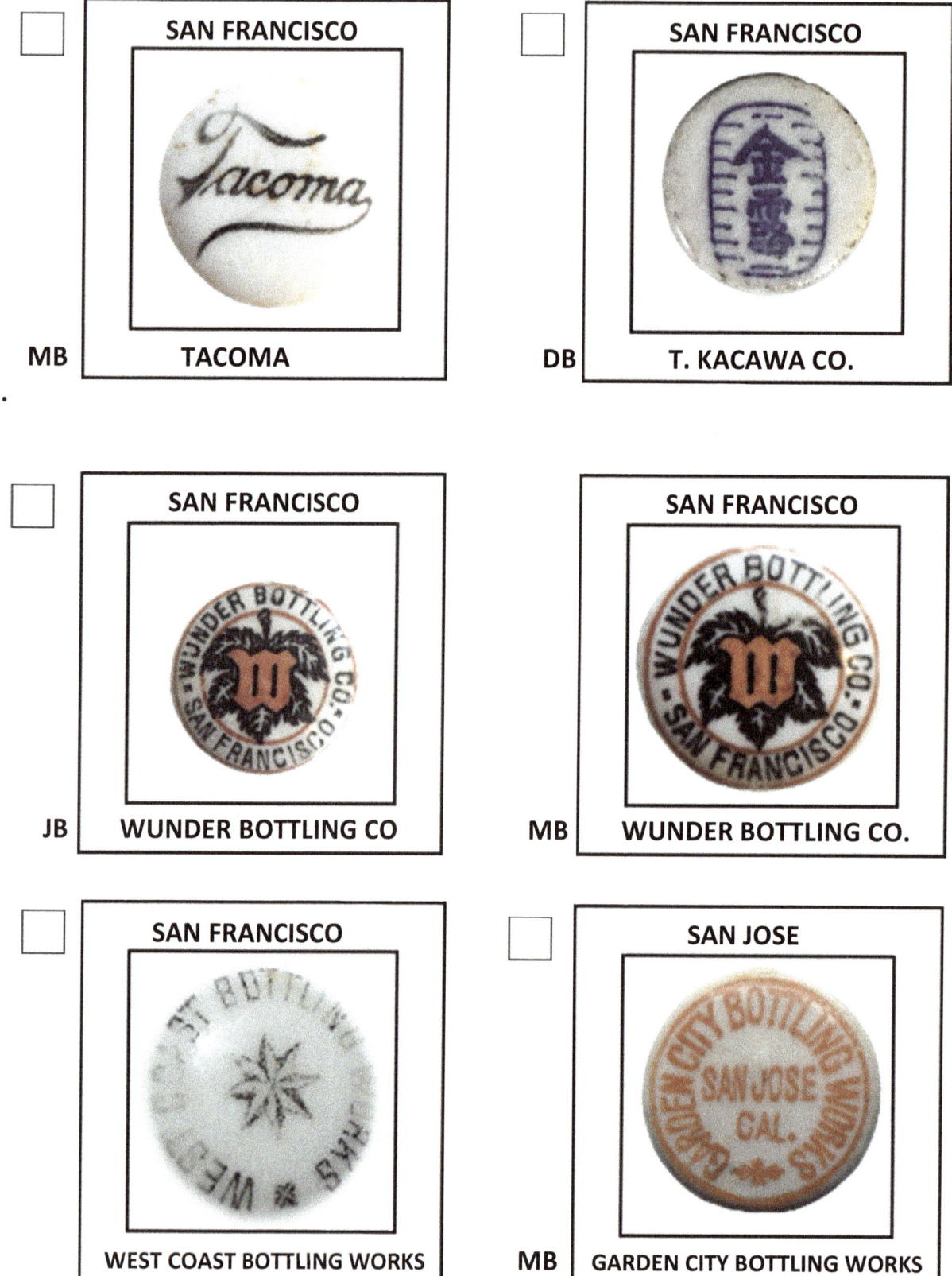

	SAN FRANCISCO		SAN FRANCISCO
MB	TACOMA	DB	T. KACAWA CO.

	SAN FRANCISCO		SAN FRANCISCO
JB	WUNDER BOTTLING CO	MB	WUNDER BOTTLING CO.

	SAN FRANCISCO		SAN JOSE
	WEST COAST BOTTLING WORKS	MB	GARDEN CITY BOTTLING WORKS

MB	SAN JOSE — RUDOLPH SCHERF	MB	SAN JOSE — W. SCHIMMEL
MB	SAN JOSE — SANTA CLARA BOTTLING CO.	MB	SAN LUIS OBISPO — McCAFFERY BROS.
JB	SAN RAFAEL — FREY & COMPANY	MB	SANTA CLARA — CASCADE BOTTLING CO.

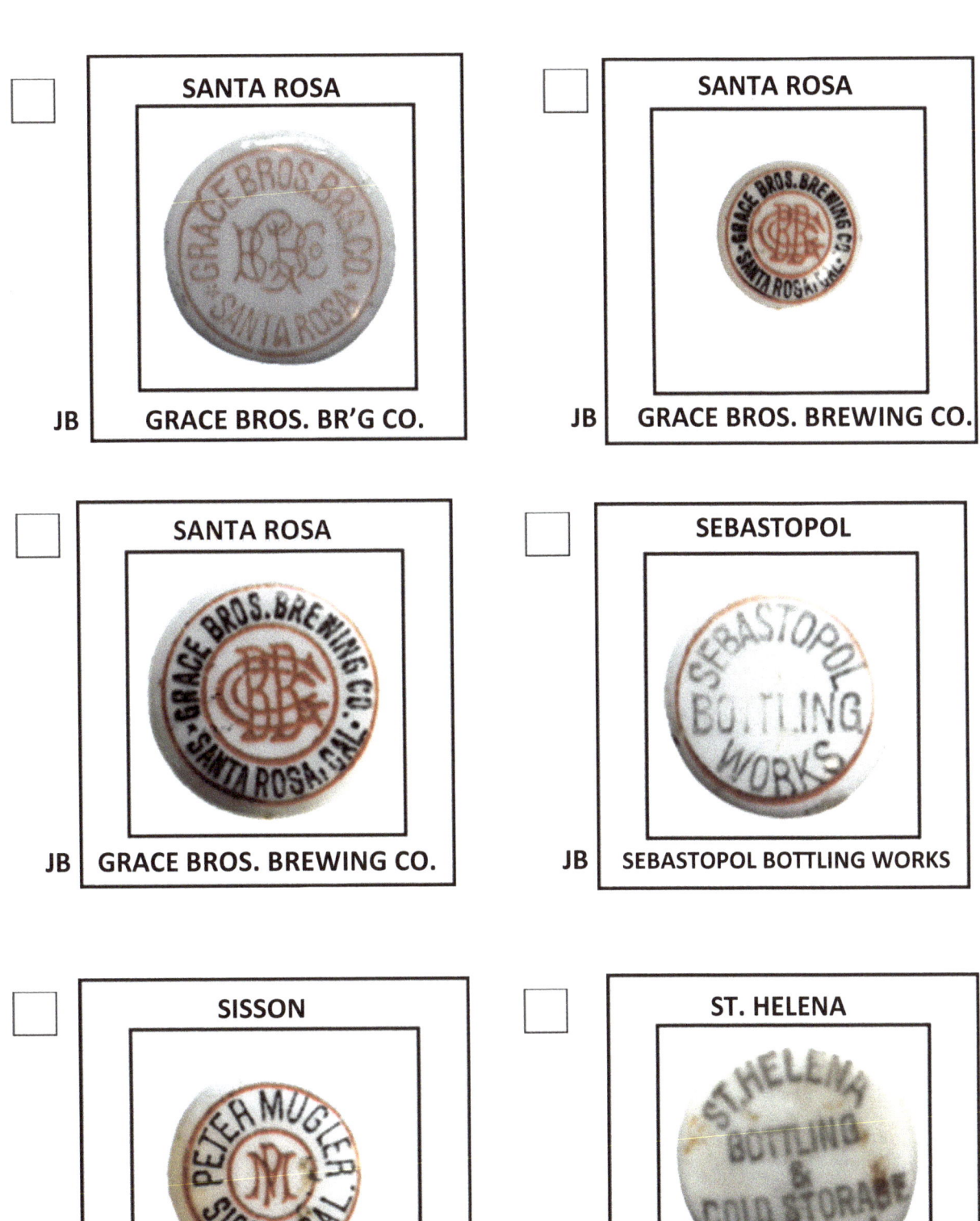

	SANTA ROSA		SANTA ROSA
JB	GRACE BROS. BR'G CO.	JB	GRACE BROS. BREWING CO.

	SANTA ROSA		SEBASTOPOL
JB	GRACE BROS. BREWING CO.	JB	SEBASTOPOL BOTTLING WORKS

	SISSON		ST. HELENA
MB	PETER MUGLER	MB	ST. HELENA BOTTLING & COLD STORAGE CO.

	St. HELENA		STOCKTON
JB	ST. HELENA BOTTLING & COLD STORAGE COMPANY	MB	EL DORADO BREWING Co.
	STOCKTON		STOCKTON
JB	EL DORADO BREWING CO.	JB	EL DORADO BREWING CO.
	STOCKTON		STOCKTON
BW	EL DORADO BREWING CO.	JB	D. W. McCARTHY

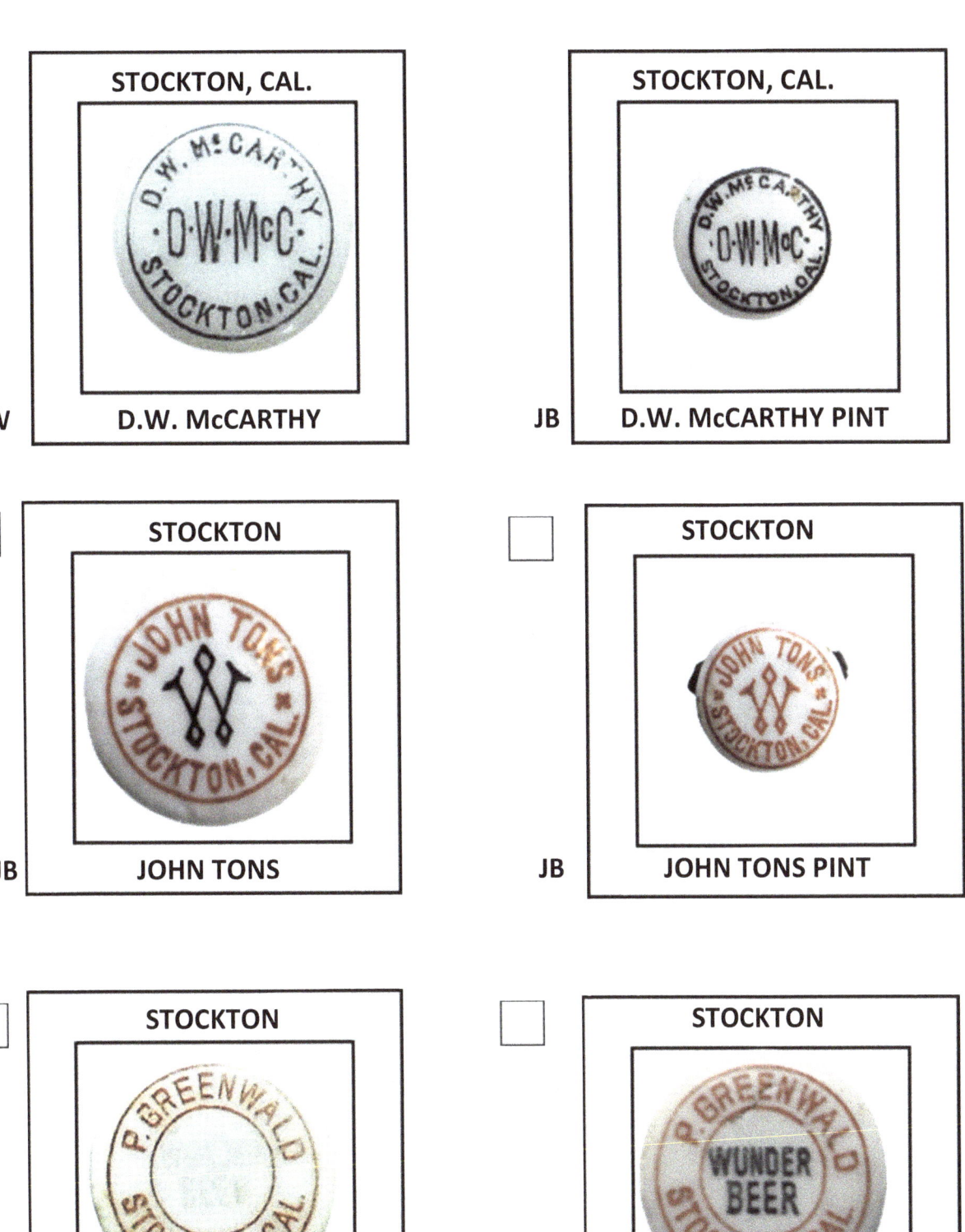

MB	STOCKTON JOHN TONS	JC	STOCKTON, CAL. JOHN TONS
RH	STOCKTON, CAL. H. ROHRBACHER	MB	STOCKTON, CAL. VALLEY BREW
RH	STOCKTON, CAL. VALLEY BREW	RH	VALLEJO DANIEL MINAHAN

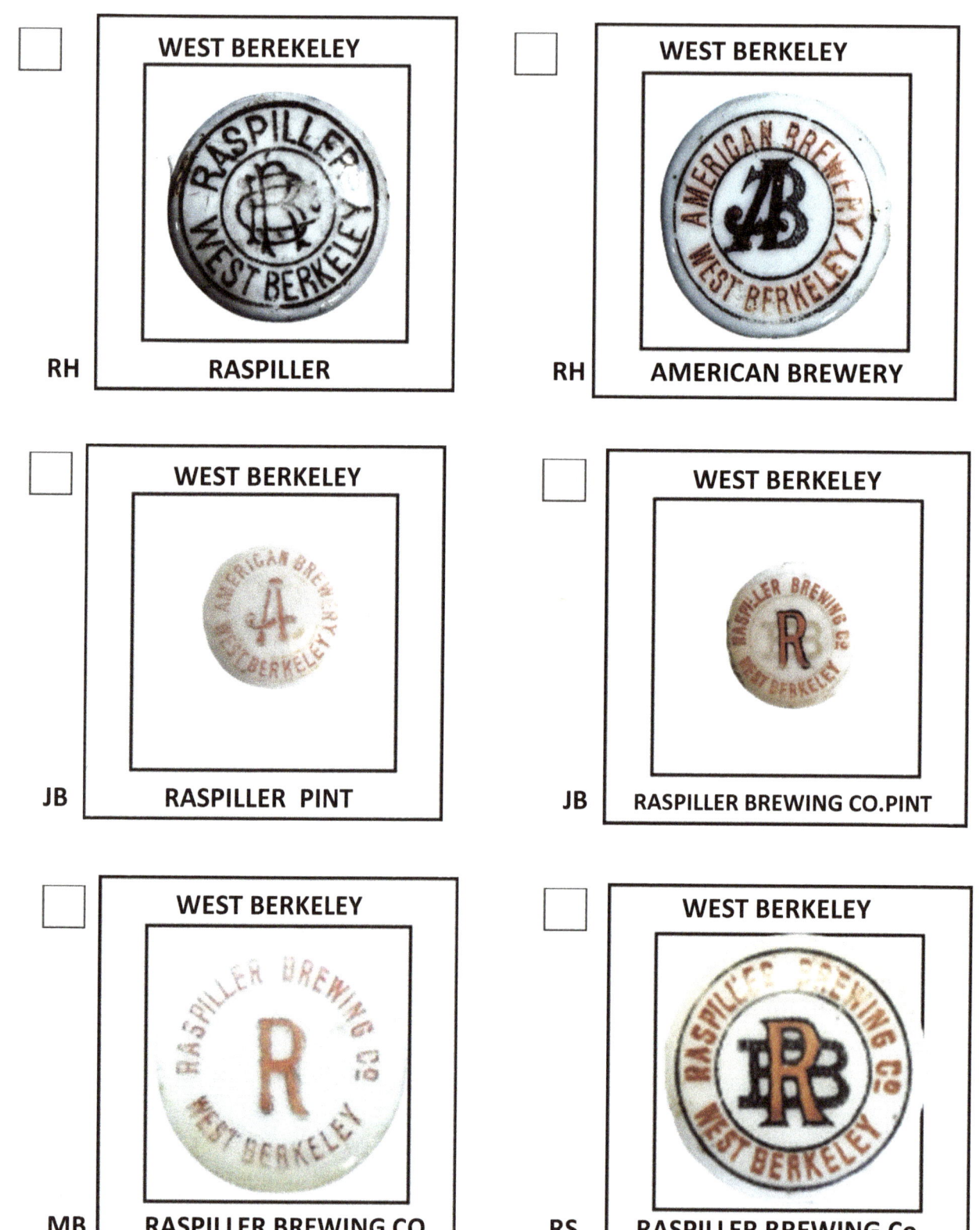

Entry	Page
Albany Brewery San Francisco	1
Ahrens Bottling Company Oakland	
Aberdeen Brewing Co. Washington	2
Albany Brewing Co. Albany, Oregon	3
Albion/Burnell Brewery San Francisco	
American Brewing Co. West Berkeley	4
Alabama Brewing Co. San Francisco	5
American Brewing & C. I. Co. Baler City	6
Anchor Brewery Oakland, Cal.	7
Anderson Bottling Co. San Francisco	
Angels Brewery & Soda Works	8
Anheuser Busch Bottling Works L. A.	9
The Anheuser Busch Beer	
Anheuser Busch Bwg. Assn. S. F. Agency	
Barner & Riebe Bottlers Redding, Cal.	10
The Bay Bottling Co. San Francisco, Cal.	
Barnolds B Seattle, Washington	
Bay View Brewing Co. Seattle, Wash.	11
Bellingham Bay Brewery Whatcom, Wash	12
Benicia Brewery G Benicia, Cal.	14
C. Beck Santa Cruz	
Borello & Porter B&P Madera	16
Val Blatz Brewing Co. Denver, Co	
Boca Brewing Co. Boca Cal.	17
Breckenfelder & Jochem Oakland, Cal.	18
Frank Bucher Redding Cal.	
F. O. Brandt Healdsburg, Cal	19
Celebrated B & S Lager Beer	
George Braun Bottler San Francisco	20
Henry Braun Beer Bottler Oakland, Cal.	21
Henry Braun Los Angeles, Cal.	
John J. Buck San Francisco	22
Buffalo Brewing Co. Sacramento, Cal.	23
Buffalo Brewing CO. S. F. Agency	25
Cal. Bottling Co. Wieland's Export S.F.	29
California Bottling Co. S. F.	
Cal. Bottling Co. John Wieland Sac.	
Cal. Bottling Co. Export Beer S. F.	
Sample of Wieland's Labels	30
California Bottling Works T. Blauth Sac.	35
Capitol Brg. Co.	
Cardillo & Lamb Pueblo, Colo.	
The L. Serf Co. Ventura, Cal.	
Capitol Bottling Works, Petaluma, Cal.	36
Consolidated Milwaukee Beer Montana	
A. Cappelli & CO. Bottle Beer S. F.	37
Cascade Lager S. F.	38
Cascade Bottling Pereira Bros. Santa Clara	38
M. Casey Gilroy Brewery, Cal.	39
N. Cervelli 615 Francisco St. S. F.	40
Chicago Brewery 1434 Pine San Francisco	41
Chicago Bottling Works D. Meinke	42
Clausen Brewing Association, Seattle	43
Clausen/Sweeney Brewing Co. – Seattle	44
Columbia Brewing Co. Tacoma, Wash.	45
Consumers Bottling Co. Redwood, Cal.	46
Consumers Bottling Co. San Francisco, Cal.	
C. Conrad & Co. Original Budweiser	47
Coors Golden Beer Pueblo, Colorado	48
Coors, Adolph Coors Golden, Colorado	
Cripple Creek Bottling Works, Boulder, Co.	51
Cuneo, J. B. San Francisco	52
Delaney & Young Eureka, Cal.	
Del Norte/Crescent City Bottling Works	
Deucher & Kalben	53
Denver Ale Brewing Co. Denver	
Jacob Denzler San Francisco	
F. A. Dohrmann San Francisco, Cal.	54
Thos. Downing, Hanford, Cal.	
Eagle Brewing Co. San Francisco	55
J. F. G. Eggers, San Francisco	
Etna Brewery, Etna Mills	56
El Dorado Brewing Co. Stockton, Cal.	57
Enterprise Brewing Co. Kern, Cal.	60
Enterprise Brewing Co. San Francisco	
Eureka Ginger Beer Co. San Francisco	63
Frank Bros. San Francisco	64
Fresno Brewing Co. Fresno, Cal.	
Chris Feldman & Co. San Francisco	
Fink & Mugler Bottlers, Keswick, Cal.	65
Frey & Co., Property of, San Rafael	
Frey & Lenz San Rafael	
Fredericksburg Bottling Co. San Francisco	
Fredericksburg Bottling Co. San Francisco	66
Fredericksburg, Property of, San Jose	
Fredericksburg, Ventura, Cal.	67
Fredericksburg, Seattle, Washington	
Gambrinus Brewing Co. Portland, Or.	74
Gambrinus Brewing Co. San Francisco	75
D. Germanus Bottling Co. Portland, Or.	
Garden City Bottling Works, San Jose	76
Goeppert, Wm. Beer Steam Bottling Co.	77
Gier, Theo. Oakland & San Francisco	
Gold Edge Bottling Works, Vallejo	78
Golden Gate Bottling Works, S. F.	79

Golden Gate Bottling Works 79	Philadelphia Bottling Co. Lager Beer 99
Chas. Roschmann San Francisco	Lang Bros. Props. S. F.
Golden Gate Bottling Works	I. F. Larson S. F. 101
McGrath & Mahoney San Francisco	Lemp's Bottling Works S. F.
Grace Bros. Brewing Co. Santa Rosa, Cal. 80	Lemp Meuhlausen C. C. Dist. Beer St. Louis
Gold Medal Agency, C. Maurer San Jose 83	Lemp's St. Louis Lager Beer
Goux, A. Bottlers Co. Santa Barbara	T. W. Wright & Co. Pueblo Agents for Lemp's
Property of Jos. Hammer Visalia, Cal.	St. Louis Beer
Hanford Ice Co. Hanford, Cal. 84	Livermore Brewery D. F. Bernal 102
Hansen & Kahler, Oakland, Cal. 85	Carl A. Lind Oakland, Calif.
Hoefer & Mevius Bottlers Redding, Cal. 86	M. Leonardini Mc Cloud, Cal.
Ferd Heim Brewing Co. Pueblo	Los Angeles Brewing Co. San Francisco 103
Henry Hock 224 Turk Street San Francisco	Los Angeles Brewing Co.
Honolulu Brewing & Malting Co. LDT.	Theodore Lutge & Co. San Jose 104
Honolulu Brewing Co. Honolulu, H. T.	MacFarland & Co. Honolulu HI.
Haub, John Sacramento, Cal. 87	Maier & Zobelein Brewery 105
F. A. Heim's Bottling Works, Los Angeles	Los Angeles Cal.
Hermes Vintages L. A. Goodman & Co.	Majestic Bottling Co. San Francisco 106
Marston Higgins & Co. Milwaukee Beer	Milwaukee Bottling Works, Tacoma, Wash.
Hoefer & Burgbacher Bottlers Redding Cal.	Mokelumne Hill Brewery E. Lagomarsino
Humboldt Brewing Co. Eureka 88	The Mathie Brewing Co. Los Angeles 107
Independent Brewing Co. Seattle, USA 89	Marysville Bottling Works Marysville 108
Japan Brewing Co. S. F. Cal. 90	Martin Bros. Angels
Japan Brewing Co. Limited Yokahama	McCaffrey Bros. S. L. O.
Jackson Brewing Co. S. F. Cal.	D. W. McCarthy Stockton, Cal.
V. Jones San Diego, Cal. 91	G. W. McIntyre Stockton, Cal.
Kanhy & Burgbacher Bottlers Redding, Cal	Meamber Bros. Bottlers Yreka, Cal.
A. W. Kenison Co. Auburn, Cal.	H. Mehlman S. L. O. Cal.
T. Kagawa Co. San Francisco 92	M. Meyer Astoria Brewery
Kalispell Malting & Brewing Co.	M. Metzler San Francisco 109
Kalispell, Montana	Geo. T. Maginnis & Co. Seattle, Wash. 110
Kamm, S. L. O.	D. Meinke San Francisco
Kern County Bakersfield Cal. Bottling	Henry C. Meyer San Francisco, Cal.
Kessler Brewing Co. Helena, Montana 93	Daniel Minahan Vallejo, Cal. 111
Kirchner & Manti, Oakland, Cal. 94	Mirrasoul Bros. S. F.
M. Kriss Redwood City 95	Chas. Mutz White Beer & E. Rammelmeyer
Fred Kostering San Francisco 96	Mt. Shasta Bottling Works 112
Geo. Ladd & Co. Stockton, Cal.	Mugler Bros. Sisson, Cal.
John Lagomarsino, Ventura, Cal.	P. Mugler Sisson, Cal.
Lagomarsino Parma Co. Santa Barbara	Peter Mugler Brewer Sisson, Cal.
C. A. Lammers Denver, Colorado 97	National Brewing Co. San Francisco 113
Aug. J. Lang San Francisco, California 98	National Lager Jos. Bickel Martinez
Lang Bros. 1318 Scott St. San Francisco	National Bottling Co. Adolph B. Lang 115
Aug. Lang & Co. S. F. Lager Beer	National Bottling Co. San Francisco AD. B. Lang
Aug. Lang & Co. S. F. Cal.	National Bottling Co. San Francisco
Aug. Lang Brewing Ass'n. S. F. Lager Beer	National Bottling Co. San Francisco, Cal.
Philadelphia Bottling Co. Lager Beer 99	524 National Bottling Works 116
Lang Bros. Props. Depot 1318 S. F. Scott	San Francisco

525 Grove Street National Bottling Works 116 San Francisco, Cal.	Salinas Brewing Co. Salinas, Cal. 144
National Lager Beer H. Rohrbacher Agt. 117 Stockton, Cal.	Salinas Valley Bottling Co. Salinas Cal.
	Santa Clara County Bottling Co. 146
Neff Bros. Brg. Co's. Wiener Maerzen 118 Bottled By H. A. Schwinhorst Pueblo, Colo.	Salt Lake Brewing Co.
	Santa Cruz Brewing Co. Santa Cruz, Cal. 147
New York Brewery, Spokane, Wash. 119	San Diego Brewing Co. San Diego, Cal.
North Pacific Brewery Astoria, Oregon	San Jose Bottling Co. C. Maurer 148
North Star Bottling Works S. F. Cal. 120	San Jose Bottling Co. San Jose, Cal.
North Yakima Brewing & Malting 121	San Jose Bottling Co. C. Maurer Prop.
Frank O'Grady Vallejo, Cal.	Property of C. Maurer San Jose, Cal.
Ohio Bottling Works 122 N. Main St. L. A.	Santa Rosa Bottling Co. 149 Hudson & Palmer
Oakland Bottling Co. Oakland, Cal 122	Toni Schmidt San Jose, Cal.
Olympia Beer Oakland, Cal. 123	L. L. Schuler Palace Brewery Alameda, Cal.
Olympia Beer Co. S. F. Cal.	Santa Fe Bottling Co. C. V. & Co. S. F. 150
P. B. Milwaukee 124	Rudolph Scherf San Jose, Cal.
Pacific Bottling Co. S. F.	Schlitz Milwaukee Beer Wm. Lagemann
A. Palmtag Eureka, Cal. 125	Schlitz Milwaukee Beer Nadeau & Waller Agts. Portland
James Pereira Santa Clara, Cal.	
Pearson Bros. Placerville	Wm. Schimmel San Jose, Cal.
H. A. Peterson, Watsonville, Cal. 126	Jos. Schwartz Brewing Co. S. F. Cal.
Tony Phillips S. F. Cal. 127	C. Schneer & Co. Sacramento, Cal. 151
T. F. Phillips Colusa, Cal.	PH. Schneider Brewing Co. Trinidad, Colo.
A. & R. Postel S. F. Cal. 128	S. F. Stock Brewery S. F. S. B. 152 San Francisco, Cal.
T. D. Postel S. F. Cal.	
Preble & Jones Calif. & Oregon Cider	S. F. Weiss Brewery Stuber & Co.
Charles R. Puckhaber Fresno, Cal. 129	S. F. Beer J. Strauss Agt. O
Pueblo Brewery Pueblo, Colorado	Sebastopol Bottling Works Cal.
J. Proll Bottling Works U. S. Lager S. F.	Seal Rock Bottling Co. John Kroger 153 San Francisco, Cal.
Puget Sound Brewing Co. Tacoma 130	
Pacific & Puget Sound Bottling Seattle	John R. Seifert Bottler San Diego
Rainier Beer Bottling Works Reno, Nev. 131	John R. Seifert Bottler San Diego, Cal.
Rainier Beer Fresno	S. F. Bottling Co. Freitas & Rodgers S. F. Cal.
Rainier Beer Fresno Bottling	Seattle Brewing & Malting Co. Seattle 154
Rainier Beer Seattle U. S. A. 132	Sierra Bottling Co. Wieland's Best 156 Jamestown, Cal.
Rainier Seattle Brewing & Malting	
John Rapp & Son S. F. Cal. 133	Silver Bow Brewing Co.
Raspiller Brewing West Berkeley 134	Swan Brewing Co. XXX Ale
Red Lion Brewery San Francisco 136	Sonoma Brewing Co. Sonoma, Cal. 157
Red Lion Lager Beer	Southern California Beer Bottling Ass'n. Los Angeles
Red Lion Beer S. F.	
Reno Brewing Co. Reno, Nev. 137	Southwestern Lager Beer Bottling 158
Richmond Bottling Works 138	Southwestern Brewery & Ice Co.
W. Reynolds & Co. Herb Beer Salt Lake	Standard S. F. Bottling Co. 159
Jacob Richter Fresno, Cal. 139	The Standard Bottling & Mfg. Co. Cripple Creek Colo.
Roseburg Brewing Co. Roseburg, Or. 140	
Ruhstaller Gilt Edge Lager Sacramento 141	J. R. Spellacy Star Bottling Co. S. F.
S Schmidt & Lowell Stockton 143	J. Geo. Steiger 5 Cedar Ave. S. F.

Star Brewery Vancouver, Wash.	160
St. Helena Bottling and Cold Storage	161
St. Helena, Cal.	
St. Louis Bottling Co. Vallejo, Cal.	162
Stockton Wholesale Liquor Co. Stockton, Cal.	
H. W. Stoll & Co. Los Angeles, Cal.	
John Strohm Jackson, Cal.	163
Sunrise Bottling Co. E. Stirnkorb	165
San Francisco	
Sunset Bottling Co. San Francisco	
Suessdorf & Layman Mokelumme Hill	
Tacoma Beer Co. Oakland, Cal.	166
Tacoma Bottling Co. S. F.	
Property of Otto Tullman Bottling Works	
San Luis Obispo, Bottle is not to be sold	
Geo. A. Ticoulet Sac.	167
Ticoulet & Beshorman Sac. City	
Tobener Bros. Bottlers Vallecito, Cal.	
John Tons Stockton, Cal.	
C. Thomas Truckee	168
D. Tweedie Red Hand Trade Mark	169
San Francisco This Bottle Never Sold	
Ukiah Bottling Works Ukiah	170
Ukiah Brewing & Ice Co. Ukiah, Cal.	
Union Brewing Co. Anaheim, Cal.	
Union Brewing & Malting Co. S. F. Cal.	171
U. S. Bottling Co.	172
John Fauser & Co. S. F.	
U. S. Bottling Co. John Fauser Co.	
San Francisco	
Little Fauser U. S. Lager	
U. S. Bottling Co. Trade Mark	173
Rapp & Debarry S. F. Cal.	
This Bottle Not to Be Sold	
U. S. Bottling Co. Rapp & Debarry S. F. Cal.	
U. S. Bottling Co. Trade U. S. Mark	
J. Rapp & Son S. F. Cal.	
Bottle Not to Be Sold	
United States Bottling Works J. B. Cuneo	
S. F. Bottle Not to Be Sold	
Vallejo Bottling Works	175
H. & K. Vallejo, Cal.	
Vallejo Bottling Works C. E. Doty Vallejo, Cal.	
C. J. Vath & Co. San Jose	
Viking Brewing Co. San Francisco, Cal	176
A. L. Van Valey Bottling Works	177
Everett, Washington	
The Walter Brewing Co. Pueblo, Colo.	

Henry Wagener Brewing Co.	178
Salt Lake City, Utah	
Henry Weinhard Export Beer	179
Portland Or.	
Henry Weinhard City Brewery Portland, Or.	
Henry Weinhard Portland, Ore.	
H. Weinhard Brewery Portland, Ore.	
Bottle Not to Be Sold	
W. B. & Co. S. F. Trade Mark	182
G. W. Angels (George Werly)	
Western Brewery Neff Bros.	183
Denver, Colo.	
Western Bottling Co. D. & K.	184
San Francisco	
Western Bottling Company S. F. Cal.	
Wiener Bottling Co. 914 Ellis St.	
San Francisco	
Property of Geo. Wissemann	
Sacramento, Cal. This Bottle Not To Be Sold	
Wieland Advertisement Jacob Adloff	185
John Wieland's Export Beer S. F.	186
Wieland's W Little Pop Cal. Bottling Co.	
John Wieland's Export Beer John Tons Agent	
Ira Wilber Lewistown, Mont.	188
W. E. Williams & Co. Stockton	
Claus Wreden Brewing Co. S. F.	189
Wreden's Lager Oakland, Cal.	
T. W. Wright & Co. Pueblo Agents For	190
Lemp's St. Louis Beer	
Wunder Bottling Works P. Greenwald	
Stockton, Cal.	
Wunder Bottling Co. W. Noethig	
Sacramento, Cal.	
Wunder Bottling Works J. Eschelson	191
Oakland, Cal.	
Wunder Bottling Works Oakland, Cal.	
Wunder Bottling Works Henry Till	
Oakland, Cal.	
Wunder Bottling Co. San Francisco, Cal.	192
Nick Zuck San Francisco	193
Porcelain Beer Stoppers	194

www.ingramcontent.com/pod-product-compliance
Lightning Source LLC
Chambersburg PA
CBHW061118070526
44583CB00028B/3331

Table of Contents

Introduction 01

DEVELOPING PRACTICAL LIVING SKILLS
To Honor (Lesson 1) 04
To Honor (Lesson 2) 07
Be Polite (Lesson 1) 08
Polite (Lesson 2) 10
Polite (Lesson 3) 12
Teamwork (Lesson 1) 14
I Long to Live in a Neighborhood Again 17
Teamwork (Lessons 2 & 3) 19
Express Yourself (Lesson 1) 22
Oh, Say Can You See—or at Least Play Guitar 24
Express Yourself (Lesson 2) 26
Humble Yourself (Lesson 1) 28
The Cow Patty Cruiser 31
Humble Yourself (Lesson 2) 33
Let's Get Organized (Lesson 1) 34
Let's Get Organized (Lesson 2) 35
Commit to Excellence (Lesson 1) 39
Section 1: Summary (Lesson 1) 42
Section 1: Summary (Lesson 2) 45

BUILDING STRENGTH OF CHARACTER
Building Strength of Character (Lesson 1) 48
Letter of the Law (Lesson 1) 50
Sweet Potato Pants 51
Law and Order (Lesson 2) 54
Be a Leader (Lesson 1) 56
Think Unique (Lesson 1) 58
First Day of School and a Furry Bathroom Rug 60
Think Unique (Lesson 2) 62
Section 2: Summary (Lessons 1 & 2) 63

CLEARING THE CLUTTER
Mind Is the Matter (Lesson 1) 68
Fear Is Failure (Lesson 1) 70
Prejudice Is to Prejudge (Lesson 1) 73
Prejudice Is to Prejudge (Lesson 2) 75
The Harley Hogs of Amish Country 76
The Problem with Pride (Lesson 1) 77
You Wouldn't Dare 79
Better or Bitter (Lesson 1) 81
Envy Is Your Enemy (Lesson 1) 83
Section 3: Summary (Lesson 1) 86
Section 3: Summary (Lesson 2) 87

ESTABLISHING HOPE AND VISION
Strength of Character Completes the
    Vision (Lesson 1) 92
Gotta Have Vision (Lesson 1) 94
Gotta Have Vision (Lesson 2) 95
Gotta Have Vision (Lesson 3) 97
The Bow-tie Drummer Boy 98
Camaraderie (Lesson 1) 101
Big Boots, Big Heart 103
Camaraderie (Lesson 2) 105
Honor Brings Relationship (Lesson 1) 107
Barefoot on a Banana 109
Section 4: Summary (Lessons 1 & 2) 111
From Honor to Glory (Lesson 1) 115
About the Author 117

BONUS
Anger 119
Harassment: Beating the Bully 120
Stuck Up On the Way Up 125
Jack an Eye 127
Harassment: Cyber Style 129
Cyber Harassment (Lesson 1) 129
Cyber Harassment (Lesson 2) 132
The Summer of Regret and the Fist I Met 134
Ode to the Party Line 136

This product includes copyrighted and proprietary material and is not to be reproduced in whole or in part without explicit written permission from TROY… Pure Blue Creative, LLC. We believe that the packaging and design of the materials strongly enhance the effectiveness for students; therefore, there is no licensing opportunity to make copies of the LA4™ material. Copyright 2000–22 TROY… Pure Blue Creative, LLC.

LA4

Look around. Quite a few folks are out there sittin' in mud puddles. On occasion they may muster up enough energy to splash a bit, but that's about it. If that's you, like it was me, then know this: You have the power to change. You have the power to get out of the puddle and get on with life.

Life's too precious to sit around in the puddle of boring routine and meaningless habits. Life is change, knowledge and growth. So get up and make a run for it. Running is the best way to get away from those people who are too lazy to get out of the puddle themselves. Besides, running is also the quickest way to dry those soggy britches.

That's exactly what LA4 is all about … to not only help you get out of the mud puddle but to empower you to run the race of life and win.

© 2000 – 22 TROY… Pure Blue Creative, LLC LA4™